THE US-TURKISH-NATO MIDDLE EAST CONNECTION

Also by George McGhee

AT THE CREATION OF A NEW GERMANY
DIPLOMACY FOR THE FUTURE (*editor*)
ENVOY TO THE MIDDLE WORLD

The US-Turkish-NATO Middle East Connection

How the Truman Doctrine Contained the Soviets in the Middle East

GEORGE McGHEE

former US Ambassador to Turkey

St. Martin's Press   New York

First published in the United States of America in 1990

Printed in Hong Kong

Library of Congress Cataloging-In-Publication Data
McGhee, George Crews, 1912–
The US-Turkish-NATO Middle East Connection: How the Truman
Doctrine Contained the Soviets in the Middle East/ George McGhee.
p.   cm.
ISBN 0–312–03540–3
1. United States–Foreign relations–Turkey.   2. Turkey–Foreign
relations–United States.   3. North Atlantic Treaty Organization–
Middle East.   4. United States–Foreign relations–1945–53.
5. United States–Foreign relations–Middle East.   6. Middle East–
Foreign relations–United States.   7. Cold war.   I. Title.
II. Title: US-Turkish-NATO Middle East Connection.   III. Title: How the
Truman Doctrine Contained the Soviets in the Middle East.
E183.8.T8M33   1990
327.730561–dc20   89-34298
                                                              CIP

To my mother

Contents

List of Maps

Foreword

Turkey's decision to join NATO was one of the most important and far-reaching decisions taken for the defence of Western Europe and the free world. Forty years on we can see that even more clearly than did those who made that decision.

George McGhee is in a better position than anyone else to chronicle the events of that time. He was an outstanding American Ambassador and had the vision and good sense to realise the importance that Turkey has geographically and politically for the free world.

Today we accept Turkey's membership of NATO as a matter of course and fact. This was far from true in the late 1940s, in the aftermath of the Second World War and in the economic and political upheaval which ensued. It is all the more creditable, therefore, that there were far-seeing statesmen both in Turkey and in the United States who recognised the importance to the West of Turkey's active participation in our common defence. Since then many years have elapsed but the importance of the Southern flank and, in particular, that part of it which embraces Turkey, is as evident today as ever it was.

Turkey has special relations and ties with the other countries of the Middle East as it does with its neighbours to the West. A hostile Turkey or a neutral Turkey would indeed have posed problems for us which would have greatly complicated our defence posture and our foreign policy and weakened the credibility of our strategy.

Ambassador McGhee has chronicled the events which led to Turkey's accession to NATO with great clarity and in a most interesting and readable fashion. He throws a fascinating light on the relationship between the United States of America and Turkey and the personalities involved.

This book not only deserves to be read, but it deserves study by all of those who are interested in Defence and Foreign Affairs.

Peter Carrington
Former Secretary-General, NATO

Acknowledgments

When I left Ankara following my resignation as US Ambassador to Turkey in May 1953, I could not take with my any classified official documents. However, over the years I had put together in one file those I considered most important, including memorandums of conversations, telegrams, letters, reports and internal communications. I asked the State Department to keep them intact in its archives so that I could seek access to them later. In my early years at the State Department, I developed the technique of taking notes surreptitiously on a small piece of paper concealed in my left hand, so as not to inhibit the frankness of my interlocutor. After the meeting, while the information was still fresh in my mind, I dictated an expansion of my notes into a full minute of the conversation.

When I became interested a few years ago in writing my memoirs of this period, I found the file intact. The officers in charge of Foreign Affairs Information Management were generous in making them available to me, and the members of the Classification Center in declassifying most of them. Since most of these documents had not been otherwise available, they along with my own recollections constitute the principal new information on which this volume is based. These are now available for scholars in my papers in the Georgetown University Library in Washington, DC.

In choosing the focus of this book, I have elected to avoid duplicating material covered in several noteworthy publications that contribute to the study of postwar US-Turkish relations and that I recommend as further reading on the subject: *The Origins of the Cold War in the Near East*, by Bruce Kuniholm, which explores in depth the developing postwar Soviet threat to the Middle East through 1946; *Troubled Alliance*, by George Harris, which perceptively analyses the vicissitudes of US-Turkish relations from 1960 to 1972; and *Turkey: America's Forgotten Ally*, an excellent Council on Foreign Relations publication by Dankwart Rustow, who highlights Turkey's role in saving the Middle East countries from the fate of Czechoslovakia, Hungary and Afghanistan. Other source materials include *Foreign Relations of the United States* and other unpublished documents in the Department of State archives, as well as published private works listed in the bibliography.

Before starting my writing I asked several experts of this period in whom I had particular confidence – Parker Hart and Raymond Hare, both former ambassadors to Turkey, and Dr Heath Lowry, Executive Director of the Institute of Turkish Studies in Washington, DC, to look over my material and discuss with me the plan of a book making the best use of it. After I had prepared a draft, I circulated it among this group for comment, also to Dr George Harris of the Historical Office of the State Department's Bureau of Public Affairs, to former British Ambassador to Turkey Sir Bernard Burrows for a British viewpoint and to a number of other former colleagues on particular questions. From each I received valuable corrections and comments for which I am grateful, most of which I was happy to include. Views expressed in the volume are, however, my own and I accept full responsibility for them. I also wish to express appreciation to Alison Raphael and Nancy McCoy for valuable assistance in editing my work, and to my secretary, Katherine Masyn, and Peggy Smedley for typing and further screening of material.

I am particularly appreciative to Lord Carrington, recently retired Secretary-General of NATO, for writing a foreword for this book. Peter Carrington has had a brilliant public career apart from his service in the House of Lords, having held the positions of Secretary of State for Defence and for Foreign and Commonwealth Affairs in the British Government. No one is in a better position to appreciate the importance of Middle East defence, and the role of Turkey and NATO.

Preface

THE RATIONALE FOR MIDDLE EAST DEFENCE

World interest has in recent years continued to focus on the security of the Middle East and particularly, as a result of the eight-year Iran-Iraq War, on the Persian Gulf. Concern over the war, which resulted in a major naval commitment by the United States and some of its NATO allies, arose from not only the regional threat that a victorious Iran would pose for the Gulf states, but the perennial fear that the USSR might try to take advantage of the situation to attempt to extend its power into the Middle East, including the Persian Gulf area. This account will explain why a Soviet threat has not materialised.

The fact that the Soviet Union today appears to offer no serious danger to the Middle East results directly, I believe, from policies adopted by the United States under the Truman administration soon after the close of World War II. At that time the threat of an armed Soviet invasion through Turkey, Iran and Iraq seemed very real. When the United States decided in 1947 to provide Turkey with massive military assistance under the Truman Doctrine and in the early 1950s to help Turkey gain admission to the NATO alliance, the door to a Soviet invasion of the Middle East was slammed shut.

I will describe, from the viewpoint of a central participant in the process from 1947 to 1953, how this took place. I joined the Department of State in 1946 after service as an air combat intelligence officer in the B-29 air war against Japan under General Curtis LeMay. I viewed the 'cold war' that quickly developed between the USSR and the West as a continuation, in different form and focus, of World War II. As an assistant to Under-Secretary of State for Economic Affairs Will Clayton, who saw clearly the developing storm, I soon learned that the Soviet Union had changed from an ally to Hitler's successor as an enemy. Later, as administrator of Greek-Turkish aid, I became one of the first acknowledged 'cold warriors'. To my satisfaction, the Soviet media directed to the Middle East often cited me in this role. I considered that my duty and that of my associates was to 'hold a finger in the dike' of Middle East defence to protect the newly emerging nations there from Soviet aggression.

Turkey's importance to the security of the Middle East is based first of all on the strength of its 600 000-man army and the unity and democratic inclinations of its people. It is also based on geography. The mountain passes of northern Turkey, Iraq and Iran provide the only land access routes to the Middle East and the Persian Gulf area that invading Soviet forces could have followed. Following their unsuccessful attempts to gain access to the region during the early cold war, I believe that the Soviets have concluded that it would be too risky for them to expose a long line of communications starting at their Iranian border, to the threat of a Turkish military intervention. Without a prior Turkish commitment to neutrality, the Soviets would first have had to attempt to neutralise Turkish forces by gaining control of Turkey's air space and attacking air fields, military bases, transportation facilities and supply depots. This is what I was told by the Turkish foreign minister back in 1952, as I will later recount.

If the Soviets ever had reason to believe that Turkey would remain neutral under such circumstances, the possibility was, I believe, foreclosed by Turkey's entry into NATO. Moreover, the United States, with or without NATO, has been committed since the enunciation of the Carter Doctrine of 23 January 1980, to a military reaction to a Soviet invasion of the Middle East; if this occurred NATO would seek, and I believe receive, the co-operation of Turkish forces and the use of Turkish bases.

If Turkey is attacked directly by the Soviets, of course, Turkey would mobilise in its defence, and the United States and other NATO members would become automatically involved in fulfillment of their NATO commitments. Although Turkey is not committed to react to a Soviet attack on Iran, which would be outside the NATO area, the evidence is clear that Turkey could not under such circumstances remain neutral, as Turkish Foreign Minister Köprülü assured me back in 1952. Turkey has, at every stage of negotiations for a Middle East defence structure, including the ill-fated Middle East Command and the Middle East Defence Organisation, been eager to commit itself to an active role. According to a JCS report of June 1952 discussed later, Turkey had promised six divisions as part of the defence of the Iranian mountain passes. Pursuit of a neutral role after 1952 would have endangered Turkey's NATO guarantee and hope for US support both within and outside NATO. If the Soviets had ever been able to seize the rest of the Middle East as a result of Turkish passivity, Turkey would have been surrounded by the Soviets and its position made untenable.

No indigenous Middle East defence without Turkey would have

been adequate to deter or stop the Soviets during this period, and outside aid has always been uncertain. The Middle East, I believe, has been protected since 1952 by Turkish forces ready to act as a 'trip wire' to draw in other NATO forces under Turkey's NATO guarantee. In October 1986, at a meeting in Istanbul of top NATO and Turkish military and political officials sponsored by the Atlantic Institute, I asked whether anyone present thought the Soviets believed that they could launch a ground invasion of the Middle East without first engaging Turkey. The unanimous reply was that they could not.

I do not believe that any Soviet objective in the Middle East after Turkish entry into NATO in 1952 was to the Soviets worth the risk of a world war. The Soviets could always have started a war in the Middle East, but they must have known that their only chance of winning one was in Europe. No Soviet move against either, however, ever materialised and is today even more improbable.

Nevertheless, NATO security must provide for all possible scenarios, and NATO must be ready to fight on its northern, central and southern European fronts, and on its southeastern flank, even simultaneously. NATO forces are, of course, not committed to defend non-NATO territory. Although it is not clear that other NATO forces, now concentrated on the central front, would be forthcoming in time to stop a Soviet attack against Turkey, it is my belief that the Turkish force would be formidable enough to delay any Soviet advances until some NATO reinforcements could arrive. I emphasise Turkey here over Greece because it is five times more populous and much stronger militarily than Greece, because Greece's northern mountains are not a probable Soviet invasion route to the Middle East and because it is generally agreed that Greek troops could fight Soviet forces only in Greece and would not deter an invasion through Iran. Greece is, however, a valuable NATO ally and could provide important air and naval support and bases for logistical support for the defence of the NATO south flank and the Middle East region as a whole.

Today, the strategic importance of the Middle East and its role as the world's greatest repository of oil continue to provide an ample basis for temptation for the Soviets. The many Middle East regional problems create weaknesses that the Soviets could be expected to try to take advantage of. These include the 40 years of Arab-Israeli hostilities over the Palestine issue, involving unfulfilled UN resolutions, the disputed status of Jerusalem, rampant terrorism, three million Arab refugees and the 1.3 million stateless prisoners of war in the West Bank and Gaza Strip.

These problems contributed to the threat of an armed Soviet intervention in 1956 following the British, French and Israeli attack on Egypt. The Middle East now faces the results of the long disastrous Iran-Iraq War, the possibility that the Syria-Israel confrontation could precipitate Soviet armed assistance to its Syrian ally and the destabilising internal religious differences between moderate and fundamentalist Islamic groups. Taken together these problems require the West to remain alert to the vulnerability of the region and to be ready to assist in its defence, particularly in light of the demonstrated inability of the Middle East states to unite in a co-ordinated defence of their own.

The Iran-Iraq War is but one example of this lack of unity. The surrounding Arab states consider Israel an enemy comparable to the Soviet Union, an attitude that would make it difficult for Israel to contribute to a Middle East defence. Not only would the Arabs not co-operate with Israel to repel a Soviet invasion, they might even seize the opportunity to attack Israel. However, the Arab states did not succeed in co-ordinating their own past wars against Israel.

As it was in 1952, the deterrent provided by Turkey in NATO still provides the single greatest protection to the Middle East and US interests there against Soviet aggression. As the Soviets become increasingly reconciled to the improbability of ever being able to achieve domination of the Middle East, and this source of Soviet-Western tension recedes, one may reasonably expect an improved Middle East climate in which, it is hoped, progress can be made in solving some of the remaining acute regional problems.

In this memoir I focus attention on Turkey during the period 1947–53, from the promulgation of the Truman Doctrine through the initiation of massive US aid that enabled Turkey to strengthen its economy and armed forces to meet its NATO responsibilities. The source material I use includes my conversations with the president, prime minister, foreign minister and other high-level officials of Turkey during my successive roles as Co-ordinator of Aid to Greece and Turkey, Assistant Secretary of State for Near East, South Asian, and African affairs and US Ambassador to Turkey. During this period I was the State Department official most directly concerned with Turkey and felt the heavy responsibility of blocking a Soviet takeover of the Middle East.

James Webb, Under-Secretary of State (a position later to be called deputy secretary), strongly encouraged the decentralisation of responsibility in the State Department. When I served as Assistant Secretary, Webb told me, 'George, I want you to consider that you are the Secretary of State for the Middle East, South Asia and Africa [at that time about a quarter of the world's population]. Any decision you feel comfortable in making, you make. If not, bring your problem to me and I'll help you get a decision'. With that he would simulate a coach giving me a pat on the back before sending me back into the game.

1 A Middle East Historical Overview, to 1947

The Middle East* has historically been of great strategic importance as a land bridge between three continents – a traditional route of empire. To this already key position was added [in 1869] the Suez Canal, permitting sea passage across shorter routes and, more recently, were made available landing and transit rights for intercontinental air flights. The area is also the single greatest repository of oil in the world, possessing 70 per cent of proven world reserves and yielding 34 per cent of world production. The importance of Middle East defence results from the unique combination of these strategic factors.

Civilisation as we know it began in the heart of the Middle East, in the basins of the Tigris, Euphrates and Nile rivers where man had access to fertile land and water. The Middle East saw the beginnings of literature, the arts, science and the law. The recording of history, which began with the discovery of writing in the third millenium BC, chronicles a series of conquering races – the Sumerians, Babylonians, Assyrians and Persians, who created empires spreading to the east and west of their Mesopotamian heartland. The Phoenicians of the Levant coast established colonies all around the Mediterranean and began trade by ship with Britain, India and West Africa. Carthage, the most important Phoenician outpost, exercised a hegemony over the western Mediterranean until it was successfully contested by the Greeks and Romans.

It was the Greeks who, by founding city-states, first colonised the eastern Mediterranean and endowed it with their Hellenic culture, an enormous contribution to the merging of civilisations in the Middle East. The Persians came next, controlling the Fertile Crescent and all of Asia Minor and nearly conquering Greece, until Xerxes' fleet faltered at Salamis in 479 BC. In return, Alexander of Macedon invaded Asia Minor in 334 BC and, after subjugating Egypt and Persia, went on to conquer the eastern world as far as the Indus River

---

*The British term 'Middle East', which encompasses the Arab states west through Egypt, Israel, Cyprus, Turkey and Iran, will be used in favour of the American term 'Near East', which usually includes only Israel and the adjacent Arab states.

and the mountain barriers of south central Asia. Three great empires centring in Syria, Greece and Egypt, which were created by Alexander's chieftains after his death, dominated the Middle East for centuries.

By the end of the first century AD, the Romans had extended their rule over the Middle East to the gates of Persia. Jerusalem, centre of Jewish resistance to the Empire, was taken in AD 70. In AD 330 the emperor Constantine, beset by invasions of new hordes emerging from barbarism in northern Europe and central Asia and by a revived Persian Empire in the east, transferred his seat of power from Milan to the ancient Greek city of Byzantium, renamed Constantinople. Here, protected by almost impregnable walls and by the Golden Horn, an inlet of the Bosporus, the Byzantine Empire controlled the wealth and manpower of Asia Minor and ruled over the Middle East for eleven hundred years, preserving and enhancing the civilisations it had inherited. Byzantine power declined, however, after the seventh century and ended with the conquest of Constantinople by the Turks in AD 1453.

Meanwhile in the seventh century the Arabs, aroused by zeal for Muhammad's new and powerful religion, burst out of their desert heartland in the Arabian peninsula and conquered lands from India to France, including the Middle East, where they converted its people to Islam. Islamic science, law and culture made an important contribution to the Middle Eastern civilisations. Islam remains today a powerful influence as a religion, a basis for government, a way of life and an inspiration for literature and the arts.

From their homeland in Turkestan in the heart of central Asia, the Turks entered the world of the Middle East relatively late in history, starting in the ninth century. The Seljuq Turks forced their entry into Asia Minor in 1071 by defeating the Byzantine emperor at Manzikert, in what is now part of eastern Turkey. The Ottoman Turks, starting in the thirteenth century from northwest Anatolia, became over several centuries the rulers of the Middle East and lands beyond, conquering what remained of the Byzantine Empire and the older Arab kingdoms. At its zenith in the sixteenth century, the Ottoman Empire stretched from Morocco in the west to the Black Sea and Persia in the east, and from the Danube River and the Balkans in the north to the Sahara Desert and Egypt in the south.

The Turks were strong rulers who held their empire together over long periods of peace and progress, a remarkable feat, since it comprised diverse peoples normally at war with each other. The

Turks generally respected the rights and religions of the minorities they conquered and preserved their indigenous cultures, particularly that of Persia. By the time the Ottoman Empire collapsed at the end of World War I, the Turks had made an indelible impact on the Middle East.

European colonisation came to the Middle East at the turn of the nineteenth century, as it had to Africa and south and southeast Asia and to other isolated states around the world that had not shared in the progress made in Europe since the industrial revolution. Starting in 1798, when Napoleon occupied Egypt as a part of his efforts to dominate Europe, this most important Middle Eastern state became increasingly drawn into the Middle Eastern power struggle. After 1801 British interests gained increasing importance in Egypt, with the British later becoming major shareholders in the Suez Canal Company.

The British, since the beginning of the nineteenth century, had a special interest in the Middle East because of its strategic location for keeping open the sea route to India, Britain's most prized colonial possession. Even before the demise of the Ottoman Empire, the British ensured their right to station troops and maintain military bases in Egypt, and after the collapse of the Ottomans through treaties with Iraq and Transjordan. Particularly important to the British was their Fayad base in the Suez Canal Zone, which included air fields, supply depots, workshops and power stations and gave the British access to the Mediterranean and the Red Sea, as well as the manpower and facilities of Cairo. Two air bases in Iraq, Habbaniya and Shu'aiba, were also of vital importance to the British.

After a series of nationalist outbreaks resulting from anti-British, pro-Muslim sentiments, Britain occupied Egypt in 1882. Despite Egypt's formal declaration of independence, Britain continued to control the country until after World War II. In 1936 an Anglo-Egyptian treaty provided for the end of British occupation in return for British rights to maintain troops at the Suez Canal, Cairo and Alexandria for 20 years. Both countries also made a pledge of mutual assistance, and Egypt agreed to respect British rule in the Anglo-Egyptian Sudan, which Egypt coveted.

France had re-entered the Middle East through League of Nations' mandates over Syria and Lebanon after World War I, at the same time that British influence was enlarged by a mandate over Palestine. The French had made a determined effort to increase their political and cultural influence and their economic involvement. When France gave up its mandates over Syria and Lebanon after World War II, Britain was left as the only remaining European power in the region.

During their exercise of power in the Middle East, England and France attempted to rule through puppet regimes, the British in the end through Farouk in Egypt and the descendants of the deposed Saudi Arabian Hashemite dynasty in Iraq and Jordan. However, both England and France were unable to maintain their influence againt the rising tide of post-World War II nationalism, which in Syria and Iraq was represented by the Ba'th political party. King Abdullah of Jordan was greatly weakened and eventually assassinated as a result of his failure to cope with the Arab defeat in the war with Israel and, reportedly the fact that he had engaged in private discussions with Israel. Decreasingly representative of their people, and challenged by the success of Gamal Abdal-Nasser (the nationalist prime minister of Egypt after Farouk's exile), the Arab dynasties along with British and French influence lost ground. Except in Jordan, colonial regimes yielded to the forces of nationalism.

*   *   *

It is 24 February 1947. In the Middle East a dangerous power vacuum has replaced colonial rule. Amid the wreckage of World War II the newly emerging, mostly Arab nations struggle to attain self-government and achieve economic stability. As a region, they are seriously divided by religious and cultural differences, unprepared to unite in a regional defence – a region strategically placed, rich in oil reserves, and vulnerable. From behind the shadow of fascism, another threatening force is emerging. Communist movements, which began to grow on the open wounds of Europe, probe incessantly for weaknesses in Greece, Turkey and Iran, seeking to control the Turkish Straits and to open the way for expansion into the Middle East.

The British, who have valiantly borne the burden of preserving the Middle East from Hitler's war and the Soviet threat that succeeded it, are forced to reassess their commitment to providing Greece and Turkey with economic and military assistance. Their own wartime losses have placed an unbearable strain on their ability to defend their interests in the Middle East and finance postwar reconstruction at home. The uncertain fate of the Middle East has approached a crisis point. Communist-led guerrillas have gained control over most of Greece outside major cities, and the Greek royalist government could fall within weeks. Turkey, which lies athwart the land route for any Soviet invasion of the Middle East, has been weakened economically by its risky policy of neutrality and its isolation during the war. Turkish weaponry is too limited and obsolete and Turkish communications facilities insufficient to defend the country against the increasing Soviet threat. For the moment the security of the entire Middle East region depends on the survivability of Greece and Turkey.

At 9.00 a.m. on that morning of 24 February, the British ambassador in Washington officially informed the Truman administration that the United Kingdom could no longer continue its postwar assistance to Greece and Turkey; the major share of the burden would have to devolve to the United States. If the Middle East is to be saved from Soviet domination, the United States – the only country to emerge from the war with a strengthened economy – must accept the responsibility. That decision will be expressed in the Truman Doctrine. To understand why this decision was made, we will consider a brief overview of the postwar history of Middle East defence and the special role played by one country – Turkey.

*   *   *

In the exhaustion of the postwar period and amid a ground swell of condemnation of colonialism, it was inevitable that the new Middle East nations would proceed toward self-government. At the same time the vast empire of the Soviet Union begun to evince its determination to expand further – in particular, to gain assured access to the Black Sea through control of the Turkish Straits and to gain influence in the area between Russia and the oil of the Persian Gulf. Its tradition of military conquest begun by Peter the Great, through which it had assembled much of its empire under the czars, had gained the Soviet Union through postwar occupation most of Eastern Europe as well. Now, in the power vacuum of the newly liberated Middle East, the region appeared to be there for the taking.

To me and to others in the administration responsible for the Middle East at that time, there appeared to be a clear threat that the Soviet Union and its Balkan allies, which had been probing for weaknesses in Iran, Turkey and Greece, would also attempt to penetrate the weak new Arab states. If they succeeded, Western Europe would have to come to the USSR for Middle East oil supplies and the gates to Asia and Africa lying beyond would be wide open.

By the irony of fate, the most imperialistic of all empires – the USSR – had for so long denounced the 'imperialism' of the West that it was in a good position to capitalise on the growth of nationalism in the Middle East. A wave of militant adventurers came to power in Middle Eastern countries. Stirred by hysterical demagogues, 'the street' became the source of power for Mohammed Mossadegh of Iran and Gamal Abdal-Nasser of Egypt. The anti-colonialism was a wave on which the Soviet Union could ride. And it did.

Hard-pressed by its burgeoning commitments in Europe and Asia, the United States was relying on the British to defend the newly emerging Middle East nations. The British, however, even with US help, had proved unable to organise the weak and divided Middle Eastern nations for the purpose of regional defence (either with or without British participation). Because of Britain's imperial legacy, moreover, many of these nations were unwilling to follow Britain's lead. Of the indigenous states only Turkey was truly independent, with a strong national tradition and sufficient military strength both to defend itself and to contribute to the defence of the region as a whole. Consequently, the British attempted to use Turkey as the anchor of their Middle East policy, channelling as much military assistance as they could to the Turks and, to a lesser degree, the Greeks.

The British, however, had suffered more than most from the war. The financial demands of rebuilding Britain's own society were enormous. Britain had little choice but to start relinquishing its responsibilities for Middle East defence and transfer some of this responsibility to the United States.

Having never been an important colonial power, America was suspect in the Middle East largely because of its European associations. The Middle East was, however, now desperately in need of US help, and America responded. Flushed with the confidence of having led the coalition that defeated Germany and Japan, Americans were willing to make the additional effort required to save the new countries of the Middle East from communism. Our increased presence in the Middle East just as the British were relinquishing power created tensions. There was suspicion that the United States was accelerating the turnover unduly and for its own benefit, that we were attempting to influence peoples whom we ourselves did not fully understand. Nevertheless, a mutual spirit of co-operation between ourselves and the British prevailed.

2 Turkey in Perspective: Historical Background

Turkey's emergence as a full and responsible member of the Western alliance represents one of the most significant political and stragetic developments in recent history. The initiation of large-scale US aid to Turkey in 1947 under the Truman Doctrine and Turkey's admission to NATO in 1952 ushered in a new phase of US foreign policy that made communist aggression anywhere a matter of US security. There also began a relationship between the United States and Turkey that has developed into a strong bond of increasing confidence and respect.

Perhaps it would be appropriate to describe my own impressions of Turkish people and their leaders with whom I have dealt privately and as a government official for more than 40 years. For 25 years my wife and I have had a second home overlooking the small town of Alanya on the beautiful Mediterranean coast of southern Turkey. We feel very close ties to the people of Alanya, which we have developed as neighbours over the years.

The Turks are the most recent of people of Asiatic origins to become European and are still in the process of doing so. In many ways, however, Turks still reflect their central Asian origins. The Turks are, of course, not Arabs but are almost all Muslims, as a result of their mass conversion more than a millennium ago. Many Turks, however, do not carry out all Muslim precepts or attend religious services regularly. My own impression of Turks with whom I have developed friendly relationships based on shared interests is that they have moral and ethical standards quite similar to those of Americans of similar stations in life.

Turks differ, of course, individually and in accordance with their Turkish backgrounds. During the rule of the sultans Anatolian peasants were looked down on by the high officials and aristocracy of Constantinople, often being treated as mere pawns of empire. The élite of Istanbul included, besides Turks, minorities from a variety of sources, the Balkans, Soviet Georgia and the Turkish imperial capitals. Many Western Europeans had settled in Istanbul for business or for service in the imperial courts. The modern Turk is a mixture of these peoples, who have been melded increasingly into a democratic whole.

Turks, apart from their physical courage and martial skills, possess many admirable attributes – dignity, self-reliance and faithfulness to their undertakings. They are polite, friendly without being intrusive, and under proper circumstances are hospitable even to strangers. Having ruled much of the world for five centuries, Turks are a proud people. However, having lost their empire, they have no desire or expectation of restoring it. Many Turks still live on the Anatolian plateau and in the Taurus Mountains under conditions that Europeans would consider spartan. Although modern Turks make tough soldiers who can withstand pain and hardships, there is no longer the willingness to accept the harshness that characterised their life under the rule of the sultans. When I gazed at the stern, bronzed faces of the Anatolian conscripts' honor guard in the rays of a dying sunset, as I passed to present my credentials as ambassador to the president of Turkey, I was glad they were our friends – not our enemies.

Collectively the Turks seek to perfect a parliamentary democracy on the ashes of 600 years of autocratic rule by the sultans. Although they have in recent years had interludes of near anarchy, which led to three military takeovers, Turkey is today, I believe, back on a stable democratic path. When the Turkish military have taken power, it has been, I believe, reluctantly and on a collective basis, as a result of responsibilities they consider they have inherited from the sultans and Atatürk.

Turkey's decision to join NATO and the West was not, I believe, the result of a temporary convenience or opportunism. It can best be described as the meeting of historical trends that were operating in both Turkey and the West. The West, particularly the United States, recognised after the last war the aggressive and expansionist nature of Soviet communism and determined to protect themselves and the free world against it. This was a conclusion the Turks reached about Russia long ago, as a result of their almost 300 years of sporadic conflict with Russia. In the early nineteenth century the Turkish people began a course toward Westernisation that has today gained their country a respected place among the democratic nations of the world. This has been particularly characteristic of US-Turkish relations, which have revealed a remarkable similarity in national aims and policies. We also share many difficult problems, including continuing differences with the Soviet Union.

*   *   *

The Turks first coupled their economic and political development to the stream of Western progress under Mahmud II, who ruled Turkey from 1808 to 1839. During Mahmud's reign the army was reorganised, a medical school opened with the aid of European experts, Turkish students travelled to Europe to study and a newspaper and official printing office were established. Mahmud's successor, Abdulmecid I, continued and built upon these reforms. Most significant, he oversaw the preparation of the Tanzimat, an all-encompassing series of reforms that effectively transformed Turkey from a medieval to a modern state.

The Tanzimat decreed the equality of all citizens before the law; established the right of trial by due process; granted equal protection of life, dignity, honor and goods; and created a levy of uniform taxes and instituted payment by salary for all officials. A democratic foundation had been firmly laid. When the 'Young Turk' movement emerged to oppose and overcome the repressive regime of Abdulhamid II (1876–1909), nationalism revealed itself to be a powerful political force as well. Freed after World War I from the autocratic rule of the sultans and the burdens of empire to concentrate on their adopted homeland in Asia Minor, the Turks emerged as a nation state.

As rapidly as the Turkish people adopted Western laws, dress and customs, they assimilated the principles of democracy. In 1924, under the powerful leadership of President Kemal Atatürk, they accepted a constitution inspired by the ideals and institutions of Western democracy. Although Turkey remained under one-man rule during this formative period, the Turks have consistently demonstrated their political maturity in sharing and transferring power. In 1938 Ismet Inönü assumed the presidency and gave substance to the democratic process by legalising opposition political parties.

In 1950 Celal Bayar, the founder of the major opposition party (the Democratic Party begun in 1945), won an overwhelming majority in an election in which almost 90 per cent of eligible voters participated. This peaceful transition of power constituted the final proof that Turkey had joined the democratic countries of the world. In 1960, 1971 and 1980 the military stepped in to control the government following the outbreak of political violence, or, in one case, the rejection of a regime considered to have deviated from its constitutional powers; power was returned after each crisis subsided.

Determined to protect their sovereignty, the Turks have refused to be bullied by the ceaseless demands and pressures of the Soviet

Union, and they have done so while maintaining correct dilplomatic relations. They have shown the United States that it is possible to live in equanimity without yielding, alongside an implacable enemy. Their ability to do this attests to their strong national unity and high degree of military preparedness.

Tensions between Turkey and the Soviets have focused on control of the Turkish Straits, the narrow lands facing the Bosporus, the Dardanelles, and the Sea of Marmara that control the only access to the Black Sea, which is in effect a vast inland waterway and the terminus of great rivers that penetrate deep into Russia and central Europe. This strategically important gateway gained symbolic significance when the Byzantine capital of Constantinople was located there in AD 330. For more than a thousand years it flourished as a leading city of the Christian world and the traditional centre of the Orthodox religion adopted by Russia in the tenth century. Strategically and symbolically important, Constantinople became an object coveted by Russian leaders.

The Turks have in modern history fought 13 wars with Russia. Arriving late on the European scene, Russia challenged the Ottoman Empire when Turkish power was already in decline. In 1677 Grand Vizier Kara Mustafa led an attack against Russia, following raids by the cossacks. Despite some early successes on the battlefield, the Turks lost most of the Ukraine and were obliged to give the cossacks trading rights in the Black Sea. In 1683, after the Ottoman Empire's defeat at the siege of Vienna, the Russians joined an alliance of European leaders bound to throw off Ottoman rule. Taking advantage of the empire's weakness, the czars expanded to the south and southwest with the ultimate objective of controlling the Turkish Straits.

The Russians have pursued strategies of either resorting to overt aggression, developing alliances with Turkey's enemies, developing spheres of influence over buffer states, or undermining Turkey's internal stability by encouraging independence movements and disaffecting religious and other minorities. Despite Soviet gains, Turkey was never totally defeated or penetrated. Moreover, it never relinquished control of the straits.

Since the Bolshevik Revolution of 1917 the Soviets have pursued a consistent course, despite the many tactical twists and turns of their objectives in the Middle East. They have employed methods of co-operation and assistance and resorted to aggressive expansionism. For example, in 1920 the Soviet Union promoted people's revolutions against the 'imperialist' regimes of the Middle East, and between the world wars it actively sought to subvert nationalist regimes, such as that of Shah Reza Pahlavi in Iran, at the same time that it superficially co-operated with them.

In 1920 the Soviets and the Turks were brought together by a common opposition to the European powers, particularly the United Kingdom. On 26 April Kemal proposed a military and political alliance between the two countries which the Soviets declined. They did, however, find it to their advantage to 'collaborate'[1] with the Turks and established diplomatic relations with them in 1920. On 16 March 1921 the two countries signed the Treaty of Moscow, giving Turkey its present provinces of Kars and Ardahan, with Batum going to the Soviets. The USSR furnished arms that helped Turkey defeat Greece in 1921–22. When Mussolini revived Italian demands on Turkish Anatolia, the Soviets lent the Turks $18 000 000 for technical military assistance with no interest.

A 1925 Treaty of Friendship and Neutrality, renewed in 1935 for another ten years, committed each party to abstain from participating in alliances, coalitions or hostile actions of any kind directed against the other. Starting in 1935 Turkish-Soviet relations started to deteriorate, being exacerbated by Soviet efforts to establish a communist party in Turkey. In 1939 the Soviets demanded unacceptable revisions of the Montreux Convention of 1936, the ensuing talks between the two countries broke down and Turkey joined Britain and France in a Mutual Assistance Pact.

The first real Turkish communist party, according to Karpat, was established in Istanbul on 22 September 1919,[2] by a group of intellectuals under the name of the Turkish Workers and Peasants Social Party. The party, which was based on the Marxist-Leninist interpretation of social classes and the political struggle, supported the Ataturk government. The socialist Green Party, which was formed in 1920 with government approval, never materialised. The Peoples Participation Party, founded as the political branch of the Greens in the same year, attempted to elect members of Parliament. It was abolished by the Turkish government in 1921 and in 1922 all communist propaganda was forbidden, when Ataturk secretly sponsored his own communist party. The original Turkish Workers and Peasants Social Party came into the open again when it was legitimised by the Turkish government after the war.

During its wartime alliance with the Western powers, the Soviet Union pursued its aggressive territorial ambitions toward Greece,

Turkey and Iran while establishing diplomatic relations with numerous Arab states. Stalin also sought an alliance with Bulgaria and demanded a Soviet land and naval base along the Turkish Straits. Further Soviet objectives were a base in the Dodecanese Islands off the southern coast of Greece and Turkey, a trusteeship in Tripolitania and a foothold in Eritrea and Ethiopia.

After the threat of Hitler's Germany became apparent in the early 1930s, the Soviets entered into uneasy treaties with several Middle Eastern states, ostensibly for their protection. These states in turn sought loose alliances among themselves for protection against the Soviets. Events would soon show, however, that Russian and German objectives in the Middle East were in conflict.

In 1939 Stalin, anxious to avoid a two-front war, and Hitler, preoccupied with acquiring Poland, signed a non-aggression pact. Stalin, no doubt, also looked forward to the possibility that Germany and the Allies would wear each other out. Such a situation would enhance the USSR's leverage in staking territorial claims, particularly in the Balkans. Stalin wanted the Turkish Straits and control of the eastern Mediterranean. Hitler wanted Soviet aid and neutrality, but not at that price. It was, in fact, the competition between Germany's military objectives and the USSR's territorial ambitions – especially Russia's interest in the area of Batum and Baku south to the Persian Gulf – that caused Hitler to renege on his agreement and attack the Soviet Union in 1941. Stalin's interests were interfering with Hitler's desperate attempts to widen the theatre in which to defeat the British.

The German invasion of Russia helped Turkey to maintain its chosen position of neutrality. Early in the war President Inönü, mindful of the disastrous consequences of Turkey's alliance with the Central Powers during World War I, had attempted to keep peace in the Mediterranean by signing treaties of alliance with Britain and France. However, after Italy's entrance into the war, the fall of France and Hitler's threat against the United Kingdom, Turkey began to shift toward a neutral course and refrained from taking military action when Germany and Italy invaded Greece and the Balkans. It did, however, provide foodstuffs to the hard-pressed Greeks after receiving a shipment of arms and food from the US lend-lease programme. Turkey's neutrality, nevertheless, seemed to work in favour of Germany, especially as Turkey signed a commercial agreement with Germany following their mutual non-aggression pact. Only in August 1944 did Turkey finally break off relations with

MAP 1   *Training Camps and Supply Routes of the Greek Guerrillas*

SOURCE   Bruce R. Kuniholm, *The Origins of the Cold War in the Near East: Great Power Conflict and Diplomacy in Iran, Turkey, and Greece.* Copyright © 1980 by Princeton University Press. Reprinted with permission of the author and Princeton University Press.

Germany, largely because of British pressure on Ankara to fulfill the terms of its earlier treaty of alliance.

With the German surrender on 7 May 1945, Turkey found itself in a greatly weakened position, even though it had not actively engaged in hostilities. Turkish war expenses had seriously damaged the economy, leading to an unpopular capital levy. By taking men from their farms, the war had depleted Turkish foodstocks. Turkish factories, railways and other transport facilities were in a precarious state due to lack of spare parts and replacements. Moreover, the German surrender left Russia free to concentrate its energies on pursuing its Middle East interests. The Turks were aware of Soviet interest in establishing a strong presence in the Batum-Baku area and in the general direction of the Persian Gulf. Turkish suspicions had been confirmed at the time of the Nazi-Soviet alliance, and Moscow's refusal to withdraw Soviet forces from Iran in 1941 had only reinforced Turkish concerns. (After joining with British forces to expel German agents from Iran, the Soviets seem to have considered Iran as conquered territory.) When the Russians participated in an assassination attempt against the German ambassador to Turkey, Russo-Turkish relations further deteriorated.

Thus it came as no surprise when, on 13 March 1945, Moscow announced its intent to renounce its 1925 Treaty of Friendship with Turkey. As relayed to Turkish ambassador to the USSR Selim Sarper, the preconditions for a renewal of the treaty were that: (1) Turkey must cede the frontier Kars-Ardahan district (gained by the Russians at the Congress of Berlin but lost again to Turkey after World War I) to the Soviet Union; and (2) the convention governing the Turkish Straits must be revised to allow the USSR to participate in a 'joint defence' of this waterway and establish bases in the area during wartime. In addition, the Soviets wanted Turkey to break its ties with the United Kingdom and to sign a treaty similar to those the Soviet Union was concluding with the nations of eastern and southeastern Europe.

Sarper rejected these demands on the spot; the Turkish government in Ankara quickly supported his stance, making Turkey's rejection official. The Istanbul journal *Vatan* commented at the time – with great foresight – that the only way to influence Soviet policy was through a firm and unified free world: 'Otherwise, the Soviets will attempt to trap, one by one, the nations they succeed in separating from the free nations of the world, and they will thus assume the initiative'.

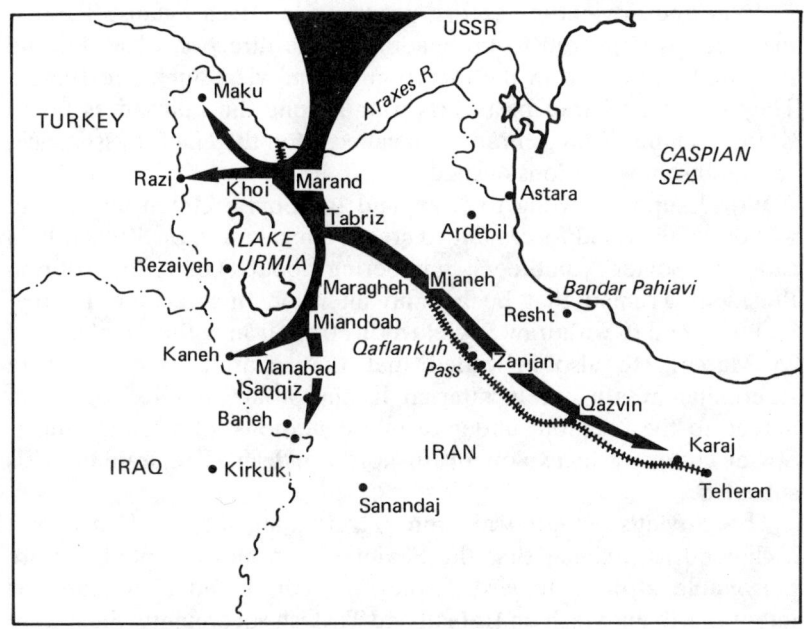

MAP 2   *Soviet Armoured Thrusts into Northern Iran (1946)*
SOURCE   As in MAP 1.

On 3 March 1946 the Soviet Union launched its first major postwar thrust against the 'northern tier' of Greece, Turkey and Iran. Its objective was the annexation of the Iranian province of Azerbaijan, where a so-called separatist movement had formed. In November of the previous year the Iranian government had dispatched a relief column toward Azerbaijan, but this was stopped by Soviet tanks outside Tehran and not allowed to proceed. In December an autonomous Azerbaijan state was declared, led by former communist agents and supported by a militia organised and armed by the Red Army.

Deeply concerned, the United States on 6 March issued a strong protest to the Soviet government on the basis of the US-UK-Soviet tripartite treaty of 1942. The message expressed hope for the withdrawal of Soviet troops, to whose presence the United States could not remain indifferent.

The United States representative in Tabriz reported that by 19 March a minimum of 235 Soviet tanks and 3500 trucks had passed into Azerbaijan through the railhead at Tabriz.

While the Soviets initiated a propaganda attack against Turkey, their troops appeared to be heading in the direction of Maku and Razi in Turkey, and in the direction of Iraq via Kaneh and Baneh. They penetrated Iran past Qazvin and along the railroad as far as Karaj, 18 miles from Tehran. Iran called upon the UN for assistance, and intense negotiations ensued.

World support swung to Iran, and the Soviet Union decided to withdraw its armed forces but to create a local militia, stiffened by a cadre of Soviet 'volunteers' numbering about 800. After assuring President Truman that he had no intention of attacking Turkey, Stalin agreed to withdraw Soviet troops from Iran within six weeks of 24 March. He also conceded that the separatist movement in Azerbaijan was a purely internal Iranian affair. For its part, Iran agreed to the creation, under certain conditions, of a joint Iranian-Soviet company to exploit oil in northern Iran. The Iranian crisis subsided.

The Soviet's withdrawal from Azerbaijan, however, was not acclaimed as a signal that the Soviet Union had accepted a more reasonable attitude toward Turkey or that it had abandoned its intentions to encroach on Iranian and Turkish sovereignty. Such were the feelings of Walter Bedell Smith, US ambassador to Moscow, who suggested that Russia's determination to gain a foothold in the region reflected the Soviet's conviction that their security interests were at stake and their desire to gain independent access to the Mediterra-nean and the Arab world by severing the British Empire's 'jugular' at Suez. Smith insisted that if the Soviets portrayed a friendly face to Turkey, it would be a purely tactical and temporary move, as the Russians since the time of the czars had linked advances in the Near East to their domination (or 'liberation', in Soviet parlance) of Turkey.[3]

Meanwhile, guerrilla warfare in Greece escalated with an attack on Litokhoron on 20 March 1946. The UN Security Council responded to the deteriorating situation by voting to conduct an investigation, which later confirmed the guerrilla threat. On the basis of reports from the US ambassador to Greece, Lincoln MacVeagh, the US Department of State concluded in December that communist move-ments from Yugoslavia, Albania and Bulgaria – with at least Soviet acquiescence – were recruiting and training Greek dissidents in an attempt to overthrow the Greek government and separate Macedo-nia from Greece. Supply routes into Greece had been set up in at least eight key locations, covering the entire northern border of

Greece: from Argyrocastro in Epirus (Albania) to Konitsa in Greece, from Monastir in Yugoslavia into Greece; and from Petrich, Smolyan and Ortako in Bulgaria into Greece.

Although it could not ascertain the Soviet Union's full role in the insurrections, the United States was aware that the Soviets were openly propagandising against the Greek government and against US and British support for that government. With the guerrillas in control of most of Greece outside Athens and Salonika – and Greek bridges, harbours, railways, roads, homes and factories largely destroyed by the war – the possibility that Greece might be drawn behind the Iron Curtain loomed large.

On 7 August 1946 the developing crisis between the Soviet Union and Turkey reached its climax when the Soviet Union demanded that Turkey revise the Montreux Convention to place the Turkish Straits under the control of all Black Sea powers and ratify joint Turkish-Soviet defence of the Straits. (Reliable information indicates that the Soviet Union, as part of its continuing war of nerves against Turkey, also directed ground forces toward Turkish territory and held naval manoeuvres 45 miles off the Turkish coast. Turkey, suspecting a real attack, mobilised its own forces under the guise of manoeuvres.) The Turks stood firm against Soviet pressure, insisting that Turkey had fulfilled its responsibilities under the Montreux Convention 'with correctness carried at times as far as a fanaticism, disregarding even purely Turkish interests'. Ankara further asserted, 'from the national point of view the Soviet proposition is not compatible with the inalienable rights of sovereignty of Turkey, nor with its security, which brooks no restrictions'.[4]

The gravity of these Soviet demands was not lost on the United States. Urging Turkey to reject these demands, Truman (after consulting with the British and Turks) sent a note to the Soviet leadership, pointing out that the regime of the straits involved other powers and that Turkey alone should continue to be responsible for the defence of the straits.[5] In his memoirs Truman commented that if the straits became the object of Russian aggression, 'The resulting situation would constitute a threat to international security and would clearly be a matter for action on the part of the Security Council'.[6]

On 23 August 1946 the US Joint Chiefs of Staff (JCS) reported that they viewed Soviet actions in the Middle East as 'a calculated Soviet policy of expanding Soviet de facto geographical political control' and concluded that Turkey 'was the most important factor in the Eastern Mediterranean and the Middle East'.[7] The rationale for US aid to

Turkey had been established, and in discussions with the United
Kingdom the United States gave assurances that it was prepared to
assume greater responsibility in the region.

On receipt of the JCS memorandum acting secretary of state Will
Clayton, whom I served as Special Assistant, suggested revising US
policies in favour of selling military equipment to Greece, Turkey
and Iran in order to strengthen their resolve to resist Soviet
pressures.[8] Ambassador Wilson later echoed these sentiments on
Turkey's behalf, arguing that Turkish morale would be better served
by a US agreement to send such military equipment as we had
available.[9] The State, War and Navy departments concomitantly
joined in urging the administration to protect the independence and
integrity of all three nations. A complete review of US policy toward
Greece, Turkey and Iran ensued. Clearly, Turkey's poorly equipped
army was no match for the Soviet army and, as reported by the US
ambassador to Turkey at the close of 1946, Turkey's long-burdened
economy could not indefinitely support a defensive posture against
the Soviet Union. According to Ambassador Smith in Moscow,
Turkey had no hope of surviving without long-term aid from the
Americans and British.

I well remember the heightened concern that pervaded those in the
Department involved in the Middle East area. We felt that there was
a clear threat of war – possibly even another general war. Since, if
there was to be a war I wanted to serve again with LeMay, I quietly
transferred my naval commission to the Air Force.

3 The Truman Doctrine: Origins and Significance, 1947

FROM CRISIS TO COMMITMENT

The fateful transfer was initiated officially at 9.00 a.m. on Monday, 24 February 1947, when British Ambassador Lord Inverchapel handed to Secretary of State George Marshall two *aide-mémoires* – one on Greece, the other on Turkey.[1] In essence, the British acknowledged the importance of protecting Greece and Turkey against Soviet influence, predicted the imminent fall of the Greek government in the absence of rapid economic and military aid, and requested the United States to assume the major responsibility for providing the assistance that the British economy could no longer support.

Unofficially, the same memos had been presented three days earlier to Loy Henderson, director of the Office of Near Eastern, South Asian and African Affairs, in order to give the State Department an opportunity to consider the matter over the weekend. The governments in Greece and Turkey were not informed, on the suggestion that notification should follow a US decision on extending aid. The eventuality of a British withdrawal of aid had, in fact, been apparent for many months to US officials, who had given the British informal assurances that US assistance would be forthcoming. Ambassador MacVeagh had reported on 3 February that rumours in Athens indicated that the British were considering withdrawing most of their troops from Greece, and on 12 February he had urged immediate US aid to that country. A report from the US Embassy in London on 20 February noted the British Treasury's opposition to further aid to Greece. In fact, when Henderson convened his task force upon receipt of the British note, the working assumption was that the United States would grant the British request for assistance.

Truman consulted that day with the new Secretary of State, General George Marshall, and read the report prepared over the weekend by the State/War/Navy Co-ordinating Committee. Its working assumption had been that the administration should decide, in principle, to assume the responsibility involved. Britain's assessment of Greece's financial requirements, as reported to the president by Under-Secretary of State Dean Acheson, quoted a figure of roughly $250 million in 1947 and more the following year. Turkey's needs were more difficult to establish but were estimated to be smaller.[2] Few specifics were available on the situation in Turkey, and the British furnished no estimates on the funds needed to re-equip and train Turkish forces so that they could be in a reasonable state of readiness. The special US committee formed to study assistance requirements to Greece and Turkey agreed with the British suggestion that American and British chiefs of staff should jointly make this assessment.[3]

Based on the committee's report and after discussions with Secretary of War Robert Patterson and Secretary of the Navy James Forrestal, Marshall wrote to the president on 26 February that he was convinced of four things: the British were sincere about their financial constraints; the situation, particularly in Greece, was desperate; the collapse of the Greek government would put US interests in peril; and the United States should, therefore, immediately extend all aid possible to Greece and, on a smaller scale, to Turkey.[4]

Truman's conclusion in light of all the advice given him was the one he had already reached. Greece was in certain danger of being drawn behind the Iron Curtain, and if Greece were lost, Turkey's position would become untenable in a sea of communism. Conversely, Turkish acquiescence to Soviet demands would put the survival of the Greek government further at risk. No less sobering were the symbolic implications inherent in this challenge to the cause of freedom. Should the United States fail to meet the test, it would set a disastrous precedent, imperil free nations everywhere and encourage what Truman viewed as the tragic re-emergence of American isolationism.

In only two days the US government had acted on the vital decision of supporting Greek and Turkish forces and had immediately set the process in motion. Important work remained to be done, however, on clarifying the situation in Turkey and defining the objectives of a US aid programme. On 27 February Secretary Marshall solicited the support of congressional leaders, noting that specifics on aid to Turkey would be forthcoming upon further investigation. The next day he cabled US Ambassador to Turkey Edwin Wilson and asked for a firsthand appraisal of the situation and of Turkey's needs.[5]

In Wilson's view the Soviets had no immediate plans to invade Turkey but would continue a 'war of nerves' for the indefinite future.[6] Wilson theorised that the Soviets' intent was to disrupt Turkey's economy by forcing the country to maintain a large standing army. Thus, he emphasised, any military aid programme must take care not to 'unconsciously play the Soviet game by saddling Turkey with an overly heavy financial burden for the equipment furnished'. Suggesting that the United States make equipment available at a nominal cost, Wilson urged US policy-makers to consider that funds spent on military hardware would come at the expense of economic projects – such as communications, transport and port development – also needed to improve Turkey's defensive posture. The extent and type of Turkey's required military aid, Wilson noted, would depend on whether the United States hoped to enable Turkey to delay Soviet incursions until US forces could arrive or whether US objectives would be satisfied by enabling the Turks simply to 'resist as long as possible and inflict major losses on the enemy'.

Prevailing ambiguity about the Turkish situation was a principal problem for those preparing the legislation for a Greek-Turkish aid programme. The bills introduced into the first session of Congress were finally based on the findings and recommendations of a report by the Joint Chiefs of Staff: the failure of the West to prevent a communist takeover in Greece would not only put the Russians on a particularly dangerous flank for the Turks but strengthen the Soviet Union's ability to cut off allied supplies and assistance in the event of war. Combined with the Soviet war of nerves against the Turks (which the JCS agreed was probably the Soviet's short-term plan), it might influence them to make concessions to the USSR to avoid ultimate Soviet domination. Failure to aid Greece could convince the Turks that it would be less dangerous to yield to Soviet pressures, even without a direct military threat, than to try to resist. Strong Western support of Greece would reduce Turkish fears and thereby reduce the amount and extent of assurances and assistance Turkey would request.

Furthermore, citing Turkey as a natural barrier to Soviet aggression in the eastern Mediterranean and Middle East, the JCS projected a course of events characteristically similar to the Domino Theory so popular during the Vietnam War: if Turkey could withstand Soviet pressures and received the wherewithal from the West to back up its stance, the resolve of all Middle East nations to stand up to communism would be heightened. If Turkey succumbed in peacetime, all Middle East countries would rapidly fall to Soviet domination. The report concluded dramatically: 'If Russia can absorb Turkey in peace, our ability to defend the Middle East in war will be virtually destroyed'.[7]

Consequently, the JCS anticipated US objectives as, first, stiffening Turkish will and ability to resist Soviet pressures and, second, improving Turkey's military potential to defend itself and exert the maximum possible capability in holding and delaying incursions on its soil. Turkey's capacity to resist Soviet aggression, the report observed, was difficult to evaluate without a specific context to account for the level of Soviet commitments on other fronts at the time of hostilities, the season of the year, the morale of Turkish troops and allied ability to provide military aid before hostilities broke out. Any determination of the level of aid would have to be predicated on a detailed analysis of the capabilities of Turkish forces at the time of engagement in conjunction with what aid and equipment the United States and Britain could practically provide at the time. The report noted that current Turkish forces consisted of 600 000 men, 41 ground divisions, seven fortress commands, 300 aircraft and a negligible navy.

The JCS recommended that the United States:

- place the greatest emphasis on strengthening the ground army and defence against air attacks;
- design equipment that would be suitable for defensive use on Turkish terrain and that would be readily operated by the Turks;
- consider implementing a programme by which the Turks could attain arms and equipment through operation and development of their own arsenals, since 80 per cent of their present equipment was of German design;
- integrate economic and military aid to permit the Turks not only to provide their own equipment but to improve selected communications and logistical facilities, with the objective of relieving economic strains by the demobilisation of some Turkish forces;
- plan, in conjunction with the United Kingdom, to supply aircraft and other such wartime necessities, since Turkey was unlikely to develop industries in the foreseeable future that could meet all its military needs.

Truman launched into intensive consultations with government and congressional leaders. Sensitive to the reactions of Congress, particularly the Senate leadership of the opposition majority party, he carefully encouraged the support of Foreign Relations Committee

Chairman Arthur Vandenberg, whose backing would prove essential to overwhelming Congressional support. President Truman decided to request $400 million – $250 for Greece and $150 for Turkey, and preparations commenced on a presentation to a joint session of Congress that would explain the sense of Truman's position on aid and smooth the way for the requisite legislation. Marshall delegated Acheson to organise the effort, which culminated in President Truman's speech to Congress on 12 March and introduced to history the Truman Doctrine.

In his meeting with Vandenberg Truman presented his case and with his approval Acheson strengthened the case by adding, as given in the latter's memoirs, the following:

> Never have I spoken under such a pressing sense that the issue was up to me alone. No time was left for measured appraisal. In the past eighteen months, I said, Soviet pressure on the Straits, on Iran, and on northern Greece had brought the Balkans to the point where a highly possible Soviet breakthrough might open three continents to Soviet penetration. Like apples in a barrel infected by one rotten one, the corruption of Greece would infect Iran and all to the east. It would also carry infection to Africa through Asia Minor and Egypt, and to Europe through Italy and France, already threatened by the strongest domestic communist parties in Western Europe. The Soviet Union was playing one of the greatest gambles in history at minimal cost. It did not need to win all the possibilities. Even one or two offered immense gains. We and we alone were in a position to break up the play. These were the stakes that British withdrawal from the eastern Mediterranean offered to an eager and ruthless opponent.
>
> A long silence followed. Then Arthur Vandenberg said solemnly, 'Mr. President, if you say that to the Congress and to the country, I will support you and I believe that most of its members will do the same.'[8]

US foreign policy had reached a turning point. The Truman Doctrine made that departure by declaring that wherever aggression – direct or indirect – threatened the peace, US security was involved.[9] Truman's message to Congress and the nation rang with the conviction of American ideals and drew deeply on the American tradition of democracy. It could not fail to inspire:

> I believe . . . that it must be the policy of the United States to support free peoples who are resisting attempted subjugation by

armed minorities or by outside pressures.

I believe that we must assist free peoples to work out their own destinies in their own way.

I believe that our help should be primarily through economic and financial aid which is essential to economic stability and orderly political processes.

Contrasting government that is empowered by the will of the majority with a government forcibly imposed by a few, Truman pleaded the urgency of maintaining the democratic spirit of peoples grown weary in their struggles for freedom and a better life. The forceful simplicity of his words left no mistake about the new role he envisioned for America:

> The seeds of totalitarian regimes . . . are nurtured by misery and want. They spread and grow in the evil soil of poverty and strife. They reach their full growth when the hope of a people for a better life has died.
>
> We must keep that hope alive.
>
> The free peoples of the world look to us for support in maintaining their freedoms.
>
> If we falter in our leadership, we may endanger the peace of the world – and we shall surely endanger the welfare of our own nation.

When he had finished, every member of Congress, with one exception, rose and applauded. Free nations of the world joined in the acclaim, while the communist world lashed out savagely.

As Acheson, Clayton and others testified before the House and Senate Foreign Affairs committees during the following weeks, Greece followed Turkey's request for financial aid with an urgent appeal for financial, economic and military assistance. On 31 March as Acting Secretary of State, Acheson described to Congress the desperate situation caused by the British withdrawal from these countries.[10]

Greece was by far in the worse straits, attempting to resist armed insurrection by guerrillas trained and given refuge in neighbouring countries while its society lay in ruins from the war. Although the situation in Turkey was different, Turkey's economy had also been seriously strained by the continuous mobilisation of its army since the beginning of the war and languished dangerously under the burden of defending the country's sovereignty. It could not continue to carry this burden and proceed with vitally needed economic development. The threat to these countries had a destabilising effect on the countries to the east and south of Turkey, and the economies and morale of the peoples in both the Middle East and Europe would have been profoundly damaged if totalitarian regimes had succeeded in installing themselves in Greece and Turkey.

Acheson faced a barrage of questions, primarily about Greece, and together with others in the administration he addressed these concerns one by one. For example, was not America simply bailing out the British in Greece and Turkey? What was the future role of the United Nations and the World Bank in aiding these countries? Were the royalist regime and conservative government in Greece in fact legitimate? What evidence was there to support Turkey's decision to continue mobilisation of its forces?

Acheson defended the Greek government by pointing out that it had won an election declared fair by 700 foreign observers, and he justified Turkey's continued mobilisation on the basis of Soviet demands for joint defence of the Turkish Straits and for cession of areas in eastern Turkey. Moreover, he emphasised that Greek-Turkish aid would not lead to war and that it did not imply that similar aid would be given to other countries. Indeed, it was a cardinal principle in the carrying out of Greek-Turkish aid that no American be exposed to or participate in conflict. Truman himself denied the possibility that Greek-Turkish aid would draw US forces into combat, and in his memoirs he specified that the new policy was not to include aid to the Middle East generally or to Italy, Germany or France.[11]

Under-Secretary of State for Economic Affairs Will Clayton and Secretary of War Patterson further detailed Greek and Turkish requirements. Although Turkey showed a small favourable balance in international trade and a stable currency, the army – Turkey's main strength – was equipped with obsolete equipment of German design. Turkish resources and industry could neither accomplish the needed replacement of this equipment nor produce such complicated items as anti-aircraft and warning systems. Turkey further needed help and equipment to rehabilitate its port, rail, highway and other communications facilities. According to Secretary Patterson, the proposed aid to Greece and Turkey would not be a step in the direction of war but away from it.

On 3 April Senator Vandenberg, as Chairman of the Committee on Foreign Relations, concluded his report on assistance to Greece and Turkey with the statement that the committee, 'Convinced that the recommendations of the President are in the best interests of world peace, recommends the passage of the bill and urges the Senate to act upon it at the earliest possible time'.[12] Legislation granting combined assistance to both countries, not to exceed $400 million for one year, was enacted on 22 May, Later, Congress would impose the Vandenberg amendment with the reluctant approval of the State Department. This provided that the president would withhold US aid when the United Nations took action or furnished assistance that would make the continuation of US aid unnecessary or undesirable. Under the broad conceptual scope of the Truman Doctrine, however, such a restriction had little force. A new policy direction had been taken, unencumbered by the specifics of aid levels and duration in the case of Greece and Turkey or by a definition of the extent to which similar aid would have to be given to other countries.

THE PRINCIPAL ACTORS

It is interesting to review the principal actors on the American side who participated in the momentous decision of 24 February 1947, that resulted in the Truman Doctrine. First and foremost, of course, was President Harry S. Truman himself, the short, unprepossessing, bespectacled man who on 12 April 1945 succeeded the three and a fraction terms of the presidential colossus, Franklin D. Roosevelt. Truman was born in Lamar, Missouri. After studying in the Kansas City School of Law, he served in combat in France during World War I as a captain of field artillery. After several efforts at business and farming, he entered local politics, which led to a judgeship in 1922 and, in 1934, to the US Senate.

Having achieved recognition as the efficient head of the Senate war effort investigating committee that bore his name, he was Roosevelt's surprise selection for vice-president in his victorious 1944 election and took office on 20 January 1945. His Truman Doctrine decision came just short of two years after he became president.

It would be a mistake to underestimate the importance of President Truman's own cold war attitudes in his decision to come to the aid of Turkey and Greece. In *Ideology and U.S. Foreign Policy*, Michael H. Hunt traces the origins and evolution of Truman's point of view. Truman had served in 'Wilson's War', which he believed had saved Europe from barbarism. He denounced Germany, Italy and Russia as early as 1939 as having a 'code little short of cave-man savagery'. He opposed isolationism, supported the US war effort once the decision was taken and announced early support for a postwar league of nations. By early 1946 Truman said he was 'tired of babying the Soviets' and by 1948 considered them worse than Hitler.[13]

Truman came to see himself as the protector of liberty and freedom. As his cold war attitudes evolved, enhanced by the similar opinions of his most trusted advisers (Dean Acheson, George Marshall, W. Averell Harriman, James Forrestal, George Kennan and Will Clayton), Truman led an administration that characterised Russia as a 'monstrous tyranny whose command of a massive military machine menaced Western civilization' and was bent on world domination. Soviet leaders were visualised as secretive, sinister figures who relied on terror, propaganda and subversion.[14]

It was, therefore, as Hunt highlights, very consistent for Truman, when faced with the Soviet threat against Greece and Turkey, to accept the great responsibility for the United States inherent in the Truman Doctrine. It fulfilled Woodrow Wilson's hopes for collective security and consummated the geopolitical thinking of Truman's postwar advisers. In Truman's ideology Americans had no choice but to throw their weight behind the preservation of freedom against communist totalitarianism. The responsive note he struck in American public opinion would carry the country into the Korean War.

The next most important participant, General George Marshall, undertook his post as secretary of state only the month before the Truman decision. Marshall, who had risen to chief of staff of the army by 1 September 1939 – the day World War II began with the invasion of Poland – and who directed the overall US war effort, brought to his new position a wealth of related experience at the highest level. Despite an ill-fated mission for Truman to China in 1945, he also brought enormous prestige. He was ably assisted by his faithful alter ego during his Pentagon years, Under-Secretary Robert Lovett, New York banker and establishment patrician.

The months following Marshall's appointment as secretary of state were, in many respects, the most momentous in modern diplomatic history. In June 1947, four months after the Truman Doctrine decision, Marshall proposed in a speech at Harvard what would become known as the Marshall Plan, earning a Nobel Peace Prize. Before his retirement, discussions were undertaken that resulted in the signing on 4 April 1949 of the North Atlantic Treaty Organisation. Marshall, the prototype of military leadership, brought to his position the quiet, calm, dignity and firm decisiveness that had characterised his military career.

Marshall refused to consider in-depth matters rising through the decision-making process in the vast departmental bureaucracy, insisting that reports be presented to him on one or two pages. As co-ordinator for aid to Greece and Turkey, I reported (when not through Lovett) directly to him. He held few long meetings to discuss decisions and held to his routine, including an early departure for his home in Leesburg.

On only one occasion did I encounter the commander-in-chief of armies in action. Disappointed with the elimination from my budget of a $5 million roads programme that I considered to be an important part of Turkish aid, I bypassed Lovett (which nettled him) to appeal directly to Marshall. After an impassioned plea I said, 'General, our aid chief in Turkey, Ambassador Wilson, says he badly needs these funds. I would compare this to a request coming from one of your field commanders during the war. I feel we cannot let him down'.

'During the war I had many field commanders', Marshall responded tartly. 'They asked for everything. I usually gave them little. Good day, McGhee.'

One man in the Truman Doctrine decision-making group I greatly admired, the man I had come into the State Department to work with after my discharge from the US Navy, was a fellow Texan, Will (never William) Clayton, from Houston. Before his recruitment into the wartime government by Secretary of Commerce Jesse Jones, Clayton had been the single greatest factor in the world cotton markets. Self-made and self-educated, Clayton was a tall, handsome figure of a man with an unfailing courtesy and extreme modesty. The biographical statement he authorised me to release on request merely said: 'I was born on a cotton farm in Tupelo, Mississippi. I quit school at 15 to become a court stenographer; later I organized with my brother-in-law the Anderson Clayton Company. I came to Washington at the request of the Secretary of Commerce to become head of the Reconstruction Finance Corporation, later became Under Secretary of State for Economic Affairs' (a position created for him, which by chance I would later hold).

My two years with Clayton before leaving to administer Greek-Turkish aid were for me immensely valuable and inspiring. Clayton was dynamic, self-confident, independent in his thinking and better informed on most subjects he discussed than others present. I valued the privilege of seeing him make economic and political decisions on the world level. As his assistant, I followed the early development of Clayton's concern at the rising Soviet threat to the Middle East and his outspoken, valuable contribution toward the crucial decision to come to the aid of Greece and Turkey. Clayton fully understood the economic impact of the war on these two countries, to whom he had for years been selling cotton.

At all times, however, Clayton was loyal and deferential to his close friend and immediate superior, Under-Secretary of State Dean Acheson. They worked together almost inseparably as a team, each representing his own field of competence. Acheson, the product of Groton, Yale and the Harvard Law School, was one of the six 'insiders' of the Eastern Establishment (which included Lovett) described in *The Wise Men* (including also George Kennan, John McCloy, Charles Bohlen and Averell Harriman) by Isaacson and Thomas. Acheson, who would go on to succeed Marshall as secretary of state was, in my judgement, the dominant leader among the other five of 'the Wise Men'. Acheson was a devoted friend to Clayton, and between them there was no rivalry or jealousy. A leading Washington international lawyer, he had received valuable experience in the Treasury Department and as State liaison with Congress.

Acheson also has his downs, particularly over his 'let the dust settle' China policy. He did not 'suffer fools gladly' and made this clear on many occasions. From my viewpoint he was stimulating and inspiring to work for, and loyal to those who served him well. He has, I believe, now been recognised as the outstanding international policy-maker of the postwar period, with a genius that must be comparable to that of Metternich and the other great figures of history for being able to take a complex situation and come up with a strategy for a solution, which he could 'sell' to others.

There were also in these challenging postwar years the professional foreign service officers and junior officials in many agencies of government who had been trained during the war. Typical and outstanding was Loy Henderson, veteran career foreign service officer with both Russian and Middle East experience, who headed up the working group to do the staff work following the 24 February 1947 British *démarche*. Skilled in their trade, perceptive, untiring, not seeking credit, the members of this committee knew by instinct what they had to do and did it. The way was cleared for a decision at the top, which was the right decision.

THE SIGNIFICANCE OF THE TRUMAN DOCTRINE

The Truman Doctrine's pledge to support 'free people who are resisting subjugation by armed minorities or outside pressure' significantly signalled attitudinal shifts that would drastically change US policy. The USSR could no longer be perceived by Truman, and Americans in general, in terms of the wartime alliance. The Soviets had refused, despite their Yalta commitments, to permit the creation of a democratic government in Poland. They encored this by attempting to seize Azerbaijan, supporting the communist-led guerrilla attack on Greece, and threatening Turkey's straits and eastern provinces.

Moreover, the imminent danger of a communist takeover came into sharp focus as US policy-makers came to recognise the grave weakness of postwar Europe as a whole. As Clayton observed while attending a meeting of the European Economic Commission in Geneva, relationships between the farm and urban economies of Western Europe had broken down and there existed critical raw material shortages for which means of payment were not available. Clayton wrote his analysis of the critical situation Europe faced and what the United States should do about it on his return flight from Europe. Since a severe flu attack had forced him to bed on arrival he asked me, when I visited his bedside to brief him and show him important papers, to take the memorandum to Acheson. Although the authorship of the Marshall Plan has been much disputed and was obviously shared among Acheson, Bohlen, Kennan, and Marshall himself, Clayton's memorandum set the case more definitively than any single statement up to that time.

I believe that the doctrine, defined by Acheson and decided by Truman, faithfully represented the consensus of the American people, who were genuinely sympathetic to the plight of the Western allies. Still suffering from the wartime destruction of their economies, Europe faced a life or death struggle against a totalitarian regime that Americans believed had deliberately deceived them. Only America had emerged from the war with a stronger economy; only America was in a position to help.

Truman's was an intuitive, uncomplicated response that to champion the cause of freedom was the right thing to do. Moreover, Dean Acheson – in whom Truman reposed complete confidence – had told him that it was right. The president's trust in Acheson never flagged, as I observed in many later meetings between the two men. On such occasions Acheson would present his brief in a quiet, respectful way. Truman would ask a few general questions – usually very incisive. He never appeared greatly concerned about the expected reaction of the press or public opinion polls, although he was sensitive, in particular, to the reaction of the Senate leadership of the opposition majority party. In the end, after careful deliberation, Truman would conclude the meeting by saying, 'I believe you're right, Dean – you go ahead'.

The Truman Doctrine has, in addition, been associated with what is called the containment policy enunciated by George Kennan in his famous Mr X article, 'The Sources of Soviet Conduct', which appeared in *Foreign Affairs* in 1947. Since according to Kennan the article was written in December 1946, and distributed at that time in an earlier form to Defense Secretary James Forrestal and other high officials, it was in the background of thinking of many of the president's advisers on the eve of the Truman Doctrine decision on 12 March. Whether it had a direct influence on the president himself is unknown. He is reported to have presented a draft which was not accepted. Kennan was not mentioned in Truman's memoirs as being among those he consulted before making his decision on the Truman Doctrine.

Only recently, in *Foreign Affairs* (Spring 1987), Kennan himself denied advocating the universality generally claimed for his containment policy, or that it recommended US military aid or force at any and every point of Soviet pressure. Kennan says[15]

> So when I used the word 'containment' – what I had in mind was not at all the averting of the sort of military threat people talk about today.

Kennan says that he meant a politico-ideological threat.

> . . . What I was trying to say was, 'don't make any unnecessary concessions to these people. Make it clear to them that they are not going to be allowed to establish any dominant influence in Western Europe and in Japan if there is anything we can do to prevent it.'

This is quite different from the Truman Doctrine. Kennan did not consider the USSR, exhausted from the war, the military threat that Truman did. He perceived the Soviet threat only in terms of the bids national parties were making for power in Western Europe and elsewhere. This described Greece but was not relevant in Turkey, where communism had little support and was outlawed. Kennan says that 'in 1946 the military aspect of our relationship to the Soviet

Union hardly seemed to come into question at all' – in fact aid to both Greece and Turkey was principally military.

Kennan was obviously influenced in his later interpretations of his Mr X article by the strong attack against it launched by Walter Lippman, one of the most respected political commentators of his time, writing in the *New York Herald Tribune* in 1947. Agreeing with the danger of our conflict with the Soviet Union, which could not be avoided, ignored, or easily disposed of, he also agreed that the USSR would expand unless confronted by US power, which it must respect.

Lippman lashed out, however, at Kennan's presumed strategic concept (which Kennan later denied) of allowing the Soviets to take the initiative and being willing to contain them at relatively weak points (such as Greece and Turkey, which Truman first chose), rather than concentrating on strong countries, such as those in Western Europe (which Truman got around to in three months and later, militarily, in NATO). Weak countries – and Lippman mentions Greece, Iran, the Arab states and China – cannot, he says, be expected to coalesce.

Lippman also criticised Kennan's optimistic assumptions about an early decline in the power of the USSR, calling the policy of shifts and manoeuvres implicit in Kennan's containment policy more suitable to the Soviet than the US system of government. Lippman was not sure the American people would be willing to pay the huge cost of hit-and-miss containment, assuming that this was what Kennan meant (which Kennan later denied), and that it was the equivalent of the Truman Doctrine (the essence of which Kennan did not advocate in his original article which antedated it, and which he did not mention in his recent article).

Lippman supported US aid to Greece and Turkey; however, he was critical of our failure to discuss this fully with the United Nations before acting. Whether or not Kennan supported the Truman Doctrine at the time – it was just before he became head of the Policy Planning Staff of the State Department – he is not claiming to be its author. Acheson in his memoirs says that Kennan thought the draft of the president's speech to Congress was too strong and might provoke the Soviet Union to aggressive action.

In his memoir of Prime Minister Clement Attlee, Kenneth Harris highlights American irritation at the speed of the British withdrawal: 'Acheson . . . conveyed to them that they should not set such "short and arbitrary deadlines, especially for the withdrawal of their troops." By now, "short and arbitrary deadlines" had become a feature of Attlee's style of government'. Harris states that Attlee 'did not create the Truman Doctrine, but the speed with which he announced Britain's withdrawal from Greece precipitated it'. He further credits this action with forcing US policy-makers to sit up and take notice of the serious postwar problems Western Europe still had to overcome.[16]

Harold Macmillan (British prime minister, 1957–68), in his memoir, *Tides of Fortune*, gives this appraisal of the Truman Doctrine's début:

> All through 1946, British troops overseas were equal in numbers to the American forces, and in spite of all our economic difficulties there was talk of still more rapid American withdrawal in the autumn of 1946. At that time the American mood was that in the event of Russian aggression, Europe should be abandoned, not defended. But in the spring of 1947 – largely as a result of the futile arguments in Moscow – there was a radical change in policy.[17]

According to Ernest Bevin's most recent biographer, Alan Bullock, Foreign Secretary Bevin identified British firmness and the tough US stance manifested in the Truman Doctrine and subsequent Marshall Plan as the reasons why Stalin did not attempt a Middle East takeover.[18]

The two years of the Greek-Turkish Aid Act, Public Law 75, aided to a considerable extent by Tito's rift with Stalin, launched the Truman Doctrine with a great victory. By 1949 fewer than 2000 guerrillas were fighting in Greece, compared with 28 000 two years earlier. The US aid programme helped to defeat the Greek insurgents and assist Turkey in rearming, restoring its economy, and regaining its confidence and stability without the loss of one US soldier.

The Truman Doctrine is rightly credited with leading directly to the promulgation of the Marshall Plan four months later, which cost the United States a bargain $14 billion; to the Berlin airlift, which broke the Soviet blockade of West Berlin; and to the success in July 1949 of the US initiative in creating NATO. Ultimately, the impetus of the Truman Doctrine engendered programmes of military and economic aid to most of the non-communist world. The United States currently supplies such aid at an annual rate of approximately $14 billion and continues to provide substantial military aid to Greece and Turkey.

The Truman Doctrine, nevertheless, has been criticised for compelling the United States to lead the defence of South Korea and

South Vietnam. It is true that we reached only a stalemate in the Korean War and the US forces were withdrawn from South Vietnam after they were militarily defeated. Would Truman have continued his policy over all those years and under such varying circumstances? We will never know. Both he and Acheson denied its permanence. Nevertheless, with the fall of the South Vietnamese government in April 1975, the Truman Doctrine reached the end of its 26-year life.

There was a time when Truman was the subject of derision, as an ex-haberdasher and product of the corrupt St Louis Pendergast Machine. Later he became the cocky, outspoken, 'Give-'Em-Hell Harry', who wrote unpublishable letters to his critics and himself. People had ignored his law degree, his expertise in American history, and also his excellent record as a senator and chairman of the wartime Truman Committee.

In 1982 a poll of historians and political scientists recognised Truman's many accomplishments by ranking him eighth among the 39 presidents evaluated. Indeed, he was a president willing to take on the hard decisions (an attribute typified by his slogan 'The buck stops here'), able to make up his mind and stick with it. He had the courage to fire the popular hero General Douglas MacArthur. The Truman Doctrine, I believe, must be held among his finest trophies, along with the Marshall Plan and creation of NATO to which it led.

4 The Beginnings of Greek-Turkish Aid, 1947–51

THE FIRST STEPS

It was necessary, of course, to determine how the new aid package would be administered. At the request of the president, the State Department took the lead among the executive agencies in co-ordinating the implementation of the policy underlying the Greek-Turkish aid programmes, in drafting the necessary legislation and in preparing its presentation to Congress. The duties of the Washington 'back-stop organization', according to a State Department analysis, 'seem to be primarily those of planning, organizing, and reporting'. For this purpose the department created the Interim Greek-Turkish Assistance Committee on 7 April 1947. Letters were sent to the departments of Treasury, War, Navy, Commerce, Agriculture and Labor, as well as to the Bureau of the Budget, inviting their participation. At the same time, a State Department committee with the same name was created to co-ordinate the activities of the ten departmental units involved with the new initiative.

The Department of State was formally delegated responsibility for the administration of the act by executive order dated 22 May 1947. The testimony of the executive agencies before the Congress and the reports of the House Foreign Affairs and Senate Foreign Relations committees envisaged small but competent advisory missions in both Greece and Turkey. Each would have a chief of mission, who would exercise a large part of the responsibility for the execution of the programme. It was also made clear that the State Department would utilise fully in the execution of the programme the agency or agencies of the government best qualified.

The difficulties and perils of conducting foreign assistance operations within the vast bureaucracy of the government, and with Congress, are well known. In 1946 the new bureaucracy for foreign operations was only beginning to emerge from the remnants of that left from the war. The Greek-Turkish aid programme was the first of the postwar aid programmes, succeeding the war-end United Nations Relief and Works Agency (UNRWA). It was later to be absorbed by the much larger Marshall Plan and Mutual Security Agency.

Little thought had been given during the effort to get approval of Public Law 75 (Greek-Turkish Aid) as to how it would be administered. When this was finally decided in favour of the State Department and myself, there was no precedent to go by. There was, however, a plethora of former participants in the war effort who were eager and ready to take part in the new crusade unleashed by the Truman Doctrine to save Greece and Turkey and other countries threatened by the Soviets. They called me and wrote me by the hundreds. I knew many of them from war days and was able to recruit excellent candidates for the Greek and Turkish aid missions.

Although the State Department had never administered anything like an aid programme, it was naively expected to do this through its normal administrative structure, which had been largely involved in leisurely policy-making and only in administering itself. It was decided, therefore, that a small central administrative staff was required, which was placed inconspicuously in a wing of the department basement.

I and my single purchasing officer, with the assistance of the Army Corps of Engineers, opened negotiations with a consortium of American engineering firms the Corps had selected to rebuild the docks of Piraeus, the harbour for Athens, which had been destroyed by the retiring Nazis. Contracts on the usual Corps cost plus fixed fee basis aggregating several tens of millions of dollars were ready for signature. When I presented the contracts for approval by Under-Secretary Robert Lovett, a leading Wall Street financier who had been a senior partner in Brown Brothers Harriman, he hit the ceiling. 'You mean you want to sign contracts for these amounts in the name of the State Department? The Department has never done anything like this before. We'll be crucified by criticism. No way.'

Feeling that I had committed myself and the Department I spent a sleepless night. Early the next morning I called the chief of the Corps of Engineers who had been helping me and explained my problem. Would he take over the projects and administer them if we would provide the funds? He would. I was off the hook. This increased the cost of the projects and imposed a delay while the Corps formed an Athens District, but the docks were built without scandal.

This being the first of the postwar aid programmes, Congress, after putting up token resistance to appropriating the funds, took little interest in how they would be spent. I kept the appropriate committees informed but found no tendency on their part to interfere with administration. They had not yet discovered, much to the increasing distress of government administrators to this day, how interesting and politically profitable it was to second-guess the government's decisions. I well recall the day, after the Greek guerrillas had blown up several of the bridges we had just built, that I quietly without getting anyone's approval outside of the department sent the Treasury Department a check transferring $50 000 000 from the Greek economic programme to the Defense Department to apply against defeating the guerrillas. No one ever complained or questioned. I concluded that the best way to survive in the Washington bureaucracy was, when you had the authority, to 'lie low'.

Pursuant to this policy the army, navy and air force departments assumed responsibility for the execution of the military aspects of both programmes. The numerous other responsibilities were divided along the following lines: *Department of Agriculture*, the agricultural rehabilitation programme envisaged as part of Greek recovery; *Department of Commerce*, the development of trade and procurement policies; *US Public Health Service*, execution of the Greek public health programme; *Bureau of the Budget*, the development of plans for the reorganisation of the Greek government calculated to increase its effectiveness; *Department of the Treasury* (although primarily interested in the development of financial and monetary policy), through the Federal Bureau of Supply, the procurement of all non-military supplies not purchased through private channels; *Department of Labor*, all matters affecting Greek labour; *Federal Security agency*, Greek social insurance; and the *Public Roads Administration*, road building under the Turkish programme.

When the missions began their work in Greece and Turkey, each of the substantive divisions developed direct lines of communication with their corresponding agencies in Washington. Although policy matters came from the chiefs of mission through embassy and Department of State channels, there was direct interchange at the working level of substantive information, ideas and instructions. Many of the departments had furnished some of their key personnel for the aid missions and maintained a keen interest in their segments of the programme. It was believed that one of the most important elements in the success of these missions was the bringing into play of all the potential contributions of the other executive agencies.

Both the Greek and Turkish aid programmes involved close co-ordination with the three service departments and with the National Military Establishment. Recommendations on important policy decisions were obtained from the secretary of defense, who, when appropriate, was to refer them to the JICs. However, day-to-day operational matters were handled by direct liaison with the minimum of formality. Excellent co-ordination between and with the services was achieved both in Washington and in the field. The size of the military missions, 450 in Greece and 363 in Turkey, at the end of 1948, gives some indication of the complexity of the problem. (Although original estimates had assumed only a small military mission in Turkey, the total number of US personnel, including civilians, was to reach at its peak almost 25 000. The large increase included many maintenance specialists but principally personnel engaged in radio intelligence, for which Turkey was ideally located.)

Important as co-ordination in Washington is in the execution of a foreign programme, co-ordination in the field is more important. This was successfully achieved, I believe, in carring out the programme, and any lapses that occurred served only to highlight the importance of a united effort. Co-ordination between the economic and military aspects of the Greek aid programme, which was vital to the success of the effort since each impinged directly on the other, was originally assured by the fact that the chief of the American Mission for Aid to Greece was responsible for both segments of the programme. Even though the responsibility for the economic side was transferred on 1 July 1948, to the Economic Co-operation Administration, co-ordination of the overall effort was effected in Greece by the US ambassador, who was also chief of the American Mission for Aid to Greece (then largely a military mission). Field co-ordination was effected through daily meetings of the ambassador with his executive committee, which was composed of the director of the Military Mission, the chief of the ECA Mission and the counsellor of embassy.

As special assistant to Under-Secretary for Economic Affairs William Clayton, I had been advising him on the Greek-Turkish aid issue and had become deeply involved, particularly in the government-wide effort to prepare for the presentation to the Appropriations Committee that would follow passage of the enabling legislation. As a result, I was asked to assume the chairmanship of the interim State Department committee. Shortly thereafter, this led to my being named as co-ordinator for aid to Greece and Turkey, a statutory position created when the enabling legislation, Public Law 75, was enacted on 22 May.

The rationale for creating such a position resulted from the personal experience of Secretary Marshall during his China Mission days. He had been in charge in the field but had requested a trusted Washington aide to serve as his channel of communications with the president, government agencies and the Congress. In the current situation the heads of the two missions were in the two countries involved. In Turkey for the two-year duration of the programme was Ambassador Wilson, and in Greece, initially, former Nebraska Governor Dwight Griswold, who was chosen by President Truman for the post. A letter of instruction was sent to Wilson in July, giving him complete authority over the military mission insofar as he wished to exercise it.

As co-ordinator, I was their representative in Washington. I was to fight many battles on their behalf – in large part because the lines of authority between Griswold and Ambassador MacVeagh tended to overlap – until we realised that the two jobs had to be combined, and Ambassador Henry Grady was chosen for the task. Since Grady reported as ambassador through the regional assistant secretary, I had fewer occasions to intervene on his behalf as chief of mission. During the initial phases of planning and co-ordination of the broad policy of Greek-Turkish aid and its shepherding through the congressional process, there had been little time to focus on the details of the programmes, which agencies of government would be involved with each aspect of the programmes, and how suitable personnel would be selected and trained.

All of these problems fell into my lap at once, before I had been able to select my own staff. On my first day as co-ordinator I received 137 telephone calls, of which I could return only a few. As quickly as I could I filled the slots in my own staff of about 20, bringing in Walter Wilds, an experienced administrator who became my deputy, and William Rountree, a very capable and experienced foreign service officer who would later become my deputy in Ankara and go on to assume important ambassadorships.

*   *   *

During the two year duration of Public Law 75 I made regular visits to Greece and Turkey, every several months, to meet with the heads of mission, staff and high officials of the host governments. In Athens I always visited King Paul and Queen Frederika, as well as the Prime Minister. I once accompanied General Van Fleet to view, at a respectful distance, the battle between Greek army and guerrilla forces for the Grammos Mountains. The Greek army won but our elation was destined to be short. The defeated guerrillas, having a sanctuary available in nearby Yugoslavia, wheeled along the border and entered Greece again unexpectedly, inflicting a crushing defeat which represented a major setback to our aid programme. I had, unfortunately, included the claim of victory in my quarterly report to Congress. When it became public coincidentally with the ensuing defeat, Walter Lippman wrote a scathing editorial accusing us of attempting to mislead the public.

During my visits to Turkey I had the opportunity of getting to know Turkish officials who would rise to high positions during the seven years I was to be associated closely with US-Turkish relations. These visits also gave me a 'feel' for the Turks, operating under what was almost a wartime situation, which was to be very helpful to me later. My friendship with Kasim Gülek who would become head of the Republican Peoples Party during my ambassadorship, and with Nuri Birgi, who would rise to the highest Turkish diplomatic posts, date from this period.

* * *

Because of the lack of information regarding Turkey's precise military needs, the State/War/Navy Co-ordinating Committee (SWNCC) prepared to send a small military mission to Turkey.[1] Its goal was to assess the situation on the ground and recommend to the State Department how much of the $400 million authorised for Public Law 75, but not yet appropriated, was required that year by Turkey. It was decided that the mission should work under the authority of the ambassador, since it was feared that the presence of an independent military mission might be construed as interference in Turkish affairs.

The Turkish government had already expressed concern that the United States would try to exercise 'control' in Turkey. In response, US Ambassador Wilson had assured the Turkish government of the limited and co-operative nature of any such control: The US government 'after consultation with Turkey, will determine what military equipment and other aid should be provided to Turkey ... All that will take place on Turkish territory will be 'observing' by US officials as to [the] manner in which Turkey utilizes assistance given'.[2]

The SWNCC group was also empowered to examine the needs of the Turkish armed forces for equipment and supplies and to suggest priorities; to assess the need for a reorganisation of the Turkish armed forces and for staff training by the United States or Great Britain; to make suggestions as to Britain's future role in aid to Turkey and how the two countries could work together if British aid were to continue; and finally, to make recommendations regarding supervision of the use of US aid.

The team arrived in Turkey on 2 May, and on 6 June Ambassador Wilson reported to Washington on its progress.[3] He stressed that the Turkish government and people welcomed US aid wholeheartedly, noting that a failure to produce the aid could be widely misunderstood. The Turks, and Wilson himself, were more convinced than ever that the aid could play an important part in maintaining peace in the Middle East and in strengthening the United Nations. The SWNCC investigations thus far, Wilson said, had revealed 'extensive need' for equipment, supplies, and training – even greater than had been anticipated. He also confirmed that the aid programme under development could have an immediate impact on some urgently needed projects. Aid from the United States, he concluded, in conjunction with economic assistance that Turkey was hoping to obtain from international lending agencies, 'Should be able to carry out successfully the development of the country's economic resources against the background of strengthened national security'.

The following is a summary of the Aid to Turkey agreement signed on 12 July 1947, which provided the basis for carrying out the Turkish aid programme.

Article I. The agreement states that aid is being supplied by the United States at the request of Turkey to strengthen its security forces and maintain economic stability. The aid will further the basic objectives of the UN Charter and strengthen ties of Turkish-American friendship. Turkey will make effective use of such aid as the president of the United States authorizes in accordance with acts of Congress.

Article II. Aid, including needed information and technical assistance, will be furnished as determined by the U.S. chief of mission to Turkey, in consultation with representatives of the Turkish government, financial conditions being decided directly between the two governments. Turkey will furnish full reports, information, and observations concerning use and progress of the aid program.

Article III. To assure full information to the people of Turkey and the United States, representatives of U.S. media will be permitted to observe and report on aid and the Turkish government will report fully on all aspects of the aid program.

Article IV. Both governments will take such measures for the security of articles, services, and information furnished under the aid program as the other judges necessary. Turkey will not transfer title to the foregoing, permit use by anyone not an official Turkish representative, nor use for any purpose other than that intended without U.S. consent [raised in connection with Turkish occupation of North Cyprus].

Article V. Turkey will not use any proceeds from aid to pay on a loan or interest to any other government.

Article VI. Aid furnished will be withdrawn if requested by either government or if the UN Security Council or General Assembly finds that UN action or assistance makes it unnecessary or undesirable [the so-called Vandenberg Amendment].

Wilson's final report, including the recommendations of the SWNCC team, was received by the State Department on 23 July.[4] In essence the report urged that a five-year assistance programme be implemented in order to modernise the armed forces while at the same time reducing their size by two-thirds, at an estimated five-year cost of $500 million. Such a programme, the report stated, would enable Turkey to defend itself against aggression for a period of months until US and British help could arrive on the scene. In its reply on the same date the department dissociated the continuing aid recommendations from the rest of the report.[5]

In his recommendation for a five-year programme, Wilson gave his firsthand impression of Turkish attitudes toward the Soviet Union:

> Few nations in the world are at present as free from communistic influence as Turkey. . . . There is a hatred of Russia and anything savoring of Russia, which has been passed down by the Turks from father to son for generations. The determination of the Turks to resist any communistic influence will be strengthened, as well as the means to accomplish this end, by a continuing five (5) year aid program.[6]

In late September the Turkish government advised the US embassy in Ankara that, for budget reasons, it intended to demobilise a whole class of recruits – reducing the size of the army from 485 000 to 350 000.[7] At the same time, the government requested $100 million in

US aid funds to cover an anticipated deficit in its military budget. Neither the State Department nor the British Foreign Office opposed the force reduction, but Wilson and the department agreed that US aid should be limited to supplying military equipment and that funds should not be allocated for meeting the budget deficit, although US purchase of equipment should help to ease the deficit.

It is interesting to note an aspect of the British view of the situation:

> Russian pressure upon Turkey has been, and will continue to be, conditioned by their estimate of the probable action of other powers, and not by the size of Turkey's armed forces. It follows that Russian intentions towards Turkey will not be affected by a reduction in the strength of the Turkish armed forces, provided the present British and American policy is maintained.[8]

There is no doubt that the Soviet Union was acutely aware of Western assistance to Turkey. As reported by Ambassador Wilson in November, the Soviet minister of armed forces commented to the Turkish ambassador in Moscow that in the past 'he had admired Turkey ... but now Turkey had placed herself under American hegemony, was allowing [the] US Army [to] create bases in Turkey', and was serving as a tool of the United States in that country's 'plans to prepare war against the Soviet Union'.[9]

As noted by a later State Department report, the breakdown of the $100 million furnished to Turkey was as follows:

Ground Force	$48 500 000
Air Force	26 750 000
Naval Force	14 750 000
Arsenal Improvement	5 000 000
Highway Improvement	5 000 000
	$100 000 000

The report stated that these funds had been used largely for modernisation, including the purchase of heavy defensive ordnance, vehicles and other army equipment as well as aircraft and naval supplies. The US aid mission to Turkey under the act in March 1948 comprised 182 personnel, including 51 civilians, 71 Army Group, 34 Air Force Group, and 13 Navy Group. Through programmes conducted by US specialists, the Turks received intensive training in the fields of supply, communications, ordnance, aircraft flight and maintenance, medical care, highway construction and machine operation and maintenance.

As a June 1948 report on the Turkish aid programme indicated,[10] substantial aid cargoes had been delivered by that time to Turkey and training programmes were proceeding apace. At Turkish army service schools the emphasis was placed on the firing, maintenance and transport of all types of the new American aid weapons. Many officers included in the ground force programme had completed training by the end of June, and some were sent to study in the United States. About 64 per cent of the intended air force equipment and about 75 per cent of the scheduled aircraft had also arrived by this time. American instruction in this aid equipment included more than 50 courses. Regarding the naval programme, four US submarines and 11 minor naval vessels had been turned over to the Turkish navy. The highway improvement programme, critical to our military assistance programme, showed marked progress on 127 miles of high priority roadways. As congressional hearings on a renewed aid package unfolded, however, it was clear that the need for assistance continued.

TURKISH CONDITIONS IN 1948

It should also be useful at this point to comment on economic and living conditions within Turkey in 1948. At the time the Greek-Turkish Aid Act had been passed, Turkey had been spending more than 50 per cent of its annual ordinary government revenues on national defence. The need to maintain a large standing force created serious financial and manpower problems. Although there was little inflation, the budgetary drain of Turkey's defence effort had reduced capital available for Turkish agriculture, industry and transport.

This prevented an increase in exports of agricultural products, an industry that in 1948 employed 80 per cent of Turkey's 20 million people. It also did not allow for development of promising exports in coal or light manufactures. Per capita consumption of consumer goods was far below European levels, although the Turkish individual's daily food consumption was adequate at 2500 calories and there was little unemployment in 1947. By late 1947 Turkey had been forced to borrow $40 million from the United States to compensate for the drop in its export surplus and foreign exchange reserves.

Living conditions by 1948 had improved slightly in some ways for the Turkish people. As a result of land reform laws, 50 000 families could be classified as landowners. Industrial workers in large factories alone numbered 300 000; owners of small businesses aggregated about the same number. Opportunities for education at the village level, beyond rote learning, were being increased, as by 1948 25 000 teachers had graduated from Village Institutes largely to teach in village schools. In addition, such goods as sugar, cigarettes, shoes, clothing and a few luxuries were becoming available at the village level as a result of government initiative under Atatürk's etatism.

Yet in many ways the Turks were far from sharing in a European standard of living. In 1948 75 per cent of Turks, 36.6 per cent of whom were officially classed as illiterate (actually, according to some experts, 80 per cent), still lived at the village level, tending their fields in the traditional way, little affected by the modern world. Women, despite Atatürk's efforts to liberate them, had achieved few rights outside the home. In addition, a primitive version of Islam still enforced a general subservience to tradition and authority.

Every Turk, during his two- to four-year term of almost unpaid compulsory military duty, was subjected to a harsh discipline that discouraged initiative. Because of his limited education, he was difficult to train for responsibility in the operation of small units using modern weapons. When I came to Turkey as ambassador in 1952 I discovered that the Gendarmerie, essentially a police force, had a call on the first 40 000 school graduates among those inducted into the Turkish armed forces for each year (approximately 135 000, many of whom had not finished school), the Navy 16 000, and the Air Force 20 000, with the Army taking what was left. This created a great handicap for the Army in training those required as a result of the modernisation of tanks, trucks and electronic communications equipment. Thus although progress was being made, the Turkish people in 1948 had still not made sufficient progress to interface freely with the modern European-American world with which their political leaders had joined them.

THE CONTINUING NEED FOR ASSISTANCE

On 9 January 1948 the Turkish ambassador in Washington expressed concern over the delay in the arrival of US shipments of military equipment to Turkey, noting that this had begun to affect the morale of the Turkish people.[11] At that point the delay had reached 60 days, a delay that the department explained as being the result of the US decision to use Turkish vessels for the shipments. The Department of War advised the State Department that planning had taken more time than anticipated and pledged that the first shipment would be sent in February, even though Turkish ports were not up to maximum capacity.

Later that month, as the president's request for additional foreign assistance funds from the Congress was being prepared, Walter Wilds, as acting co-ordinator for aid to Greece and Turkey in my absence, reported to Under-Secretary of State Lovett on Turkey's needs for a second year.[12] The situation in Turkey had changed little since Public Law 75 was enacted, and the modernisation and strengthening of Turkey's armed forces could not be accomplished without continued funding. The aid was required, he stressed, to bolster the confidence of Turkey's people and discourage the Soviet Union from taking any aggressive action.

Wilds reported that the missions sent to investigate the Turkish situation felt that aid given in 1947 only began to fulfill US security interests. Turkey's military budget had strained the country's economy, reducing government services and economic productivity. Without improvement in the living conditions of Turkey's workers and peasants, Wilds warned, the nation's will to resist aggression would surely be weakened and the way would be opened for communist subversion. Although the Turks were known to be strongly nationalist and ready to defend their sovereignty, he said, they were aware that, without allied support, they were not in a position to resist an all-out Soviet invasion.

Secretary of State George Marshall and I appeared before the Committee on Foreign Relations on 15 March, accompanied by Major General Horace McBride, representing the mission to Turkey, and Major General A. M. Hooper, representing the mission to Greece. In his opening testimony Secretary Marshall said that aid furnished to Greece and Turkey had been of great importance in helping these countries preserve their freedom and independence. He described the desperate economic and military situation still existing in Greece; Turkey was mainly burdened by the large sums required to maintain such a large army in the face of Soviet threats against the Turkish Straits and demands for cession of Turkey's eastern province. He highlighted the urgency of the situation thus:

The hour is far more fateful now than it was one year ago. By intimidation, fraud, and terror, Communist regimes have been imposed upon Hungary [the Soviets' first challenge to the Truman Doctrine was made – just nine days after Public Law 75 was enacted – when the communists seized power in Hungary on 31 May 1947] and Czechoslovakia. Totalitarian control has been tightened in other countries of eastern Europe, and these states have been linked together in a network of alliances. Other European peoples face a similar threat of being drawn against their will into the Communist orbit.[13]

In my prepared remarks I pointed out that all of the $100 million allocated to Turkey from the initial appropriation under Public Law 75 was for military assistance. The special problem of the Turkish programme necessitated a long planning period in order to assure the most efficient use of funds available for increasing the defensive power of the Turkish armed forces. Considerable time had been required to send a military survey group to Turkey to develop a specific list of requirements and to establish a programme based on this list in the light of funds and supply availabilities. The final programme had been completed in December 1947, and procurement had been actively prosecuted since.

Normal procurement lags, superimposed on the rather protracted planning period, had delayed the first important shipments to Turkey in the early months of 1948, and as a result, some of the supplies would not be ready for shipment until after the end of the fiscal year. It was estimated, however, that the bulk would be ready at US ports before the end of July 1948, and if the capacity of Turkish ports and internal transport permitted, as was then believed to be the case, nearly all 1948 programme cargoes would be received in Turkey by the end of September 1948.

At the current rate of commitments virtually all funds in the present programmes for Greece and Turkey would be exhausted by 31 March 1948, although deliveries would continue through the fiscal year. In order to initiate procurement for military requirements during the next fiscal year, it was necessary that funds from the proposed supplementary appropriation be authorised for use at the earliest practicable date. It was for that reason that the State Department had requested the Congress to incorporate in the bill extending Public Law 75 authority for the advance by the Reconstruction Finance Corporation of $50 million to be reimbursed to the corporation after enactment of the related appropriation bill.

Both Greece and Turkey were included in the proposed European Recovery Program then before the Congress, and it was assumed that any additional economic requirements of these countries would be met from that programme. Although the war did not result in destruction of Turkey's production facilities, the cutting off of normal sources of imports and the necessity of maintaining a large standing army had seriously affected the country's domestic economy. Industrial and transportation equipment suffered from disuse and under-maintenance, agricultural production was hampered by the diversion of manpower and animals to the army, and stocks of consumer goods had been drastically reduced. If Turkey was required to spend substantial amounts on military equipment beyond the American aid programme, a gold and dollar drain might be created that would prejudice its participation in the European Recovery Program on a cash basis.

One small but important component of the initial aid programme was $5 million for highway improvement. The Turkish highway system at that time was limited, modern paved roads scarce, and construction and maintenance forces primitive. Since the Turkish aid programme was strictly for military assistance, road building had to be justified on military grounds. This included strategic roads to transport military forces and supplies to key defensive positions – including a highway from the port of Iskenderun to Kars and Erzurum on the eastern Russian front. Roads to Edirne in Thrace could be used to meet an attack from Bulgaria. Of course, road improvement for military purposes met other demanding Turkish needs, including raw materials for industry as well as armament production. Roads also provided a great boost to the development and movement to market of Turkish farm and forestry products.

Five million dollars is a relatively small sum to spend for highways for a large mountainous country such as Turkey. It went, of course, to pay for the foreign exchange costs of highway machinery and salaries of US highway experts. Stone, cement and local labour were furnished by the Turks. To manage the programme, I was able to recruit the deputy director of the US Public Roads Administration. In addition to being an outstanding highway expert, he was a friendly, outgoing individual who admired the Turks and became a Turkish legend.

Soon there appeared all over Turkey highway equipment compounds with strong iron fences and locked gates painted the same distinctive orange colour as the equipment, just as depots are built in the United States. Equipment was on rigid maintenance schedules and protected from theft. Highways appeared for the first time where none had been before. I had the pleasure of making the first trip on the first highway along the south coast of Turkey since Roman times – from Gazipasha to Alanya. One of my greatest disappointments was that, because of the imminent availability of Marshall Plan funds, the $5 million for highways was eliminated from the second year's budget under Public Law 75 aid, after my personal appeal had been turned down by Secretary Marshall. I was concerned that the programme would be interrupted or discontinued by the inevitable delay in setting up new aid administration.

On 22 March 1948, a little less than a year after the first act providing aid to Greece and Turkey, the Committee on Foreign Relations met to consider the appropriation of an additional $275 million (S.2358), strictly for military assistance, for the fiscal year ending 30 June 1949.[14] The $275 million was requested as a single sum, without allocation between the two countries, because the State and Defense Departments believed it was essential, 'if maximum benefits are to be derived from the expenditure, that a complete freedom of transfer of funds from Greece to Turkey, or from Turkey to Greece, as may be required, shall be provided for'. The amount for Greece, however, was tentatively set at $200 million, with Turkey's share to be determined after more information could be obtained on Turkish requirements.

The anticipated division of funds was as follows:

Ground Force	$202 357 363
Air Force	50 642 637
Navy	22 000 000
	$275 000 000

As noted earlier, an additional $50 million was requested to prevent an interruption of aid during the period that new appropriations would be made and come to take effect.

After completing its deliberations on the bill, the committee unanimously voted to recommend it to the Senate for favourable action. The committee apparently agreed with Secretary Marshall's estimation of the threat of totalitarian groups 'whose aggressive aims have thus far been frustrated by the continued existence of a free

Greece and a free Turkey' and 'who are convinced that time will play into their hands' as the West wearied of providing assistance. In its recommendation the committee noted that the goal of preserving Greek and Turkish freedom was only 'half won', and 'as a result of the constantly increasing totalitarian pressure in Europe the need for assistance in 1948 is even more imperative than it was in 1947'.[15]

5 The United States Develops a Middle East Policy, 1948–52

BEGINNINGS

Despite the progress achieved, many in the US government, including me, felt that we should not underestimate the seriousness of the Soviet cold war threat or overestimate our apparent initial successes in containing communism. The conflict was drawing heavily on our resources and on the strength of other threatened nations around the world. There was no room for complacency or relaxation of vigilance. However, it was clear that the Soviet threat was by no means the only problem facing the weak new nations of the Middle East, who were struggling for security and political and economic viability in the face of traditional rivalries.

Iraq, an artificial British creation, and Egypt, had achieved independence from Britain only in the 1920s. After World War II, Lebanon, Jordan and Syria followed suit. These nations were still struggling to overcome the effects of colonialism and were just beginning to think in terms of economic development and social reform. The creation of the new State of Israel in 1948, following a recommendation by the United Nations, drastically changed the political and geographical landscape of the Middle East. Not only did large-scale Jewish immigration take place, but some 800 000 Palestinians became refugees from their homelands as a result of the ensuing war between Jews and Arabs, which was terminated by a military stalemate and an armistice.

In the late 1940s and early 1950s the warnings of the US administration to Middle East states about the Soviet threat it perceived seemed to have little effect. Attempts to persuade Middle Eastern leaders to reverse their trend toward neutralism fell on deaf ears. The response of the newly emerging nations to the impact of the two superpowers on the global political scene was the non-aligned movement. Nasser of Egypt, then the leader of the Arab nations, was a co-founder of the movement, which sought to avoid association

51

with either superpower and to work against political polarisation and bloc rivalries.

Such policy provided no basis for comfort to the United States, although it could, if faithfully carried out, help protect the Middle East against undue Soviet influence. Our early efforts with the Middle Eastern states also, I believe, contributed to this goal. Although some states were from the beginning willing to accept and profit by favours from the Soviet bloc (as was the case in Egypt with the Aswan Dam), no important lasting ties between the Soviet Union and Middle Eastern states seem to have resulted from these contacts except in the case of Syria. Middle Easterners, most of whom are devout followers of Islam, demonstrate more tolerance for states with other religions (except in the case of Israel) than for a country such as the USSR that denies the basis for any religion.

The Soviets have also made themselves a less appealing ally by the nature of their own actions. They have established a reputation as loners in the world, without natural allies, and they show little generosity in their dealings with others. The Soviets face fierce foreign opposition, even within the international communist movement. Realpolitik has brought the Soviets into opportunistic alliances, such as that with Syria, and they have profited in the Middle East from the Arab-Israeli conflict. In general the Soviets have given more military than economic aid to other countries, and then only by sale and when they earned strategic advantage. It has been shown that Soviet imperial interests will always take precedence over other considerations, as in the case of the Soviet invasion of Afghanistan.

Along with the US foreign policy establishment, the US Joint Chiefs of Staff had by 1947 concluded that the security of the Middle East was vital to US security.[1] It became US policy that we should be prepared to make full use of our political, economic and, if necessary, military power to defend this region. Our air force had rights to use the Dhahran air base in Saudi Arabia and Wheelus Field in Libya, but we had no assurances of permanent rights at these bases or elsewhere in the Middle East.

Yet the Mutual Defense Assistance Act of 6 October 1949[2] made no reference to a future extension of military aid to the Middle East, nor did the US-UK Middle East talks held in Washington a month later specifically discuss increased US military responsibility in the region.[3] A conference of US chiefs of mission in Near Eastern countries, held in Istanbul in late November, and over which I presided, made no recommendation for drastic changes in US military policy toward the Middle East.[4] Military preparedness for countries not contiguous to the Soviet bloc countries was simply not part of US cold war strategy. Furthermore, Washington saw no need for security pacts between the United States and the countries of the Middle East, with the exception of Saudi Arabia, with which it was felt the United States should develop special ties.

As the cold war and the apparently growing Soviet threat to the Middle East grew more intense, I sought to modify this policy. To the Joint Chiefs of Staff, who argued that US forces were more needed elsewhere, I countered that even if military aid could not be justified on strategic grounds, it should be extended on the basis of providing these countries with at least their minimum requirements for meeting internal security and self-defence needs. Otherwise, I pointed out, we could not hope to gain their co-operation in combating communist encroachment.

Testifying at a congressional hearing in March 1950, on behalf of the Foreign Assistance Act, I argued that in the context of the cold war the strategic location of the Middle East assumed greater importance than ever before.[5] The political loss of the area in time of peace would be just as disastrous as its loss during a war. The USSR would be immeasurably strengthened and the cold war prolonged if the Middle East were to fall under Soviet influence. The House Foreign Affairs Committee shared my concerns and agreed in a subsequent report that the US strategic interests in the area warranted the proposed expenditures for military and economic assistance.

Saudi Arabia had, even in 1950, shown evidence of possessing the single greatest oil reserve in the world. Because of this fact, its geographical position, and its importance in the Arab world as 'Keeper of the Holy Places', we sought to establish closer relations with the venerable patriarch King Ibn Saud and help alleviate his internal problems as well as his feeling of insecurity *vis-à-vis* the Hashemite family he had deposed, and which he felt had British backing.

I visited the king in March 1950 to assure him that we would fulfill military requirements recommended by General Richard J. O'Keefe in his report submitted to the Joint Chiefs of Staff in January. I also urged the negotiation of a long term agreement for US use of the Saudi Dhahran air base and a US-Saudi Treaty of Friendship, Commerce and Navigation. I assured Ibn Saud he had nothing to fear from the British and that if anyone menaced him aggressively or subversively we would take strong action. My visit helped reinforce the special relationship with the Saudis initiated by President Franklin Delano Roosevelt in 1945, which has continued with varying vicissitudes until today.

A series of US-UK talks were held in 1950 to discuss the situation in the Middle East and how the two allies could co-operate in defence matters.[6] The United States had increasingly been forced to support the British in other parts of the Middle East than Greece and Turkey, as the military value of British treaty rights in Egypt, Iraq and Jordan declined. The British, whose goal was to hold on to these rights for as long as possible, perceived the defence of the Middle East as a means of continuing British influence in the region – a strategy they called 'Inner Defence', centred on the 'Inner Ring' whose locus was Suez. The United States, however, saw Middle East defence as a way to defend the region as a whole from Soviet aggression by bolstering the military strength of Turkey, Iran and Iraq (the 'Outer Ring') in an 'Outer Defence' strategy, with 'Inner Defence' as a backdrop.

These conflicting goals were most evident in the case of Turkey, whose armed forces the British sought to put under their command for the purpose of organising both types of defence. The Turks were aware of and resented the British effort to 'use' them largely to prevent popular opposition against those Arab regimes that supported Britain's 'Inner Defence' treaties. The US goal was to incorporate Turkey's forces into NATO, where they would serve as the Middle Eastern anchor to the defence of Europe and contribute to whatever comparable regional organisation could be created for an 'Outer' and 'Inner' Middle East defence as well.

In September 1950 the British prepared a report suggesting for the first time that small US ground forces might be stationed in Dhahran, in Saudi Arabia and Tripolitania, in Libya, and that a joint US-UK Middle East arms policy might be worked out.[7] The report also stressed that 'to retain the countries of the Middle East in the Western orbit is a vital cold war objective, and the Allies must be prepared to make military sacrifices to that end'.[8]

In a memorandum to Ambassador Philip Jessup, Washington's envoy in these discussions, I pointed out that the British view was contrary to JCS opposition to any moves that might commit US forces to the Middle East in the event of war.[9] I also introduced my own view that the United States should give consideration to stationing forces at the Dhahran air base, if this was acceptable to the Saudis. I argued that even if the force committed was small, it would help to bolster Middle Eastern confidence in the United States. In addition, I said, it would provide reassurances to US oil company representatives in the Persian Gulf area and could assist in denying oil to the enemy in the event of war.

In October 1950, during a high-level US-UK political and military meeting, US Army Chief of Staff General Joseph Collins agreed to consider US participation, with Britain and Egypt, in supporting a military base in Egypt.[10] Consideration was also given at the meeting as to how to support Britain's already waning defence treaty rights in the Middle East. The latter discussion resulted, in September 1951, in the presentation of a new defence concept: the British Middle East Command, based in Cairo with Egyptian representation.[11] However, as will be discussed in detail later, the idea was rebuffed by Egypt's prime minister, and the Egyptian parliament proceeded to abrogate the country's 1936 treaty with the United Kingdom, which included its base rights.[12] The command idea was revived in 1952 under the more attractive name of the Middle East Defence Organisation (MEDO).

The Middle East was throughout the early postwar era rife with rumours of pacts and alliances intended either to improve the area's precarious stability (the perception of the West), or to maintain the influence of the former colonial powers (the Middle East perception). As a result both sides gave careful consideration as to what form these arrangements should take. For example, pursuant to a suggestion by Prime Minister Tsaldaris of Greece in April 1949, the US administration was asked its opinion of a possible Greek-Turkish declaration that would outline the basis for a pact to include the Arab states and to be supported by the United States and the United Kingdom.

The State Department advised the Greeks and Turks that it raised no objection to their making such an announcement but that it did not believe the Arab states would join as long as hostilities with Israel continued. The United States did not wish to encourage the project. The Turkish government also did not believe that such a 'grandiose scheme' could be realised until the Palestine question was resolved, and it feared that such a pact might engender a false sense of security and incur a Soviet reaction against Greece and Turkey.

While the United States continued to view piecemeal aid to

Greece, Turkey and Iran as a necessary response to the Soviet threat in the Middle East, it gave priority to the defence of the countries of the North Atlantic region.

TURKEY SEEKS REASSURANCE AND A NATO ROLE

Progress toward a North Atlantic alliance, however, became a major issue for Turkey, which would continue to press for its inclusion until it succeeded in 1952. The dialogue began in force in early May of 1948, when the Turks expressed concern that the United States might extend guarantees against aggression to the Western European countries in NATO without including Turkey.[13] Such steps, they feared, would give the Soviets the impression that the United States would leave Turkey undefended. The State Department, however, explained that it had made no final decision as to whom it would extend security guarantees (NATO was not established until 24 August 1949) and that Turkey, in the meantime, was profiting from military assistance under Public Law 75.

In August of the same year Secretary of the Air Force Stuart Symington visited Ankara. During his stay he became impressed with the Turks' serious need for reassurance. He reported that he sensed that Turkey was in danger from Russia and that although the Turks would fight in any event, they did not want to face the conflict alone. They desired increased sympathy and understanding from America, as well as assurance that US aid to strengthen their armed forces would continue.[14] On 30 August I requested a decision from the National Security Council as to long-range US interest in the military establishments in Greece and Turkey. I pointed out that our military mission in Ankara had stated that the future aid programmes to Turkey should be integrated with strategic concepts to achieve maximum benefit.[15] On 9 September Turkish Ambassador Feridun Erkin asked for a declaration of US interest in Turkey 'somewhat bolder than in the Greek-Turkish Aid Bills'.

Turkish demands for reassurance, it should be pointed out, coincided with ambiguity in the US administration over whether the military establishments in Greece and Turkey figured in our long-range strategic interests. US policy under the Truman Doctrine had envisaged support for Greece 'to the extent required to achieve internal security' and for limited military assistance to increase 'Turkish confidence in her ability to resist Soviet pressure'. Funding for this assistance was due to run out at the end of the year. Consequently, in October, the State Department urged the Joint Chiefs of Staff to define on strategic grounds whether 'any assistance to those countries in the form of U.S. military equipment and/or advisory personnel is justified'. In its memorandum the department noted: 'There is involved of course the question of priority of such assistance in comparison with other strategic demands, [the] relationship to U.S. policies with respect to the so-called "Western Union" countries, any "Eastern Mediterranean Bloc" which may develop, possible plans for defense of the Persian Gulf oil area, and policies of the United Kingdom'.[16]

In late October my office pointed out to Under-Secretary Lovett that the Turks, throughout the summer and autumn, had requested security assurances from the United States comparable to those given to countries similarly exposed. They preferred that assurance come through participation in a regional group, such as the NATO grouping envisaged by the 'Vandenberg Resolution'.[17] The Greek government was exploring a similar grouping that would also include Egypt. My office was cognisant that a defensive arrangement for Western Europe, articulated in the absence of similar arrangement or declaration for countries equally threatened (such as Turkey), would jeopardise the power of pro-Western leaders in these countries and weaken their resistance to the Soviet Union. Some formula had to be found under which other friendly nations threatened by the Soviet Union would be given public assurance of US interest in their defence.

My suggestion was to consider a proposal already studied by the NSC: a US-UK declaration that an attack on Greece, Turkey or Iran would affect our own security and would bring into effect our obligations to maintain international peace under the UN Charter. Such a declaration should be made, I said, at the same time the United States made any announcement regarding a defence pact with the North Atlantic countries, this statement being in the final stages of preparation.[18] Alternatively, assurances might be given to a regional group, as proposed by Turkey.

On 17 December 1948 I officially recommended $300 million in aid for FY 1950, including $200 million to Greece and $100 million to Turkey.[19] Three weeks later, in early January 1949, Ambassador Averell Harriman, US special representative in Europe for the ECA (Marshall Plan), met with President Inönü and other officials.[20] He later said:

In my brief 24 hours in Ankara I talked with President Inönü, most of the members of the cabinet, and a number of senior government departmental administrators, as well as our people. I have renewed confidence in the determination of the Turks and in their effective use of American aid under our direction. They realize that they must expand their economy to support their army principally in agricul ture and mining and therefore they have reversed their prewar attitude toward foreigners, at least as far as we are concerned. They recognize they need, not only our physical aid, but even more essentially, our technical assistance in developing programs and training their backward people.

Ministers are largely energetic, occidentally trained young men, who understand not only the opportunities of Turkey's undeveloped resources, but the lack of training of their people. We should accept their request for guidance in the development of their program which they are now incapable of doing alone, in the engineering of specific projects and in the development of a training system for the workmen and farmers. Our people explained that from their experience the Turks learn quickly and have an enthusiasm and determination, spurred on by fear of Russian aggression. The Turks feel their security lies primarily in what they do for themselves and in their hope for American assistance and support.

President Inönü stated he believed that war could be avoided if the United States could develop unity among the free countries of Europe, which required determination and maximum effort by each country, and that Turkey would do her part. He emphasized that firm American moral support is of even greater value than material aid.

I left with the feeling that any aid we can afford to give to Turkey would be well used. The situation calls for materially strengthening our ECA mission on the technical side first to help the Turks develop a program. There are many phases which need to be thoroughly analyzed and welded into a balanced program. There are enormous opportunities in the expansion of agriculture requiring machinery for and training of the farmers and need for construction of primary and secondary roads to bring out the products. The mineral and oil potentialities require critical analysis for exploitation. The Turks earnestly plead for our advice. I urge that we supply it as a matter of urgency on the recommendations of Dorr in consultation with the Ambassador and General McBride.[21]

The signing of the North Atlantic Treaty on 4 April 1949, and the unexpected inclusion of Italy, because of its strategic location and internal communist threat, and, at French insistence, the Algerian departments of France, raised an acute problem for Turkey. Foreign Minister Necmeddin Sadak, during a visit to Washington on 12 April, outlined for Secretary Acheson the position in which Turkey found itself as a result.[22] Beginning in March of 1947, Sadak noted, the United States had begun a programme of providing support for Turkish independence and security, including very effective military assistance. Later the Western Union was formed. In the autumn of 1948 conversations between the United States, United Kingdom and Turkish governments took place in which Turkish officials sought to discover where Turkey would fit into security arrangements being contemplated for the North Atlantic area. At the time, Turkey was informed that the arrangement under consideration was strictly aimed at the North Atlantic region. Specifically, Sadak reminded Acheson, Turkey was informed that Italy would not be included.

The inclusion of Italy and French territory in North Africa was a source of consternation for the Turkish government, which had informed its National Assembly of the strictly geographic nature of the intended pact. Thus the change was evidently a source of concern to the Turkish people. The original idea of a North Atlantic pact had been acceptable to Turkish public opinion. It was believed in Turkey, Sadak noted, that a similar arrangement in which Turkey could participate would be made for the Mediterranean countries. Now a Mediterranean country was being included in the 'North Atlantic' security pact, upsetting the plans of the Turkish government and causing deep uneasiness among the Turkish public. This turn of events, Sadak said, inevitably gave the impression that Turkey – the most exposed of all the European countries to Soviet pressures and attacks – was being abandoned and excluded from the thinking of the Western powers regarding security arrangements.

This situation was all the more incomprehensible for Turkey's government and people, Sadak stressed, given the fact that Turkey had made considerable efforts to withstand constant Soviet pressure and threats since the spring of 1945. Since then Turkey had borne the economically difficult burden of maintaining a large armed force, Foreign Minister Sadak reminded Secretary Acheson. With the announcement of the NATO pact, suspicions grew that the United States had altered its strategy regarding Turkey and had ceased to take a strong interest in preserving Turkey's independence and integrity. Soviet propaganda, he added, had not been slow to make the most of this situation. Sadak bluntly asked Acheson how he could explain this situation to the Turkish parliament and people.

Reviewing the many ways in which the United States had provided concrete support for Turkish security, Acheson assured Sadak that President Truman continued to believe in the importance to the United States of Turkey's independence and integrity. Soon after, President Truman wrote to President Inönü and expressed his confidence that Turkey realised that:

> the signing of the North Atlantic Treaty in no wise diminishes the concern felt in the United States for the maintenance of the independence and integrity of Turkey and other free nations outside the Atlantic area; but rather, by strengthening the collective security of the Atlantic Treaty countries, the creation of this pact serves to enhance Turkey's security as well. Through it, the principles first enunciated with respect to Greece and Turkey are further implemented with respect to other freedom-loving peoples of the community of nations.[23]

Acheson later reported that the most difficult question Sadak asked was: 'Will the United States fight if the Russians attack Turkey?' Acheson could say only that Truman never went back on a friend and never over-promised. In the end Acheson reported that Sadak was 'relieved and satisfied that the U.S. was deeply interested in Turkey and not just using the country as a means to an end'. The Turkish government was, however, not fully satisfied and continued to press for a NATO-like security guarantee.

Acheson further explained that Italy had been invited to participate in NATO 'not merely to please that country or France', but because it was a 'logical development'. He observed, 'France had argued that Italy has been the back door into France through which throughout history attacks have been made upon it. It was only after this back door had been closed through the decision to include Italy that France's attitude had changed with reference to her own security problems. . .'.[24]

THE STATE DEPARTMENT DEFINES POLICY ON TURKEY

On 5 May 1949, as these discussions were held, the State Department was preparing a policy statement on Turkey, which elaborated on US security and strategic considerations. The statement began by laying out the broader picture of US interests in the Middle East.[25] 'Our fundamental objective in the eastern Mediterranean and Middle East is to promote peace and stability. This requires that we endeavor to prevent rivalries and conflicts of interest in that area from developing into open hostilities which might eventually lead to a third world war.' Concerning Turkey, the report continued, the administration hoped that a peaceful policy of military and economic assistance would assist that country in preserving its independence and 'maintaining its present role of bulwark against Soviet expansion' in the area. To the extent that Turkey's armed forces were strengthened as a result of US aid, the United States and its allies could rely on Turkey as a base of operations in the event of war and keep the Soviets out of what was viewed as a 'vitally strategic area'.

US military aid, the statement continued, had totalled $106.8 million at the end of January 1949. The aid was appropriated to create a 'more compact and effective' armed force that would permit decreased manpower, enabling soldiers to return to needed economic sectors, and that would increase mobility and firepower to keep the Soviets at bay. The statement noted that Turkish officials had constantly sought further reassurances of US support, and it acknowledged the negative effects within Turkey of the announcement of the final NATO pact. In an attempt to counteract concerns that Turkey was being abandoned, the statement noted that President Truman and Secretary of State Acheson, on several occasions, had publicly declared sustained US interest in protecting Turkey.

The statement also confirmed that Turkey had been under 'severe though intermittent pressure' from the Soviet Union, which desired a pro-Soviet regime in Ankara. The combination of Turkey's natural anti-communism and US and British aid had kept Turkey firmly in the Western camp. Regarding the future of US policy toward Turkey, it was underlined that Turkey's resolve to resist Soviet pressures had been infinitely increased by US aid, without which Turkey might already have been forced to make concessions to the USSR. Thus, US policy was judged to have been successful, especially in that Turkey had assumed a strong westward orientation and anticipated US aid to preserve its independence. As a result, the statement warned, 'We should be especially vigilant not to allow any situation to arise which might weaken Turkey's intention to resist because of doubts of our determination to continue our assistance'.

In order to ensure the continued success of US policy toward

Turkey, the State Department concluded that US military assistance should be continued; the United States should strongly oppose in the UN any diplomatic offensive against Turkey or any attempt to undermine its position in the Turkish Straits; Turkey should be assisted in its efforts to obtain economic aid from international sources; consideration should be given to Turkey's desire to join the NATO pact or to create a similar regional defence arrangement to which Turkey could belong. Finally, the statement urged that the American public be kept aware of Turkey's situation so that it would respond favourably to future requests for aid to the Turkish government.[26]

I AM APPOINTED ASSISTANT SECRETARY

On 8 June 1949 President Truman appointed me to the position of assistant secretary of state for the Near East, South Asia and Africa. This was for me a most welcome post, one that covered an area with 600 000 000 people in 90 political entities, most of which had been colonies before World War II. There were at that time only seven independent countries in the area; today there are almost 70. The area included Greece and Turkey, and since my former position as co-ordinator of aid to Greece and Turkey was not to be filled, I continued to be responsible for aid to both those countries.

As demonstrated by the State Department's policy statement, US defence policy in the Middle East continued to focus on Greece and Turkey. A broader defence policy on behalf of the entire region was not yet a part of our cold war strategy. This strategy was necessarily influenced by the need to balance perceived threat against limited resources. Moreover, a Middle East defence policy was greatly complicated by the desire to enhance relations with both Israel and the Arab nations, currently hostile to each other. For the time being, US military assistance would be limited to such measures as the Mutual Defense Assistance Act of 1949. This act permitted the extension of cash reimbursable military assistance to any nation whose ability to defend itself, or to participate in the area of which it was a part, was important to the United States.

CO-OPERATION WITH THE BRITISH

Because the British had historically played a predominant role in the Middle East, the United States was interested in maintaining close co-operation with London during the postwar period. When I became assistant secretary, I wrote to Michael Wright, my counterpart in the British Foreign Office with whom I had developed close relations starting with our respective responsibilities with the Arab refugee problem in 1949, outlining my thoughts for the future and suggesting that a meeting would be useful as a format for exchanging ideas on key economic and political issues facing the Middle East.[27]

We met in Washington on 14 November 1949, along with a large group of officials from both governments.[28] After our opening remarks, Wright delved into the heart of the matter from the British viewpoint. Britain, he stressed, viewed the Middle East as key to the overall struggle between the West and the Soviet Union. The removal of Western influence from the Middle East, the British feared, would create a vacuum into which the USSR would immediately advance; a move toward communism in the Middle East, he continued, would pave the way for communism in Africa as well and would negatively affect British interests in Asia. In addition, the loss of the Middle East to communism would prejudice the recovery effort in the United Kingdom, depriving the economy of oil and cotton. Wright acknowledged that the United States had to make its own decisions, but he underlined the feeling of British leaders that a strong US presence in the Middle East was highly advantageous to both countries.

I replied that despite the fact that US interests in Africa and Asia were negligible compared with Britain's, and despite our lesser dependence on Middle Eastern oil, Washington was interested in the Middle East because of its importance to Britain and because of its strategic importance. The problem facing US policy-makers, I said, was just how far the United States ought to go in accepting new responsibilities and playing a more active role in the region.

Our thoughts, I told Wright, were that warding off communism was not a sufficient strategy. It was also necessary to help improve living conditions by strengthening economic development and social and political systems. Supporting nationalist movements had thus far proved to be an effective tool against communism, I noted, but did not always result in pro-Western sentiments on the part of nationalists. Nonetheless, I said, the United States believed that helping

Middle Eastern countries to improve their economic situations could lead to increased co-operation with the West. Our dilemma was how far we could go to achieve these objectives.

Wright replied that his country was coming around to the belief that supporting nationalism could work as a tool against communism, although France, Belgium and the Netherlands did not agree. As European colonial interests in the developing world declined, Europeans might have fewer objections to US support for nationalism. But, he stressed, it was not possible to fight nationalists and communists at the same time. Therefore, it was necessary to convert the nationalism of the Middle East into a friendly force.

The discussion then turned to the question of the UN Economic Survey Mission – in particular, the mission's suggestion that a new agency should be established to administer relief and relief works projects. This mission, the so-called 'Clapp Committee' after Gordon Clapp from the Tennessee Valley Authority who headed it, had been launched in 1949 by the United States, United Kingdom, France and Turkey, in an effort to solve the Arab refugee problem. The Foreign Office, Wright said, hoped to see a rapid transition from relief to relief works and did not want the agency to be administered or controlled by the UN Secretariat. The new agency, he said, should not include Slavs and should, if possible, be composed of representatives of the same nationalities on the Economic Survey Mission. The Foreign Office also believed that, insofar as possible, local governments should be made responsible for the execution of the projects, as the new agency should not be responsible for development of the entire Middle East. I told Wright that the United States agreed with these criteria. (There is a more complete discussion of US efforts to assist the Arab refugees in my memoir, *Envoy to the Middle World*, Harper & Row, 1983, pp. 27–32.)

Our talks also covered the issue of Arab unity. According to Wright, Britain believed that one of the reasons for Arab countries' bitterness toward the West was the arbitrary division of territories made by the British and French after World War I, boundaries that the Arabs viewed as artificial. Their efforts toward unity had thus far yielded only the Arab League, whose record was on the whole unsuccessful. Difficulty had been experienced by the league in arriving at agreement on common policies for important issues. The league's policies had been extremely nationalistic and anti-Western, although they had moderated somewhat in recent years.

Wright felt that Arab extremism was likely to grow if the West continued to block efforts toward Arab unity. Since Arabs saw a linkage between political, economic and social change, they viewed any attempt to block political change as a means to prevent social reform and economic development. As Wright and I discovered through our talks, our countries agreed that change by force should be opposed, but both disagreed with the French view that the *status quo* must be maintained at all costs. The United States and Britain would not obstruct political change that was brought about in a peaceful, constitutional manner.

We also agreed that much of the region's instability resulted from a sense of national insecurity among Middle East countries. This raised the issue of a regional defence organisation, by which Turkey, Greece and Egypt had been seeking to remedy the situation. Several key points emerged. A recent Egyptian proposal for an Arab collective security pact, both Wright and I felt, was at too early a stage to be evaluated, and both our countries planned to take a non-committal stance for the time being. The United States opposed a Middle East pact based on the NATO model, which it felt would not, in itself, meet US strategic requirements.

Prudence dictated that US and British military assistance to the Middle East continue along present lines. Both Wright and I felt that bilateral treaties between the United Kingdom and Arab countries were still necessary as a stabilising factor, as was the US airbase at Dhahran. Consideration would be given to extending these treaties to other countries as well and to finding a way for the United States to provide support for existing treaties. We agreed that, because of the situation in Palestine, both our countries had to maintain a balance of favours to Arab countries and to Israel. Because of our limited resources, I said, the US military assistance programme could not be extended at that time to any of the Middle Eastern countries except Greece and Turkey, which we were already supplying. We might, however, add Saudi Arabia at a later date because of its oil and strategic importance.

Overall, the meeting made evident a spirit of co-operation between the United States and the United Kingdom, in which neither country was angling for an advantage and both were dealing with common problems from a common perspective. Happily, this spirit continued during the remaining two years that I served as assistant secretary, and also when James Bowker succeeded Michael Wright. The only strains during this period occurred during the Anglo-Iranian oil crisis and as a result of the Anglo-Egyptian Treaty. Little did we know that six years later a major divergence would occur over the Suez Canal.

THE CHIEFS OF MISSION CONFERENCE ADDRESSES US MIDDLE EAST POLICY

One of the most profitable practices of the Department of State in organising the conduct of US foreign policy is, in my judgement, the holding of regional conferences at which diplomatic and consular representatives can meet with key departmental officials and focus on regional problems. A Middle East Chiefs of Mission Conference was held in Istanbul on 26–29 November 1949; as assistant secretary, I presided.[29]

The conference lasted four days. It did not result in any startling policy recommendations or particularly newsworthy events. Rather, it represented another step forward in the development of a US Middle East policy. Aside from vigorous discussion of the Arab-Israeli conflict and the question of Palestine, the conference came to several conclusions. The basic objectives of US policy in the Middle East must be the maintenance of peace through the development of area economic stability and security; the countries of the region should be encouraged to develop closer ties with the United States and the West and away from the USSR; and every effort should be made to enhance US prestige in the region. To achieve these ends, the United States would have to maintain an active interest in the area within a framework of strict impartiality between the Arab states and Israel.

Those present at the meeting believed that the Soviet Union was attempting through subversion to gain control and influence in the Middle East. Although US policy should be to continue and extend military aid to countries that bordered the USSR, it should offer only economic and technical aid to non-contiguous countries. There was agreement that the refusal in most Middle Eastern countries by older political élites to permit younger, more liberal elements into the political system might result in a growing susceptibility to Soviet propaganda. The United States should attempt to thwart the Soviet technique of playing upon the nationalist feelings of tribal and other minority elements, such as the Kurds, to create unrest.

When the conference closed on 30 November I explained in a press conference that, to traditional US cultural interests in the Middle East, the conference had added increased economic ties and a growing recognition of the area's strategic importance, which had increased US interest in the welfare of its people's and governments. I stressed that we sought no special privileges in the Middle East, although we recognised an obvious community of interests with the countries there.

I also observed that the US diplomats assembled at the meeting agreed with a recent report by the UN Survey Mission to the Middle East, which concluded that economic and social development offered the best hope for regional stability. Since communist propaganda and agitation had not yet become a major problem in the Middle East, I said: 'We see no present need for U.S. association with any regional military or mutual defense pacts to assure greater protection against aggression'. A report on the conference in the Istanbul daily, *Vatan*, on 3 December noted: 'It may be asserted that the shortcomings of the exclusion of the Near and Middle East countries from the Atlantic pact have been eliminated by the steps taken to improve their economic situation and reinforce their resistance'. Obviously, the failure of the conference to recommend a security pact did not go unnoticed.

It can be seen from this meeting that while the United States recognised the communist threat in the Middle East and its own increasing security interests in the area, its approach was one of caution. The limited US defence budget was strained to make good our NATO commitment to save Western Europe, which had top priority. It would be another year before the United States would reach the point of offering a place in NATO to Greece and Turkey and of providing large-scale economic and military aid to other Middle Eastern states. Discussion of the issues of Palestine and relations with Saudi Arabia during the 1949 meeting were only a faint glimmer of what would soon become major questions for US foreign policy. This meeting provided an impetus for assistance to underdeveloped Middle Eastern countries by which the Truman administration hoped to lay a sounder basis for peace and security in this troubled region.

THE UNITED STATES TACKLES REGIONAL INSTABILITY

In 1949 the United States initiated efforts to promote the well-being and political stability of the developing world as a whole, including the Middle East countries, through technical and economic assistance. Social and economic development was recognised as an essential foundation for mutual security. President Truman introduced as a surprise what came to be called The Point Four Program, directed toward this end, in his inauguration address in January 1949. He said: 'Our aim should be to help free the peoples of the world, through their own efforts, to produce more food, more clothing, more materials for housing, and more mechanical power to lighten their burdens'.[30]

For this purpose the United States provided considerable funds in addition to those directed to Greece and Turkey, including $34.5 million for global technical assistance under the 1950 Point Four Act for International Development. Although this was a pitifully small amount for such an ambitious undertaking covering the entire undeveloped world, it represented a start and gave hope for the future. Although not carefully thought out, the small amount asked for made it difficult for the Congress to turn it down. Approximately $45 million by the end of 1951 was also provided on behalf of the Palestine refugees. In addition, $160 million was provided for technical and economic assistance to the Near East for the fiscal year ending in June 1952, under the Mutual Security Appropriation Act. This represented a major step forward, much larger and more significant than Point Four, the first substantial appropriations for general economic and technical assistance in the Middle East area.[31]

Point Four agreements responded to the individual situations of particular countries. The broad scope of problems the United States addressed ranged from financial support for anti-locust and anti-malaria campaigns in Iran,[32] to housing and social welfare programmes in Egypt,[33] to a programme in Libya and Eritrea designed to increase food production and reduce disease.[34] Other Point Four agreements followed with Saudi Arabia, Afghanistan, Israel, Hashemite Jordan and Lebanon.[35]

As made clear by the Truman administration's recommendation to Congress in 1951 for a Mutual Security Program, US concerns for regional security went beyond Greece, Turkey and Iran. The Arab states, although not located on the borders of the Soviet Union, were vulnerable to Soviet pressure nevertheless:

There are increasing evidences of Soviet-inspired subversion in the Arab States. An ideal target for subversion are the nearly a million

Arab refugees from Palestine who are scattered throughout adjoining Arab States and who, though they are being assisted by the United Nations, represent a dissatisfied and homeless group.

Moreover, the Arab States have been deeply disturbed by the conflict in Palestine, and despite the traditional cultural bonds between the Arabs and the West, breaches in mutual understanding and much bitter feeling have come about as a result of the Palestine issue. This bitterness, together with the growing feeling in these states that the West has no interest in their welfare, has accentuated a tendency toward neutralism.

. . . A paramount security objective of the United States and the free world must therefore be to minimize or eliminate this risk – to strive strenuously and immediately to lay firm foundations of economic progress and internal stability.[36]

US AID CONTINUES AS TURKEY CHANGES LEADERSHIP

By March 1950 total military assistance to Turkey under Public Law 75 had reached $236 million. Progress was seen both in equipping and training Turkish armed forces, which had been reduced from 500 000 at the outset of US aid to 300 000. Turkish military requirements for fiscal 1951 were estimated at $45 million, down from $81 million in 1950, but economic aid was increasing. Turkish receipts from the ECA (Marshall Plan) and ERP (European Recovery Program) for FY 1950 were $114 million, with FY 1951 aid estimated at $76 million. These funds were for economic development – to increase the low Turkish living standard and to help compensate for the heavy burden of the defence budget. The department considered that the objectives of US aid to Turkey were being achieved and that aid should be continued.

United States aid has contributed to strengthening the political stability of the country with the result that continued progress is being made in the program of democratization. These factors undoubtedly account in part for the absence of overt or violent Soviet pressure on Turkey during the past year, although Soviet radio and press propaganda, acting to undermine the Turkish government, as well as Turkish-American relations, has continued. The economic burden on Turkey of carrying out the necessary modernization of its military forces is still greater than that country can bear without direct United States military aid in addition to the economic aid extended through ECA. . . . United States aid to that country must be continued.[37]

As early as October 1949 the Turks had explored the possibility of obtaining assistance to improve Turkish air bases. In May of 1950 we agreed to assist in improving the airfields at Byerbakir, Kayseri and Eskisehir, as well as to construct housing at four other bases.

In the meantime important political developments were taking place in Turkey. In free and orderly elections held on 14 May 1950, the Democratic Party won a sweeping surprise victory over the Republican Peoples Party (RPP), the party of Atatürk, which had held power since the inception of the Turkish Republic in 1923. This was considered evidence that Turkey had become a full-fledged democracy. President Inönü had fostered this development, voluntarily turning power over to the opposition. The victory of the Democratic Party was interpreted by the Department of State as reflecting widespread dissatisfaction with economic conditions in Turkey and with the single-party attitude of many Turkish Republican Party leaders. In his letter of congratulations to Turkey's new president, Celal Bayar, President Truman paid tribute to the furtherance of democratic development in Turkey.

The Democratic Party in power largely continued Republican Party policies, seeking to remove the influence of the political left and to co-operate closely with the United States. The two countries continued a common cold war strategy in taking full advantage of Turkish aid and seeking Turkish membership in NATO. When this was finally achieved in February 1952 under Menderes – Inönü acquiesced gracefully. Surprisingly, however, Inönü was opposed to Menderes sending a Turkish brigade to fight in Korea in July 1950. Feroz Ahmed believes this was more because Inönü and the Assembly had not been consulted than because of the decision itself.[38]

The most important policy difference between the two parties in the 1950 elections concerned management of the Turkish economy. Although the RPP had taken steps toward liberalisation, it followed to the end the etatism initiated by Atatürk. When Semseltin Gunalty became prime minister in January 1949, he attempted to counter opposition criticism in light of a very weak economy; he instituted an overall economic plan under a committee to co-ordinate the plans of the various ministries.

In addition to combatting the élitist, one-party image of the RPP, the Menderes government (prodded by the Americans who administered the Marshall Plan) sought respect for private property, protection of individual economic freedom and an enlarged economic role for private enterprise. Etatism was not to be eliminated but to be confined to organising rather than running the state. State enterprise would be limited to public services and other activities monopolistic by nature. The Democratic Party opposed a state monopoly and the bureaucrats who sought to perpetuate it because they profited from it.

Their overwhelming victory gave the Democrats confidence that they had gained a clear mandate for economic change that included use of foreign capital to induce rapid growth in the private sector. The party leaders thought that much of this could be accomplished by revising existing law. In August 1951 they sought to increase foreign capital investment by liberalising the Law to Encourage Private Investment in Turkey. The response, however, was not forthcoming until further liberalisation, including oil exploitation, was added.

The Democrats did not, however, propose any radical changes in foreign policy. Foreign Minister Fuad Köprülü, noting that Turkey had since World War II been oriented to the West, said only that Turkish policy would take 'a more energetic form in that direction'. This it promptly did in sending a brigade to Korea on 18 July and stepping up efforts to gain entry into NATO. In addition, Turkey increased its support for US and UK efforts toward strengthening Middle East defence and was willing to use its influence with other Middle Eastern states to this end.

6 Turkish Entry into NATO: The United States' Role, 1950–51

TURKEY CONTINUES TO PRESS FOR NATO MEMBERSHIP

As Turkish pressure for admission to NATO grew, the matter began receiving greater attention in Washington. On 9 September 1950 the Joint Chiefs of Staff directed a memo to the secretary of defense indicating the reasons behind their disagreement with Turkish inclusion in the pact.

They argued that the timing was not right for Turkish admission and that to bring Turkey into NATO would require considerable revision of the still-new treaty.[1] Turkey's inclusion, the chiefs continued, would raise the broader question of whether NATO should be enlarged to include all of the 'anti-Kremlin peripheral area'. The Joint Chiefs saw the North Atlantic area as the focus of the United States' 'primary military commitment' and felt that including Turkey (as well as Greece) might 'adversely affect' the progress under way in the existing treaty arrangements. The memo suggested that perhaps offering 'associate status' to the two Mediterranean countries might satisfy them while at the same time serving to obtain their co-operation in co-ordinated planning efforts to counter Soviet aggression.

Regarding other proposed arrangements for Greek and Turkish defence and a broader regional defence, the JCS retained confidence in current arrangements. They did not accept the possibility of a new, separate treaty between the United States, Britain and France that would guarantee the integrity of Greece and Turkey, since there would be no supreme authority to make rapid decisions. The formation of a purely regional defence treaty arrangement was also considered inadequate, since most of the countries in the area were militarily weak.

In light of these considerations, the Joint Chiefs recommended the following policies:

(a) The United States [should] now support the granting of

associate status to Turkey and Greece in order that their representatives may participate without delay in coordinating planning; (b) as soon as the defense of the member nations of the North Atlantic Treaty Organization is reasonably assured, the United States [should] consider raising the question of full membership for Turkey and Greece in [NATO]; and (c) serious consideration [should] not be given at this time to granting Iran either consultative or associate member status in [NATO].

The end result of these recommendations would be once again to postpone the persistent and increasingly critical problem of Middle East defence.

Two days after this memorandum was distributed, Ambassador Erkin presented his country's increasingly familiar arguments.[2] He stressed that during the past year Turkish acceptance into NATO had become more urgent. Turks felt they were being treated as second-class members of European society and were growing more and more dissatisfied. Despite US efforts, such as aid through the Truman Doctrine, the perception was growing in Turkey that Washington's interests focused only on Western Europe and that Turkey was being abandoned. Once the Turkish government made it known publicly that a request had been made for admission to NATO, a dangerously bitter mood could emerge should the request be turned down, Erkin warned, reminding State Department officials that the Soviet Union would be quick to capitalise on such a turn of events.

A similar message from President Bayar was being transmitted to the US ambassador in Istanbul. Ambassador Wadsworth sent a telegram to Washington on 12 September, in which he noted that Bayar, although expressing gratitude for US military and economic aid, stated outright that a refusal of Turkey's request to join NATO would be viewed in Istanbul as 'unwillingness to accept us as equal partners in meeting jointly any threat of aggression'.[3] Bayar emphasised to Wadsworth the widespread concern and uncertainty in Turkey provoked by Washington's hesitation to agree to Turkish entry: 'We feel our very future is at stake', Bayar concluded.

For the time being, however, these efforts by Turkey's leaders proved fruitless. On 14 September Secretary of State Acheson proposed the JCS' formula to the North Atlantic Council deputies: no NATO membership for Greece and Turkey, but an invitation to become associate members and participate in planning for defence of the Mediterranean area.[4] The deputies agreed to this formulation, and Acheson so advised Ambassador Erkin on 19 September.[5] Erkin expressed grave disappointment and said the decision would be unsatisfactory to his government and people. Nevertheless, Acheson replied that the subject of Turkish entry must be considered closed for the next 12 to 16 months while NATO built up strength in the North Atlantic. The Turks accepted their limited programmes with good grace.

The same day that Acheson spoke with Erkin, I was holding talks with Anthony Rumbold and Michael Wright of the British Foreign Office.[6] They wondered if participation in planning would be sufficient to counter Turkish disappointment at not being admitted as a full member of NATO, and Wright noted that existing treaty obligations would provoke British intervention in case of an attack on Turkey. I pointed out that the United States was aware that the fall of Turkey would mean the crumbling of the entire Middle East and that we were increasing military aid to Greece, Turkey and Iran by $193 million during the next fiscal year. I stressed our government's opinion that full membership should not be extended until NATO had the military strength to assist Turkey in case of attack.

DISCUSSION OF A MIDDLE EAST DEFENCE BEGINS

In late December a high-level meeting was held in Ankara among Turkish and US military officials to discuss the defence of the Middle East. Present were General Yamut, the Turkish chief of staff, Minister of Defence Robik Ince, and General 'Duke' Arnold, head of the US military mission in Turkey.[7] During the discussions Yamut outlined the contributions that area countries could be expected to make toward regional defences. Yamut felt strongly that the Abadan-Suez areas and Cyprus should be secured as a first and essential move, before their security was threatened. He said that in the event of aggression Turkey planned to fight a delaying action in Turkish Thrace for as long as possible, and when forced to withdraw to the east it would defend the mountains in northern Turkey, fighting successive delaying actions and inflicting maximum casualties.

Yamut pointed out that Turkish forces also posed a threat to any enemy moving south through Iran. If the Russians attacked Turkey from the east, Yamut said, Turkish forces would withdraw to the Iskenderun area, which, he added, needed urgently to be built up as a port for future defensive reasons. Yamut's estimation was that Russia would need to use sizable forces to effect a quick victory over Turkey and that Turkey's ability to fight on its eastern front would require the Soviets to deploy more troops there than would be the case otherwise in order to move south toward the Middle East's oil fields.

With regard to the defence capabilities of other countries of the region, General Yamut noted that Greece, despite its goodwill, did not have the resources to play a key role. He pointed out that the Arab countries would inevitably be drawn into the region's defence. Yamut urged that plans for defence of Iran, Iraq and other countries of the area be made immediately, for if they were not, the area would be a vacuum in defence planning. To make his point, Yamut hypothesised that if Russian troops began moving south into India through Nepal, the USSR would rely heavily on the fuel and motorised transport equipment supplied by the Baku area. To ensure the area's safety, the Soviets might prod the Kurds to seize the Azerbaijan province of Iran to serve as a buffer state to the south of Baku.

Others at the meeting agreed with Yamut that the role of Egypt in Middle East defence must also be carefully considered. Egypt's situation caused considerable anxiety, since it was felt that if left to itself during the Middle East crisis, Egypt would experience turmoil and uprisings. Yamut identified Bengazi and Tripolitania, present-day Libya, as stable countries, whose people were reliable fighters and were friendly toward Turkey. However, Tunisia, Algeria and Sfax (a port in Tunisia), under French control, were considered unreliable allies.

The military men at the meeting agreed that Turkey and Greece must be considered together from the military point of view but, given their separation by the Aegean Sea, they could provide each other little assistance. Neither Greece nor Turkey could halt a concerted attack from Bulgaria on Grecian Thrace. The main Turkish forces, it was agreed, should be concentrated on the Anatolian side of the Turkish Straits.

POLICY FOCUSES ON THE TURKISH STRAITS

Soon after the conclusion of this meeting on 22 January 1951, the State Department issued a policy review paper on the Turkish Straits.[8] The issue was to determine what position the United States should take if the Soviet Union raised questions about the 1936

Montreux Convention governing control of the straits. This was not unlikely, as the Soviets (in 1939, 1940 and 1945) had sought increased rights in the straits, including the establishment of air and naval bases. On several occasions they had raised objections to Turkey's control of the straits and demanded a more active role for themselves. As mentioned earlier, the Montreux Convention gave Turkey full control of the straits, including the right to fortify the area. The convention also guaranteed freedom of passage for merchant vessels during peacetime but gave Turkey the right, if threatened by war, to specify routes. The passage of warships was restricted in peacetime as well as in war. Turkey, Greece, the USSR, Britain and France, Bulgaria, Rumania, Japan and Yugoslavia were all parties to the treaty, but the United States was not.

The previous November the United States had sent a note to the Turkish government in which it proposed several modifications intended to modernise the Montreux Convention. These included a recommendation that the straits be open at all times – including times of war – to merchant vessels of all nations and to warships of the Black Sea powers, within limits to be agreed upon. Britain and Turkey agreed to the suggested changes, but the Soviet Union demanded revisions that would put the straits under the control of all Black Sea powers, with joint Soviet-Turkish defence. Backed by the United States and Britain, Turkey rejected the Soviet demands.

The 22 January policy review concluded that the United States should not initiate any discussion of a revision and should persuade Britain and France also to abstain on this issue. If the USSR once again proposed revisions, the United States should insist that Turkey have a voice in the discussions, it was agreed, and the Soviet proposals should be rejected. Passage through the straits, it was concluded, should be denied to vessels of any country defying the edicts of the United Nations, whose continued role the United States supported.

In the meantime the Turks in April of 1950 had requested the views of the United States on their controlled mining of the Turkish Straits, under the authority given them by the Montreux Convention.[9] They proposed to lay mines near the Black Sea entrance at 20 to 30 fathoms, which could be controlled from a harbour entrance post. Together with Britain, whose advice had also been sought, the United States felt that the laying of such mines would provoke the Soviets, who would then almost assuredly demand revisions of the treaty.

THE KOREAN WAR ERUPTS

A month after the landslide victory of the Democratic Party on 14 May 1950, the Korean War broke out. For the first time communists and Western forces engaged in battle. At the urging of the United States, the UN sent out a general appeal to members to contribute troops. At this time Turkey had received no pledges from the Western powers regarding its own defences, but it showed clearly its own commitment to the West. The Menderes government, without consultation with the opposition party, decided in a cabinet meeting in Yalova to send a brigade of 4500 men to join the US forces in Korea.

Turkey was the first nation, after the United States, to respond to the UN appeal. Menderes stated at the time: 'It is only by way of a decision similar to ours, to be arrived at by other Freedom-loving nations, that acts of aggression can be prevented and world peace can be safeguarded'. Scattered opposition was soon overtaken by pride in the fighting qualities of the Turkish troops, which achieved world-wide recognition. The government's decision was approved in December by an overwhelming majority of the Turkish parliament.

The first Turkish brigade arrived in Korea on 24 October 1950. The next month would witness its greatest triumph. What the Turkish brigade had achieved, during the well-known 'Kunuri' battle, was described by General Walker, then the commander of the Eighth Army:

> The Turkish Brigade, which has been operating with the 2nd U.S. Division, has, by the great courage it has displayed and the delaying actions it fought continuously for 4 days, prevented the defeat and annihilation of the Army. In the 2 days' fighting (from November 28) the strength of the enemy forces in the sector held by the Turkish Brigade was 6 divisions. Despite this, the enemy was unable to penetrate our lines. The Turkish Brigade, together with the 2nd U.S. Division, secured the necessary time to avert the complete encirclement of the whole 8th Army.

On 27 January 1951, in a show of good faith, the Turkish government dispatched fresh troops to replace those who had been fighting under United Nations command in Korea. This was a controversial move in Turkey, given the high losses sustained by Turkish troops and the failure of Turkey to gain entrance into NATO. The Turkish brigade in Korea was replaced three times.

Turkish troops suffered the most casualties of the Korean War after South Korea and the United States, with 706 killed and 2111 wounded, 168 missing and 219 taken prisoner – 66 per cent of the Turkish representation.

The prompt Turkish contribution toward winning the Korean War gave the Menderes government a new and stronger basis for gaining entry into NATO. On 1 August the Foreign Office renewed its request to the US, British and French ambassadors in Ankara and issued a public statement through the *New York Times* that stressed NATO entry as a proof of US interest in Turkish security. No other security arrangement was acceptable. Turkey also earned British support by stating publicly its willingness to take part in Middle East security, which was then being pursued through the Middle East Command concept.

US NATIONAL SECURITY IS RE-EXAMINED

Two weeks later, in February 1951, a second Chiefs of Mission Conference was held in Istanbul, with the participation of US ambassadors and other high-ranking personnel from posts throughout the Middle East, as well as the commander-in-chief of US naval forces in the eastern Atlantic and the Mediterranean and the secretary of the air force. In 1949 JCS opposition to extending US military guarantees to Turkey had been such that no military men had attended the meeting. Under the direction of General Omar Bradley and with the advice of General Joseph Collin, army chief of staff, the JCS had been reluctant to extend a military guarantee to the Middle East until the United States progressed further in fortifying the military strength of NATO. Denmark and Norway had also been cool to the expansion of their security commitment to the volatile Middle East.

The participation of military representatives in 1951 augured well for Greek and Turkish admission to NATO. Whereas in 1949 I had been unable to obtain permission from the State Department to invite Rear Admiral Conolly (commander-in-chief of US naval forces in the eastern Atlantic and Mediterranean) to attend our meeting, both Admiral R.B. (Mick) Carney, who succeeded Conolly, and my old friend, Secretary of the Air Force Thomas Finletter, were with us. During the two years since the last conference the Middle East had become more critical to US national security. Moreover, public and intelligence sources indicated that the time was ripe to gain acceptance for admission of Greece and Turkey to NATO.

It may seem curious to those who have never participated in the policy-making process within the State, Defense and other government departments, but this can at times be made more effective by being abroad. A departmental officer in State can direct a memorandum through channels that will usually eventually arrive at its destination. Often, however, it gets blocked or amended and quite often delayed, particularly if aimed for the Secretary of State or the President.

An ambassador abroad, or a visiting departmental official who can use the embassy telegraph facilities can, if he plays his cards right, get a message on the desk of the Secretary overnight. The very fact of his being abroad adds importance and interest to his message. Emphasis can also be added by marking NIACT, Top Secret, Eyes Only for the Secretary, or Pass to White House. In my Istanbul meeting in February 1931 I had not only a dozen key Middle East ambassadors to back me up, but the Secretary of the Air Force and the Commander of US naval forces in the Eastern Mediterranean. Add to this the place of origin, the ancient city of Istanbul, and the intrinsic interest in the subject. This had all been part of my strategy which culminated in the drafting of my telegram recommending US approval of Greek and Turkish admission to NATO.

As the distinguished Middle East historian Bruce Kuniholm notes on the basis of the department reports (in *The Near East Connection, Greece and Turkey in the Reconstruction and Security of Europe, 1946–1952*), major changes had occurred in the world since October. Progress had been made in NATO and the US FY 1951 defence authorisation had risen to $48.2 billion. This represented a 257 per cent increase over the initial request of $13.5 billion. At the same time that it seemed NATO would gain sufficient strength at an earlier point than had been anticipated, the Middle East situation was deteriorating. I believed that plans there should be based not on Soviet capabilities but on estimates of the effort the Soviets were likely to exert, and on judgements about the extent to which US interests justified commitments that were necessary to deter it. I wrote Acheson that if the West were to make wartime use of Middle East oil, bases and manpower, positive political and military action was required.

Before leaving for Istanbul, I asked for a meeting with the Joint Chiefs of Staff.[10] They received me on 6 February. Present from the

State Department were Dean Rusk, Paul Nitze and others. I had distributed a paper that the chiefs had not had a chance to study fully. My purpose was to see how far they would let me go, in the forthcoming Istanbul meeting, in discussing an increased US contribution to Middle East defence. I pointed out the department's growing concern over the deteriorating political situation in the Middle East. There was a threat that the smaller states in the area, increasingly concerned over their future, might defect, even in peace, if we could not provide the security assurances they wanted.

I made it clear that I did not suggest extending a US military guarantee or relieving the British of their primary responsibility for the area, but rather an insurance to protect our large military investments in Greece and Turkey by providing political stability in depth through a regional approach. Specifically, I asked for limited material assistance, between $5 and $10 million, and small military missions to Syria, Lebanon and Israel to create at least internal security. Responsibility for Egypt, Jordan and Iran would remain with the British. I proposed creating a US-UK co-ordinating mechanism for the Middle East as a whole.

In the course of an extended discussion Admiral Forrest Sherman, representing the navy, and General Joseph Collins for the army, argued against extending our limited military strength further in the Middle East at that time. Sherman wanted to keep the defence of Greece and Turkey separate from the rest of the Middle East. Collins wanted us to concentrate first on the defence of Western Europe and not to relieve the British of their overall responsibility for the Middle East. General Omar Bradley, however, tended toward the position that, since we were already involved in Greece, Turkey and Iran on a large scale, a small diversion to other Middle Eastern countries was justified. He saw it as strictly a cold war problem. He said, 'The more solid we can keep an area the better off we are. I can see great advantages in this'. It 'would tend to increase our influence in depth'.

In the end, however, the chiefs would agree only to a National Security Council (NSC) paper to study the problem from the cold war viewpoint. All agreed, however, that the British should not be involved in military co-ordination with us in Greece and Turkey and that although the United Kingdom was nominally responsible, its capability for defending the rest of the Middle East was very limited. I had pointed out that Britain's regional defence entailed only 11 000 men concentrated on defending Suez. It was on this note that I left, soon after, for the conference in Istanbul.

Again as cited by Kuniholm, on my way to the conference I met with President Bayar. It was a meeting that would be of great significance in acquiring support within the US administration for Turkish inclusion in NATO. I began by telling Bayar that 'Turkey was the first country to which the United States had extended military assistance on any scale after World War II; the military assistance program was a forerunner to military assistance to Western Europe'. The military programme under which Turkey was receiving more military aid than any other country was growing larger and would continue to do so.

I expressed the hope that the United States and Turkey could enter into some kind of security arrangement when NATO had gained sufficient strength. According to Kuniholm, 'this statement . . . was a much more explicit indication of U.S. intentions than any previously given the Turkish Government'. Although the Korean War had diverted resources, I continued, it had also made Turkey more important in the defence of the free world.

Bayar 'dwelled at some length on Turkey's desire for a security guarantee', and he indicated that, in return, Turkey would quickly put 25 divisions under arms. Yet Bayar wondered whether military aid should not be tied to the question of a security guarantee. I promised to present Bayar's deep concern over a security commitment to President Truman and indicated that I would do everything possible to accelerate consideration of the question.

The conference began on 14 February.[11] In my opening remarks I summarised the world background of the meeting and what we should seek to achieve. Our general purpose was not to enter into a detailed review of country problems but rather to re-examine the broad area problems that confronted us. We must gain the co-operation of the states of the area to prevent a world conflict or – if war came – to win it. In the case of countries already co-operating with us, such as Greece and Turkey, we must keep them on our side. We must also create increased strength and long-term stability in the Middle East behind the Greek-Turkish barrier. To these ends we must induce all of the countries of the area to utilise their resources and manpower to the utmost.

I noted that the apparent absence of a positive US security policy for the Middle East had led to an increasing fear of its peoples that we would abandon them in the event of war. This had already created political disaffection. Our failure to halt this trend could well result in the loss of the Middle East, even without open Soviet intervention.

The Kremlin was fully aware that denial of Middle Eastern oil would profoundly affect the economic and strategic power of the West. Conversely, Soviet control of the Middle East and its oil would enormously enhance Soviet power and the Soviet military threat against Western Europe. In retrospect, these remarks can be seen as only the beginning of our concern over Middle Eastern oil, which has assumed much greater importance over the years.

I advised the conference of the recommendations the department had made to the National Security Council backed up my proposals to the JCS. These were directed at strengthening the US contributions to Middle East defence through a substantial increase in Turkey's armed forces, efforts to achieve greater political stability in the Arab states and Israel, and the improvement of local area defence through combined US-UK leadership. Military and economic aid to Greece and Iran would be moderately expanded, and Turkish participation in the defence of Iran would be explored. The department proposed that the United States declare to the world that, because of vital US security interests in the Middle East, we were prepared to assist the states of the area in their defence against aggression.

The department recommended further that the United States and United Kingdom strengthen the forces of both the Arab states and Israel on a one-to-one basis, to promote their stability and pro-Western orientation. It was also recommended that the United States join with Britain in establishing a combined military mission in the Middle East to develop plans for area-wide defence in co-operation with local states. Such a mission, a kind of Middle East security centre, would maintain primary UK-Commonwealth responsibility. I made it clear, however, that the JCS and NSC had not yet approved the department recommendations. I sought the views of the group on those proposals.

The question of Greek and Turkish entry into NATO, because of its extreme sensitivity with the countries themselves, the US Congress, and our NATO allies, was handled with great secrecy and as a separate matter during the week-long meeting. After three days of discussion and debate the conference participants agreed that our basic objectives in the Middle East must continue to be the maintenance of peace and the development of regional stability and security, the enhancement of US prestige, and the orientation of the area to the United States and the Western powers and away from the USSR. Our main goal during the cold war period was to prevent the

USSR from gaining control of any of the Middle East countries by subversion or by other means short of actual war.

In the case of states bordering on the USSR, we should continue large-scale military aid and, where necessary, economic aid, and encourage strong popular resistance to communist aims. In the case of countries not contiguous to the USSR, military preparedness, except that required for internal stability, had not yet achieved a high enough priority among other demands created by the expanding cold war. These countries, for the time being, could be given only the technical and financial assistance required to achieve political and economic stability. The United States should not attempt to negotiate security pacts with the Middle Eastern states. New arms assistance should, for the time being, be given only to Saudi Arabia on a reimbursable basis. We must maintain a policy of active interest within a framework of strict impartiality between the Arab states and Israel. We should encourage direct negotiations between Israel and the Arab states on the Palestine problem but should ourselves refrain from putting forward any specific proposals for settlement, leaving this to be determined by the relative bargaining positions of the parties.

The conference endorsed, in general, the recommendations made by the State Department to the NSC on 10 February, including the initiation of limited arms supplies and military missions on the basis of a co-ordinated US-UK effort. The conference recommended clarification of US and UK military responsibilities for the Middle East as a whole, while agreeing that the United States should retain the leading role in Greece and Turkey and a special position in Saudi Arabia. It was also agreed that the United States should issue a unilateral statement that it would, in co-ordination with the United Kingdom, help strengthen the Middle East states against aggression. The conference also recommended that an effort be made with the British to bring the policy of the Anglo-Iranian Oil Company, in its relations with the Iranian government regarding its oil concession in the country, into conformity with US foreign policy objectives in the Middle East.

A principal topic of discussion during the conference had, of course, been Greek-Turkish admission to NATO. I was thoroughly convinced that this was a vitally needed step to bring the very considerable Greek and Turkish forces, particularly the Turkish army, into the NATO defensive line. Only in this way could the Soviets be prevented from making a military 'end run' around

NATO. Turkey would be NATO's eastern anchor. No longer would the other weak Middle Eastern states be such easy targets for communist subversion or military attack. Their morale, as well as that of Greece and Turkey, would be given a great boost.

Both countries, I said, ardently desired to become full-fledged allies with us in NATO and to gain a guarantee of collective defence and access to more arms. Acheson and Bevin had been giving both countries oral assurances. Their full admission had, however, been delayed by NATO in September 1950. They had been only temporarily appeased by the invitation to become associated with NATO planning. At the end of the meeting, the most important of the conference's recommendations was that we enter into reciprocal security arrangements with Greece and Turkey, preferably through their direct adherence to NATO.

During the Istanbul meeting, after a consensus had been reached among the participants, Admiral Carney and I sent a top-secret telegram to the State Department in which we urged that the departments of State and Defense give renewed attention to Greek-Turkish entry into NATO. We cited not only the well-known arguments but also intelligence that we had received during the meeting to the effect that the Turks, although they sought strongly to join NATO, were becoming discouraged and considering alternative courses of action if their entry was further delayed. We argued that we could make a better agreement with the Turks when they were eager to join than when their interest might be declining, and we pointed out that the Turkish army was larger than that of any current NATO member. I felt confident that the conference had made a valuable, perhaps decisive contribution to the successful conclusion of my long struggle to get Turkey and Greece into NATO.

On the evening of 21 February, when the conference had ended, I held a press conference at which I issued an official statement. I noted that in light of the changed international situation the conference had focused on the security of the countries of the area. We were satisfied with progress made by Greece, Turkey and Iran in building up their security forces and appreciative of the contribution of Greece and Turkey to the UN collective security action in Korea. During the November 1949 conference, emphasis had been placed on economic and social development, I recalled, stressing that these issues were still of great importance. I saw no definite indication of war in the Middle East and refused to be drawn into any discussion of Middle

Eastern pacts. (Although the conference had reached its conclusions on this issue, our government had not.)

On 13 February A.E. Yalman, publisher of *Vatan* and later a close friend, wrote a very perceptive editorial addressed to me and my colleagues. He described the atmosphere of confidence between Turkey and the United States as 'one of the fundamental factors of stability in the midst of the present confused situation'. Turkey was blessed to 'win such a powerful fellow-companion'. He pointed out, however, that there resulted a heavy burden for Turkey, which Turkey would bear not in return for aid or to please us but to fulfill its historic role in the defence of the Middle East. Yalman described this as a national policy. He also assured us that: 'Democracy and freedom have taken root in Turkey in a manner never to be shaken again'.[12]

In late March 1951 Secretary of State Acheson, using my earlier conversation with Bayar together with the conference's recommendation to legitimate reconsideration of a security commitment to Turkey, approached General Marshall on the issue. His memo began the process by which a presidential decision was reached in May. The United States should press immediately for Turkish and Greek admission to NATO as full members.

THE FINAL STEPS ARE TAKEN

At the same time that the Chiefs of Mission Conference was taking place, in February 1951, the United States was preparing a National Intelligence Estimate (NIE) for the purposes of assessing Turkey's will and ability to maintain its alignment with the West and of evaluating the courses of action open to Turkey in the event of war.[13] The NIE had concluded that the Turks would be faithful allies and that they could play an important role in halting any future Soviet military aggression in the region. The estimate agreed with the other earlier assessments that Turkey was firm in its desire to 'resist Soviet expansion', noting that Turkey's efforts to align itself with the United States were a consequence of this commitment. As long as the United States maintained as a fundamental goal the halting of Soviet aggression, Turkey would remain closely allied; if this were to change, Turkey would probably adopt a neutral stance, the analysis concluded.

The NIE went on to hypothesise that if the straits were invaded by Bulgarian forces, the Turks could probably hold them off; in case of a Soviet invasion, Turkey was judged to be sufficiently strong to hold its own for two to three months. With substantial foreign assistance, Turkey could probably hold for some time a redoubt area in southern Turkey against Soviet forces. Moreover, the NIE concluded that Turkey would continue to support Western action under United Nations auspices, as it was doing in Korea at the time. 'The commitment of Turkish troops or provision of Turkish bases, however, would be contingent upon a firm assurance of U.S. armed support in case of attack', the report noted.

If the USSR were to take control of neighbouring countries, through military aggression or subversion, Turkey would resist aggression against itself and remain allied with the United States, although its leaders would probably be obliged to adopt a 'more cautious policy' toward the Soviets, the NIE concluded. Moreover, in case of a general war that did not involve Turkey as a belligerent, the country's leaders would probably do everything compatible with non-belligerent status to facilitate a Western victory.

This National Intelligence Estimate, which found Turkey to be a strong and faithful ally, obviously played an important role in the US decision to encourage the admission of Turkey into NATO. The participation of Carney and Finletter in our Istanbul conference and our telegram gave a powerful impetus to Greek-Turkish membership in NATO. Both countries were pressing for entry publicly. Upon my return to Washington I lobbied strongly for a favourable decision, particularly with General Collins and the other Joint Chiefs. On 15 May the United States made a formal proposal to the United Kingdom and France.

On 4 June Ambassador Erkin asked to see me immediately upon his return from Ankara.[14] The urgency of the meeting came from discussions he had held with President Bayar on the day of his arrival from Washington. Bayar had asked his ambassador to convey to the United States a matter that he considered to be of the utmost importance regarding Turkey's possible involvement with NATO.

The Turkish president had received a letter from Zekeriya Sertel, a man well known in Turkey for his pro-communist sympathies, in which he appealed to Bayar to maintain a policy of neutrality. The letter, Erkin said, had been carefully written so as not to be identifiable with any communist line. Rather, Sertel's approach had been that of the Turkish patriot, arguing that Turkey could not count on its Western allies in case of war and would therefore benefit more from a strictly neutral stance. Bayar feared that this sort of nationalist argument could become very popular within Turkey, seriously eroding support for NATO membership, unless some definite action were taken soon to remove Turkish suspicions regarding US support.

Erkin told me that even a positive decision on the part of NATO regarding Turkey's admission would be greeted with less enthusiasm than would have been the case a year earlier. He attributed this waning enthusiasm to two main factors: the Turks felt little confidence in the strength or determination of the European NATO countries, and Turkish national pride was being wounded by indications that other NATO countries were unwilling to admit Turkey as an equal partner. Erkin expressed hope that a decision on the question of Turkish admission would be forthcoming soon and asked questions aimed at enabling him to assess the views of other NATO countries.

Although the Norwegians, on 29 June, questioned this solution to the Greek-Turkish problem, the United Kingdom gradually changed its position in favour of admission. On 18 July the new British foreign secretary, Herbert Morrison, publicly announced support and so advised the Greek and Turkish governments. The question was placed on the agenda for the meeting of the North Atlantic Council to be held in Ottawa later in July. George Perkins, assistant secretary for European affairs, was put in charge of the overall conference, and I was named one of the senior advisers on the delegation to handle the Greek-Turkish question.

Bringing Greece and Turkey into NATO, however, proved to be more of a problem than we had anticipated, even with US, British and French agreement in advance. We had prepared arguments to meet the expected opposition of the Nordic members, who, having joined NATO to assure protection of the North Atlantic area where they lived, did not want to be drawn into a war in the perilous Middle East. There was much discussion. Denmark was the last to withdraw opposition.

Just at this juncture, with the other nine members waiting in the conference chamber to vote in favour, the United Kingdom and France decided to try to wring national advantage from the decision to which they were already committed. France sought to use its approval as leverage to place a French admiral as chief of a new Mediterranean naval command; the United Kingdom sought to get Turkey, as the price of entry, to agree to place Turkish troops, in time of war, under a British-led Middle East command. The latter proposal, coming when it did, was the dying gasp of an old British proposal the United States had at one time espoused. It had, however, been sharply rejected by the Arabs and Turkey. We told the British that if Turkey would accept willingly, we would raise no objection, but that we would not join in any attempt to coerce Turkey to accept wartime Britain command. I was in touch with the Turks through their representative in Ottawa and, predictably, they held firm against the British proposal.

There remained many hours of thrashing about between the three powers on these two issues, which became increasingly embarrassing *vis-à-vis* the other NATO members, several of whom had been persuaded against their better judgement to support Greek-Turkish entry. Morrison, in a clumsy way, attempted to carry out his bluff. He lectured me and other American delegates as though we were junior staff members of his Foreign Office. Although the US side attempted to be patient, we stood firm and in the end reason prevailed. Secretary Acheson and the British and French foreign ministers went back into the council meeting and the invitation to Greece and Turkey was passed unanimously. I breathed a sigh of relief. The long battle was over.

A protocol admitting Greece and Turkey to NATO was signed by the Council of Deputies during mid-October. Denmark was the last country to sign final acceptance. In a statement to the Foreign Relations Committee of the US Senate on 15 January 1952, when it considered the *Protocol to the North Atlantic Treaty on the Accession of Greece and Turkey*, General of the Army Omar Bradley, chairman of the Joint Chiefs of Staff, remarked:

> From the military viewpoint, it is impossible to overstate the importance of these two countries . . . Greece and Turkey occupy strategic locations along one of the major east-west axes. . . . Located as they are – and allied with the free nations – they serve as powerful deterrents to any aggression directed toward Southern Europe, the Middle East, or North Africa. The successful defense of these areas – any one or all of them – is dependent upon control of the Mediterranean Sea. Greece and Turkey block two avenues to the Mediterranean which an aggressor might endeavor to use should they decide upon a thrust there. . . . Greece . . . . presents a barrier along the overland route from the Balkan States located to her north. Turkey, astride the Bosporus and Dardanelles, guards

the approach by water from the Black Sea to the Mediterranean and to the Suez Canal and Egypt farther south. Turkey, too, flanks the land routes from the North to the strategically important oil fields of the Middle East.

By a vote of 73 to 2, with 21 members not voting, the Senate approved ratification of the protocol on 7 February 1952. The protocol went into effect finally on 15 February 1952. The area of the treaty was extended to include Greece and Turkey. There could no longer be any Soviet 'end run' around NATO. The defence of the Middle East was assured.

During the three years preceding the signing of the protocol admitting Greece and Turkey to NATO, Stalin had allowed relations with Turkey to remain relatively calm. On 3 November 1951, however, before the protocol went into effect in February 1952, and a month before my arrival in Turkey as ambassador and Turkish acceptance of membership in NATO, the Soviets directed a note to the Turkish government protesting participation in NATO. It said in part:

> Under these conditions it is quite obvious that the invitation to Turkey, a country which has no connection whatever with the Atlantic, to join the Atlantic bloc, can signify nothing but an aspiration on the part of the imperialist states to utilize Turkish territory for the establishment on the USSR frontiers of military bases for aggressive purposes.

Turkey delayed in replying and summarily rejected this note, attributing its NATO membership to a sense of insecurity created by Soviet threats. The Turkish reply pointed out that:

> If the Soviet Government were to carry out a sincere self-inspection, she would admit that there exist very genuine reasons for Turkey to feel anxiety about her own security. It should not be forgotten that Turkey has been confronted with demands which threaten her national independence and territorial integrity.

There was another Soviet note on 30 November, but the matter was dropped.

Another step in strengthening our relations with Turkey was made possible on 4 March 1952, when General Dwight D. Eisenhower, in his capacity as NATO commander, made an official visit to Turkey. Eisenhower displayed his usual friendly and engaging personality.

During their talks Eisenhower and President Bayar focused mainly on Turkey's role in NATO.[15] Eisenhower told Bayar that his sword was longer and stronger as a result of Turkey's admission to NATO and that he looked forward to working closely with Turkish military authorities. After his earlier conversations he foresaw no difficulties in Turkey's active involvement in NATO. He added that he hoped to maintain close liaison between NATO headquarters and the Turks, and assured Bayar that he would be particularly mindful of any logistical problems that Turkey might be facing. To that end, Eisenhower said, he would request periodic reports on Turkey's economic situation, in order to avoid putting Turkey's military efforts in jeopardy. Bayar paid a tribute to American economic and military aid to Turkey. As a result of large-scale importation of American tractors, Turkey had for the first time become an exporter of wheat – up to 100 000 tons. The visit was a brief one, but Bayar and Eisenhower got on well and the trip further cemented Turkish relations with NATO and the United States.

7 The United States Helps Turkey Assume its NATO Responsibilities, 1951–55

Turkish entry into NATO was welcomed joyously by the Turks. It represented to them acceptance by the West on a basis of equality, and it presaged a broadening of the scope of Turkey's relations with its new NATO allies, particularly the United States. US military assistance was institutionalised and put on a longer-term basis. We became Turkey's principal arms supplier under NATO, only minor amounts being available from others, principally from Canada and, after 1963, West Germany. Turkey had to adjust to directives from NATO commands in Paris, Naples and Izmir, to participation in joint military exercises, and to NATO command of its troops in time of war. Its 600 000 ground troops were expected to take the brunt of any Soviet attack against NATO's eastern flank, since Turkey could expect little reinforcement in the event of war except by air.

Although Turkey was not committed to action outside the NATO area and might be unwilling to make such a commitment in advance, to this end a network of air bases was already under construction using aid furnished under the Truman Doctrine. The most important was the Incerlik field near Adana, through which, when completed, the US Strategic Command in Omaha would rotate US air units. In 1952 Izmir was selected as the headquarters of NATO's Southeast Command, under an American commander reporting to Admiral Carney in Naples.

From a narrow military base, US-Turkish relations burgeoned in a series of bilateral agreements covering a variety of specialised fields. Turkey expected help from us and its other allies in modernising and developing its backward economy. All this was with the full support of both the Republican Peoples' Party, which had initiated Turkey's move toward NATO, and the Democratic Party in power. Turkey's development of close relations with its new NATO allies opened up a new era for Turkey.

For the first time since its abandonment of empire under Atatürk, Turkey, with US encouragement, was willing to improve its neglected relations with the other Middle East nations. Turkey not only became an important source of guidance to us in our relations with the Middle East but was willing to act as intermediary and to exert influence over its former dominions on our behalf. The trust that Turkey placed in the United States provided opportunities for both nations; however, it raised the continuing problem for us as to how far we should go in furnishing the many forms of assistance Turkey needed in every field if it was to progress toward Western standards.

The problems encountered in the administration of the diverse activities and increasing number of US civil and military personnel in Turkey were alleviated by the Status of Forces Agreement of 1954. This was followed by a drastic increase in US personnel, who by 1970 would number 25 000. They were there to complete not only the supply and training projects stated under Public Law 75 but the follow-on network of airfields, naval bases and support forces for US electronic intelligence bases, US combat and reconnaissance aircraft, and later intermediate-range ballistic missiles (IRBMs). It was only in 1960, when the US U-2 plane based in Incerlik air base was shot down over the USSR that serious concern arose among Turks over the scale of US activities in their country.

My appointment as ambassador to Turkey had come in December 1951, when Ambassador George Wadsworth announced his retirement and President Truman named me as his replacement. (I also succeeded Wadsworth as chief of the US Aid Mission to Turkey.) For me it represented a most interesting challenge; although I regretted leaving my post as assistant secretary, the idea of complementing my Washington experience with a mission of my own was appealing. Given my close involvement with Turkey during the preceding four years, Ankara was a welcome posting. I looked forward to assisting Turkey in its accession to NATO and to doing everything possible to facilitate US assistance in building up Turkey's military contribution to NATO and Middle East defence.

Soon after my arrival I was present in the visitors' balcony of the old Turkish parliament building when the Majlis voted unanimously, with one abstention, to accept the invitation to join NATO. I often wondered what happened to the member who abstained. This vote is more remarkable in light of the fact that 18 US senators had opposed America's entry into NATO, including Robert Taft. I was, of course, jubilant. My tour as ambassador had been given a good start. The Turks were very much aware of my efforts as assistant secretary to help them gain entry into the select organisation that they had coveted so ardently.

I was very fortunate, during my tour of duty in Turkey, to have such an able and loyal staff and such competent and co-operative military colleagues. I had arranged the transfer to Ankara of my deputy William Rountree, the wise and cool foreign service officer who had been with me in Greek-Turkish aid. He was to go on to an assistant secretaryship and important ambassadorships. I had also been able to arrange for my economic officer, Ted Hadruba, and my secretary officer, George Emery, to join my staff. Russell Dorr, a personable and experienced banker, continued his fine work as head of the US economic mission, and General 'Duke' Arnold as military head, a fine officer with great leadership qualities who had developed excellent relations with the Turks. 'Duke' later became commander of US forces in Austria. Although under Public Law 75 I was the titular head of the military mission, holding as ambassador four-star rank, I naturally deferred in military matters to Arnold, in whom I had great confidence.

My first Turkish contact was with President Bayar when I presented my credentials. Already in his late 60s, Bayar was one of Turkey's most respected elder statesmen. He had been a close associate of Atatürk. In 1946, with Inönü's approval, he formed the opposition Democratic party and, with the party's victory in 1950, was elected president. I had been greatly impressed by Bayar's sincerity, friendliness and sound judgement during my meetings with him during earlier visits and was to enjoy a close association with him. Bayar was a neighbour in Cankaya, a suburb of Ankara, where his official residence was next to the embassy residence. There were friendly greetings as he walked in his garden. He often spoke, through his interpreter, with our children when they were playing nearby.

On one very pleasant occasion which provided an interesting insight into his personal life, he invited my wife and myself to join him for a convivial weekend cruise on a private yacht on the Marmora Sea. We were the only foreign guests. Present also were his daughter, Prime Minister Adnan Menderes, and President of the Grand National Assembly Refik Koraltan, with whom I had some interesting conversations. Our host for the cruise was a substantial political supporter of the president, who was hospitable and provided pleasant amenities, drawing the group together at drink and meal times. I particularly enjoyed the opportunity for informal talks with Menderes, who spoke excellent English. On one occasion when the boat was anchored Menderes, who was in a bathing suit, plunged into the sea without any announcement and swam with a strong breast stroke the considerable distance in a choppy sea to a nearby deserted beach. Feeling challenged, after appraising the distance a little apprehensively, I followed him and we continued our conversation lying comfortably on the sand.

In later life I saw Bayar often during my annual visits to Turkey. I attended his 100th birthday celebration in Istanbul, where our conversation was interpreted by the same able foreign office aide, Fikret Belbes, who had interpreted for us in the 1950s.

Soon after my arrival I also called on Menderes, for whom I had developed a high regard over the past few years. A wealthy landowner from western Turkey, Menderes had attended an American college and had served in the Grand National Assembly under Atatürk before joining with Bayar in founding the Democratic Party. At 51, Menderes was a handsome, articulate and confident leader; unfortunately, he was to become a victim of the revolutionary colonels during the 1960 coup.

Finally, I made a brief courtesy call on the official who would be my normal point of contact as ambassador. Foreign Minister Mehmet Fuad Köprülü, then 61, had begun his career as a distinguished intellectual, serving as a professor of history and author at the School of Political Science and the Academy of Fine Arts in Istanbul. Turning to politics in 1935, Köprülü was elected to the National Assembly; he was a founding member of the Democratic Party and had come to the Foreign Ministry following the 1950 election.

A short, wiry man with graying hair and a friendly smile, Köprülü was still very much the scholar, possessing a keen mind and articulate views on any important issue touching upon Turkish or Middle Eastern history and politics. I had particularly looked forward to doing diplomatic business with Köprülü and learning from his vast store of knowledge of the region. During our meetings I inconspicuously took copious notes, which permitted me to reconstruct our conversations nearly verbatim.

During a series of meetings with high-ranking Turkish officials in January and February 1952, soon after I arrived in Ankara, I communicated to the Turkish government the perspective from Washington regarding both Turkey and Middle East defence, and solicited their views. As the substance of these meetings characterises the tenor of US-Turkish relations during this period, I present here a detailed account of our conversations.

I began my first official meeting with Köprülü on 8 January 1952, by expressing my hope that we could develop close and early consultation between our two governments and co-ordinate our actions regarding major world events, particularly in the Middle East.[1] I mentioned the usefulness of the consultations our governments had held on Iran, the Middle East Command and Korea, telling Köprülü that I hoped this type of consultation could take place on a regular basis. He expressed agreement and said he would welcome a more consistent exchange of information and analysis between the United States and Turkey.

I also suggested that we broaden our co-operation beyond the field of security. I noted that the broader the base of our relations, the better the chance that any unforeseen difficulties that might arise could be overcome. To this end, I suggested cultural and information exchanges and a closer working relationship between the large number of American personnel working in Turkey and the Turkish government, institutions and people. Again, the foreign minister expressed full agreement with my formulations.

The discussion then turned to a review of the events surrounding the recent NATO decision to extend an invitation to Turkey. I explained to Köprülü the reason behind the apparent US hesitation in reaching this decision – largely, our feeling that we had to give substance to existing military commitments in Western Europe before making new commitments. I also told him that a strong recommendation for Turkey's entry into NATO had gone forward from our recent Istanbul Chiefs of Mission Conference and that the subsequent delay merely reflected the length of time required to clear such important matters at all levels of our government and with our NATO allies.

I assured Köprülü that the upcoming ratification vote in the US Senate would be favourable. I reiterated that US policy, as well as that of other NATO members, was that Turkey should be admitted into NATO without any qualifications whatsoever and without any relationship to the proposed Middle East Command. I also added that I was pleased that the British had made their position in this respect very clear to the Turks and had agreed that Turkey should come under the NATO commander, General Dwight Eisenhower. These events, I said, should pave the way for better relations between Turkey and Britain. This was important to the entire Western alliance, since close co-operation was required in an organisation such as NATO.

The foreign minister expressed considerable resentment of the earlier British manoeuvres, which he felt were tied to considerations of prestige. Köprülü went on to say that, for Turkey, membership of NATO was tied to two fundamental points of principle: first, that all technical military requirements be met and second, that decisions made should be for the general good, not for the benefit of any single country. I told him that I agreed with these points and was sure the Standing Group of NATO did as well. Neither he nor I mentioned specifically the matter of a British commander over Turkish forces in time of war. It was a prickly issue.

I noted, however, that Turkey's entry into NATO would involve for the first time co-ordination of certain aspects of Turkish military efforts with the other NATO members. General Eisenhower and his successors and various NATO bodies would, of course, be making decisions on these matters in the months and years to come. Within this framework, nonetheless, I told Köprülü, the United States would continue to allocate US military equipment to Turkey as it had during the past few years. Consistent with the United States' responsibilities to NATO and taking into account its recommendations, America would see that the volume of military aid and the effectiveness of its training programmes in Turkey would not be diminished.

This point seemed to trouble Köprülü, who sensed a potential conflict between Turkey's NATO membership and its ability to take full advantage of its direct relations with the United States. I suggested that it was impossible to foresee such a problem at present and assured him that our administration was, in fact, requesting an increase in military aid to Turkey for the next fiscal year. I was sure that other NATO members would recognise the value of this aid to Turkey and approve.

We then went on to discuss the issue of the Middle East Command (MEC), originally a British concept that had been developed jointly with the United States, as I have already mentioned. I assured Köprülü that the United States had always viewed this as an issue quite separate from Turkey's admission to NATO. The decision to present the idea of the Middle East Command had come late, having been delayed until Turkey had been admitted to NATO. Now, unfortunately, it was too late to address adequately the problem of Egypt, which created one of the principal situations the command had been formulated to deal with. I explained that in spite of the setback of Egypt's refusal to join, which we had anticipated, we still considered it highly important that the four powers (the United States, Britain, Turkey and France) proceed to set up the command.

This was required to make clear to all our determination to organise a defence for the Middle East, just as failure to do so would be interpreted as a sign of weakness by the other states of the area. I expressed to Köprülü my belief that, although the details of the plan were still uncharted, its mere existence would have a positive influence in the Middle East. The United States was gratified by Turkey's expression of willingness to participate in the command. We hoped to have a headquarters established by April. Although we recognised that Turkey's greatest contribution toward Middle East defence was to build a strong Turkey under NATO, we nonetheless hoped that Turkey would make a direct contribution to the specific military objective of the Middle East Command in order to assure the defence of the region as a whole.

Because of its geographical position, Turkey naturally had a keen interest in the defence of the Middle East and the organisation of the command, Köprülü responded, especially since the Turks were aware that their armed forces were the strongest in the area. He added, with some feeling, that he believed that a number of mistakes had been made in the launching of the Middle East Command, especially along 'psychological' lines.

First, he thought, it had been a mistake to introduce the Suez resolution against Egypt in the UN Secretary Council. Köprülü told me that the Egyptian foreign minister had been scheduled to visit Turkey and that if the resolution had not been introduced and Turkey had not felt compelled to vote for it, the visit would not have been cancelled and the Turks would have been able to propose to the foreign minister something similar to the Middle East Command. He also stated that it would have been better from a psychological standpoint if things could have been arranged so that the countries of the Middle East requested the outside powers to organise the command, rather than the other way around.

Of course, I pointed out and Köprülü agreed, it would have been impossible to meet the psychological needs of all the countries of the Middle East. In approaching complicated and delicate matters such as defence, there would inevitably be objections from one country or another to some aspect of any plan that was devised. The only way to achieve progress, I suggested, was to develop the best plan possible and press ahead, knowing that there would be objections.

Acknowledging the truth of this appraisal, Köprülü nonetheless pointed out that statements by Winston Churchill and other British leaders had served to confuse the countries of the area about the real purposes of the Middle East Command. Its only chance of acceptance, he said, lay in proving it was what it purported to be – and not a subterfuge for covering up the defence of British interests in the Middle East. Before deciding what contribution to make to the command, Köprülü said, Turkey needed to know the answers to a number of basic questions, such as the obligations of the members and the geographical area to be covered. He was also curious about the planned location of the headquarters.

I had no firm answers to his questions, but I assured Köprülü that a great deal of thought had been given to these matters. The final decisions would have to be made in consultation with Turkey and the other nations involved. Given present circumstances, I said, it appeared that Egypt could not be the headquarters. As to the juridical basis for the MEC, it could not be expected to be as firm as that of NATO, since the two situations were quite different. But, I pointed out, this would not prevent the interested states from taking co-operative action. In any case, I agreed with Köprülü that the parameters of the command should be defined as quickly as possible. The United States, as well as Turkey and other potential members, could not make decisions regarding commitment of forces until such matters were finalised.

My talk with Turkey's foreign minister also covered the evolution of thinking regarding US aid programmes. I explained to him that the new emphasis in the US Mutual Security Program was on military, rather than economic aid. Congress had placed importance on short-term and military projects, making it more difficult to justify such long-term projects as dams, whose impact on the economy could not be felt for several years. I mentioned to Köprülü that I was aware of talk in Turkey that the level of US economic aid was unsatisfactorily low, and I suggested that he and others in the government might point out to critics that Turkey was the only European country to receive large-scale development assistance, since Marshall Plan aid had been conceived to help economies devastated by war. I also assured him that the United States would provide Turkey with as much aid as possible to help achieve our common objectives.

The foreign minister assured me that the criticisms being made were not shared by the government; in fact, he said, they were made largely to embarrass the government. He believed that security assistance was extremely useful and that although Turkey had many short-term projects that required outside help, the shift in Washington would not be negative for Turkey. He requested, in this regard, that I return the following week, in order to discuss economic questions in more detail. In particular, he suggested we focus on how to encourage American capital to invest in Turkey, the policy and organisational aspects of the new Mutual Security Program and how to make current US economic aid more effective.

When I returned on 1 February, Köprülü introduced me to Fatin Zorlu, secretary general of Turkey's Foreign Office, who worked closely with the Organisation for International Economic Co-operation.[2] Zorlu, member of a distinguished Turkish family, was tall, handsome, confident and articulate, although he was inclined to be rather arrogant in his dealings with subordinates – and Americans of lesser rank. He did not deserve the harsh treatment accorded him later in the 'Colonels' Revolution'.

I began the meeting by explaining that I understood that although unfettered free enterprise worked successfully in the United States, there were countries, and stages within a country's development, in which state initiative might be useful or even necessary. I was aware of Atatürk's initial use of etatism in the development of the Turkish economy. Since his original efforts to solicit private investment had failed, it could be said that he had no alternative. Turkey's Democratic Party had come to power on a platform of encouraging free enterprise, and I told the two Turkish leaders that the progress that had been achieved thus far was heartening. I felt that Turkey, with its great resources of arable land, minerals and its energetic people, stood a good chance of developing a free enterprise market stystem in which the country as a whole could prosper. However, certain steps needed to be taken.

Along with resources and people, another important variable was the extent to which the government created a framework for economic freedom. In the past the Turks had not been great traders or industrialists but, I noted, this trend seemed to be changing in recent years. I told Köprülü and Zorlu that in order to encourage American investment in Turkey, the government should demonstrate the importance it attached to success in buisness, perhaps by passing legislation further liberalising the business environment or by bringing successful businessmen into key government positions.

Another requisite, of course, was the availability of capital – and I told the two men that this was one area in which the United States might be able to play a role. With the exception of the Soviet Union, I observed, no country had developed a large industrial plant without the assistance of foreign, private capital. Although loans from governments could play a certain role, they were never sufficient to meet the needs of industrialising countries. Since the war, I explained, private American capital had mainly been available from companies that invested their surplus funds in foreign ventures in their own field. However, an advantageous pattern of partnership between American companies and local business groups had developed that brought capital, management skills and technology into the country.

The United States, I pointed out, was itself the strongest competitor for American capital, since it was still developing, and great profits could be made at home without considering foreign investment. Nonetheless, I noted that several American firms had recently invested in Turkey and others had expressed an interest, such as the Anderson and Clayton Company, a leading cotton processing and sales organisation. As US firms began to enter Turkey, if their experience was positive, other firms would follow.

Köprülü, who had at various times during the conversation indicated approval of my remarks, spoke up at this point to say that the Democratic Party was in agreement with the analysis I had laid out, and was doing everything in its power to free up the business environment, including a law passed to encourage foreign investment. There was virtually no competition from the government in the form of state firms, although he acknowledged that some in government, particularly in the government investment banks, still held on to notions of etatism. He asked what else I thought could be done to encourage foreign investment.

A number of measures could be taken by Turkey that had proved successful in other countries, I suggested, giving the following examples: the United States and Turkey could conclude a Treaty of Friendship, Commerce, and Navigation; exchange visits of leading industrialists could be arranged on invitation by the two governments; a joint commission of Turkish and American industrialists could be formed; a publicity effort could be made in the US media. The Turkish ambassador in Washington could make speeches on business in Turkey and I could make similar speeches or write articles about opportunities there. Köprülü agreed that such steps should be taken. Later considerable progress was made by US firms in Turkey in the pharmaceutical and electric light bulb industries and in petroleum production, refining and marketing.

During the same conversation I once again stressed to the Turkish officials the important changes that were occurring in Washington regarding the balance of military and economic aid; specifically, that economic aid was, in effect, to be in support of military objectives. I had heard that discussion was under way within the Turkish government regarding the possible creation of an organisation that could provide overall co-ordination between agencies dealing with military and economic aid. Acknowledging that this was an internal matter, I nonetheless suggested to Köprülü and Zorlu that such a body could play a valuable role in providing a balance between the various aspects of Turkey's development programmes. Moreover, it could be important when Turkey finally joined NATO, where a high level of co-ordination of military and economic matters would be required in order to co-ordinate with the various NATO organs. Co-ordination with Washington, I noted, could also be facilitated by such a body.

On 9 February I was requested to meet again with the foreign minister. We were to discuss Iran and Turkey's entry into NATO.[3] When I arrived in his office, Köprülü informed me that Prime Minister Menderes would shortly join us. This turn of events both surprised and pleased me; since Menderes was the unquestionable head of his government, the meeting would provide me with a direct line into government thinking at the highest level. As it turned out, three such meetings were held on three successive days. Naturally, we covered a great deal of ground.

Köprülü began by informing me that during his farewell meeting with the Egyptian ambassador he had stressed many of the points made during our recent talks. He had assured the Egyptian official that Turkey's participation in the Middle East Command would serve to guarantee that it would not be utilised as an instrument of imperialism. He told me further that the Egyptian ambassador had been optimistic that discussions over the command could commence at an early date between his country and Great Britain. I told Köprülü that it was my hope that they could first discuss the Sudan, the British treaty and British forces in Egypt. At an appropriate stage the other three members of the command could join in the discussions.

Köprülü told me that Menderes was particularly interested in the economic questions that we and Zorlu had discussed, as well as matters pertaining to NATO. When Menderes arrived, I began by expressing pleasure that four more countries had recently ratified Turkey's entry into NATO, and that the US Senate was scheduled to do so that very day. I offered to discuss briefly the status of military questions arising out of Turkish and Greek entry, the agenda for the upcoming Lisbon NATO meeting – which the two countries would almost certainly be attending – and whatever else they wished to discuss.

My understanding of the way NATO's organisation was shaping up, I told them, was that Turkey and Greece would be admitted into NATO forces under an American, Admiral Carney, Commander-in-Chief, Allied Forces Southern Europe (CINCSOUTH). Turkey's land forces would be under a Turkish general, while Greece's would be under a Greek general, both of whom would report to Admiral Carney. Both Menderes and Köprülü expressed full satisfaction with this arrangement.

Because air and naval forces were more fluid than land forces, I continued, their co-ordination was required over larger areas. The plan under discussion by the Standing Group, I told them, placed the Greek and Turkish air forces under Admiral Carney's air commander, also an American, and their naval forces under an Eastern Mediterranean Command headed by a British admiral serving under Carney, who was in control of the US Sixth Fleet. I expressed hope that the Turkish forces would not object to serving under the British admiral if that was the final decision of the Standing Group, and I stressed that it was not a matter of direct command over Turkish units but rather co-ordination and planning of available forces within the overall NATO structure. Admirals from other NATO countries, I explained, would head other commands in other areas of the world.

In response to a question from Köprülü about strategic air forces, I explained that US strategic air commands would not come under Carney in the same way, because their employment had to be co-ordinated on a global basis. I noted that the US strategic air commands were based chiefly in the United States and staged through airfields available to us on the periphery of the Soviet Union. I deliberately refrained, however, from raising the question of the use of Turkish bases in this connection, as did Menderes and Köprülü.

When this topic appeared to have been fully discussed, I proceeded to give the two Turkish officials a briefing on the agenda for the Lisbon meeting of NATO. Once Turkey was finally admitted to the organisation, I said, the country's economic conditions would be investigated and recommendations would be made about what Turkey could provide to, and what it needed from, the other NATO countries. At that point, I told them, there was the hope that considerable amounts of equipment, particularly mortar shells, could be procured from Turkey. This would benefit Turkey as well by adding to its dollar earnings. I reminded them of the need for increased trade among member nations and stated that I was certain Turkey would do everything in its power to export needed cereals, coal and metals. Prime Minister Menderes was also optimistic about Turkey's potential exports, and pointed out recent gains in the area of wheat, coal, cotton and nuts.

Also on the agenda for the upcoming meeting was consideration of plans for reorganising NATO. The United States favoured replacing existing civilian boards with permanent, United Nations-type delegations from each country that would be headed by ranking members of each government. The same type of change was favoured for the upper levels of NATO, so that a permanent secretariat would be headed by a secretary-general. The United States also favoured Paris as a permanent headquarters for NATO. The purpose of these changes was to streamline the organisation and facilitate the work of the specialised boards, which had become cumbersome. Menderes and Köprülü agreed with these changes, noting that the proximity to Supreme Headquarters, Allied Powers Europe (SHAPE) and the emphasis on European defence made the shift to Paris a sensible move.

Another expected agenda item was the formation of the European Defence Community. Although NATO was not responsible for the establishment of the community, there was an obvious confluence of interest, since the European army would come under NATO command. The Turkish officials appeared satisfied at the progress made thus far in this direction, and Menderes commented that he believed it was US backing that had made the community possible, since Great Britain would otherwise have opposed it.

We concluded with a brief discussion of the rules under which NATO operates, which were familiar to Köprülü from his experience on the European Council. Both they and I felt that Turkey would state its views fully and frankly and would accept the rule of the majority, even when it disagreed with a given decision. I told them that I was sure that Turkey would set a good example for other NATO countries, particularly because such a large portion of its resources went toward defence. Turkey's intimate knowledge of the Soviet Union, I said, would be another asset.

The conversation then turned to Middle Eastern affairs, specifically Iran and Egypt. Pakistan's foreign minister was scheduled to visit Turkey in the near future. The Turks were close to the Pakistanis and considered them good fighters and trustworthy allies. Since I had some knowledge of the Kashmir and Pushtoonistan situations that the two countries were planning to discuss, I volunteered to inform the Turks of the US point of view. Washington hoped, I told them, that Pakistan would ultimately join the Middle East Command, especially because that country had by far the greatest military potential of any country east of Turkey. In earlier discussions I had held with Pakistani officials, they had agreed that Pakistan should consider joining the command, once the threat of hostilities with India in Kashmir had been overcome.

Pakistan, the United States felt, could make an important contribution toward the defence of Iran, since the two countries not only were neighbours but had close relations. The Turkish ministers agreed that together Pakistan and Turkey could exert a positive influence on Iran, which was in the midst of its Mossadeq-Anglo Iranian oil crisis. (Additional information leading up to the situation in Iran at that time can be found in my memoir, *Envoy to the Middle World*, Harper & Row, 1983, chapters 27 and 31; also in a recent book, *Mussaddiq, Iranian Nationalism and Oil*, by I.B. Tauris, 1988, in which many recollections of the Iranian prime minister are given in pages 296–309.) I pointed out that Turkey might play a unique role in helping to resolve the Pushtoonistan problem, since it enjoyed close relations with both Pakistan and Afghanistan. Once the impractical Afghan demand for an independent Pushtoonistan state had been resolved, Pakistan should be able to play a greater role in regional problems.

When I met with Köprülü again the following day, he told me that he and the prime minister had given serious thought to our discussion about Iran.[4] They both felt that the prospect of a rapid deterioration of the situation there was too high to simply let events take their course. Turkey 'should not remain a spectator', he said, but must take some positive action. He expressed hope that he might meet soon with US and British officials to discuss what Turkey might do about the situation; we agreed to resume discussions within the week.

We were joined by Menderes and Zorlu to continue our conversation about Turkey's economic situation. Noting that I had been disturbed by criticism in the Turkish press over the levels of US aid, I told the three men that I would like to begin by outlining the current situation in the United States. Acknowledging that these criticisms did not originate with the government, which in fact had publicly expressed gratitude for the aid already received, I told them that I wanted to clarify the situation affecting US foreign aid, which was difficult for the outsider to comprehend.

I began by highlighting the tremendous pressure on Congress to reduce the United States budget, which had reached the all-time high of $85 billion. Taxes on the American citizen were crushing – nearly 88 per cent at the top rate. Budgetary deficits had already begun to produce noticeable inflation in the United States, which was worse than that in many countries, including Turkey. Congress was attempting to cut the deficit without reducing defence expenditures, which at the time constituted 75 per cent of the budget. A favoured target, therefore, was foreign economic aid; members of Congress felt that since the American people were making economic sacrifices, people in other countries should do the same.

As a result of this statement, the president's aid request the previous year had been cut by about $1 billion, which meant, for example, that Turkey had received only $45 million out of the amount initially allocated. Subsequently, it had been possible to take advantage of the provision of the Mutual Security Act that authorised a transfer of military aid to economic aid, and Turkey's share of this would raise total aid to $70 million for the year.

I told the three officials that it was my view that Turkey had done extremely well in terms of US aid, having received over $1 billion since the aid programmes began. The figures, I noted, were sometimes deceiving, since the actual totals for military aid are confidential and often gave the appearance to the general public that a country was receiving less aid than it actually was. Although Turkey would be receiving less economic aid the next year, the reduction was less than had occurred in some other countries. I also pointed out that reductions should not come as a surprise, since the Marshall Plan was scheduled to end in 1952. Both France and Britain were still experiencing serious difficulties with their balance of payments and budget deficits, but the United States recognised that these governments would have to play the key role in setting their economies to rights; Washington could not do it for them.

Tracing the history of US economic aid to Turkey, I told the three ministers that when the original calculations had been made for the first year of the Marshall Plan, many economists in Washington felt that, based on its balance of payments figures, Turkey should be willing to grant assistance to other countries. It was only with great difficulty that those of us working on economic aid to Turkey managed to obtain a token $10 million loan that first year. Subsequently, we had justified economic aid to Turkey on an increasing scale by the country's need for economic development – a rationale unique among all our aid programmes worldwide. This had proved to be a worthwhile effort, I said, because we were able to demonstrate to the appropriate authorities that the aid had assisted Turkey to support a larger military effort.

I reminded the Turkish officials that this year was the first time that the United States had undertaken a programme of development assistance, under the Technical Cooperation Act. The programme was on a much smaller scale than the aid furnished to Turkey: $50 million to India, $15 million to Pakistan, and $23 million to Iran. Since no other country except the United States had ever given aid on a similar scale, there was nothing to compare our efforts to. In any case, I told Menderes, Turkey could rest assured that I and other officials involved in Turkish aid programmes would continue to do everything in our power to ensure that Turkey's needs were brought to the attention of the proper US authorities.

Menderes' response was to deliver an extended and effective presentation of Turkey's role in the Middle East and its economic needs. He repeated the well-known fact that Turkey was the bulwark of defence of the Middle East and had, up to that point, saved the Middle East from communist aggression. If Turkey was to continue to play such a vital role, however, it would be necessary to increase the economic strength of the nation, Menderes stressed. The unfortunately low level of industrialisation and overall standards of living must be increased to ensure the survival of Turkey and the Middle East as a whole, he said.

American aid invested in Turkey, Menderes insisted, was sure to receive good returns. The country had a good resource base and great potential, especially given the introduction of new technology, such as tractors and improved means of transportation. Menderes felt that Turkey was capable of doubling and even trebling its national income within a relatively brief period, because new technology would have a strong impact, particularly in the area of agricultural production. The stronger Turkey could become in the economic sense, the stronger its military force would be, Menderes argued. Pointing out that Turkey was currently spending some 40 per cent of its budget on military preparedness, he said that as the budget increased, as it surely would with economic growth, the amount allocated for military purposes would grow proportionately, thereby enhancing the security of the entire region.

The prime minister acknowledged that from my presentation he understood that the United States was aware of Turkey's situation – both its role and its needs. That, he supposed, was why we had given Turkey exceptional treatment regarding the economic development programme. Although he and his government were appreciative, Menderes said he nonetheless hoped that we would give some consideration to increasing the $70 million allocated for the coming year.

I repeated that every effort would be made to obtain assistance for Turkey. But I also reminded Menderes that although Turkey's planned import and export programme was excellent, it included increases of 40 to 50 per cent in imports when most countries were reducing imports and introducing austerity measures. No one would deny that Turkey needed everything on its list of prospective imports, I agreed, but it was also true that a cut in the list would not have a disastrous effect on the Turkish economy. Regarding exports, the increases over the previous year were substantial and constituted a source of satisfaction. However, the US Embassy staff had noted a tendency to withhold certain goods from the market in order to obtain higher prices.

Although the desire to take advantage of normal seasonal and demand factors was understandable, I said, clearly it was inconsistent with our mutual objectives that scarce commodities be held for speculative purposes or for anticipated rises in world prices. The proceeds of these exports were needed to balance Turkey's accounts, I commented, and the grain, cotton, coal and chrome were vitally needed in other countries. Finally, I concluded by noting that an increase in the $70 million aid figure was very unlikely for that year. The total funds available were limited, I said, and would inevitably be less than what was desired in the recipient countries. I told them I was confident that Turkey would reconcile itself to this in good spirit.

I had from 6–8 May 1952 the opportunity of discussing a broader Turkish role in Middle Eastern affairs and development of Turkey's economy with President Bayar, when I was invited to travel with him on his official train to observe the military exercises at the Cankari Infantry School.[5] Guests included General Arnold, Minister of Defence Hulusi Koyman and Chief of Staff General Yamut. We were joined for the day of the 7th by the Minister of Public Works, Minister of Industries, Minister of Communications and the Governor of Cankari, Vilayet. The party stayed in the car where we held conversations and had our meals, except for the time spent in visiting the school and observing the exercises. The trip provided a pleasant and convivial atmosphere for the informal discussions that developed naturally, some of which were on subjects interesting enough to report.

I began by suggesting that Turkey should be able to play a leadership role in the Middle East analogous to that of the United States with Latin America. I pointed out that whereas these countries had previously distrusted the United States, we had now developed an important degree of co-operation throughout the inter-American system. Turkey, I said to Bayar, should, in light of its historical role, military strength, political stability, economic development and membership in NATO, consider pursuing a Good Neighbour policy in the Middle East, as we had in Latin America.

The next day Bayar told me that after giving my arguments consideration, he believed they might have some merit. He acknowledged that Turkey had in recent years for the most part ignored the Middle East, as the country put its efforts into strengthening ties with the West and joining NATO. The Middle Eastern countries were militarily weak, and he spoke of them with a certain degree of disdain. He agreed, however, that now that Turkey had achieved its main objectives, it might be time to put some effort into its relations with the states of the Middle East.

A general discussion developed between the president and myself as to the development of Turkey. I suggested that Turkey had great potential for development because of the high ratio of undeveloped land and mineral resources to population. In my judgement, only Brazil offered similar possibilities for development.

The president agreed. He believed that Turkey's development could best be achieved by increasing its agricultural production and its value through processing to as advanced a degree as possible. It was on this policy that he had based the Democratic Party's economic programme, in contrast with the previous government, which had artificially encouraged the development of industry.

I agreed, pointing out that US development had been based largely on agriculture, particularly in the south, where the cash crop had been cotton. Industry had developed naturally out of consumer demands created by the agricultural income. I commented, however, that I believed the time had also come in Turkey for light consumer industries to help fill the rising demand for consumer goods, combat inflation and save Turkey's scarce foreign exchange. I mentioned the new Squibb pharmaceutical plant and the General Electric light bulb plant, in which cases US capital had participated along with Turkish capital. I expressed the hope that other US firms would make similar investments.

The president replied that he agreed as to the desirability of such investments; however, the General Electric Company had been promoted by a middleman who was interested only in his own profit and had not made a full economic analysis of the venture. As a result, the company had been very troublesome in seeking tariff protection, of which he did not approve. I responded that we also did not approve of such protection in principle and had not supported General Electric in its request for tariff protection. I expressed the conviction that the plant could be competitive when its market had sufficiently expanded, as it was now doing.

I asked the president how many people he thought Turkey could ultimately support, to which he replied 50 million. (In 1987 Turkey's population was 55 million.) If so, this would put Turkey's resource base on a par with any country in Europe, except a united Germany (still not united). If Turkey's current rate of agricultural production and industrialisation were to continue at about 8 per cent annually, its economic potential by the time its population reached 50 million would correspond to that of the major Western powers (whose populations have increased little compared with the larger increase in their economies).

At that point, I suggested to Bayar that the advantage Turkey now enjoyed over the other states of the Middle East would be greatly accentuated. Despite the oil reserves and Arab lands that could be irrigated, none could claim the land resources, variety of minerals or the political and social stability required to develop a powerful modern state. If its development continued apace, Turkey could be the unquestioned leader of the Middle East.

Then, more than ever, I continued, it would be in Turkey's interest to have developed good relations with the other countries in the region. This need not entail transfers of large sums of money, I told Bayar, but would require other positive actions. Turkey could open spaces in Turkish civil and military schools for students from Middle Eastern countries (foretelling the Middle East Technical University in Ankara) or send professors and training missions abroad, as Turkey had already done successfully in Afghanistan. In many ways, I pointed out to Bayar, it would be easier for Turkey to play this teaching role than for the United States or the West Europeans. The development gap between the United States and the countries of the Middle East was too great; Turkey provided a much more comparable environment and would not be perceived as posing a colonial-type threat. President Bayar seemed genuinely impressed by this line of argument and pledged to raise it in government circles at the earliest opportunity.

During our talks, both Bayar and I expressed a growing feeling of trust and mutual confidence in the relations between our two countries. This was an extremely positive development, and I told Bayar that I hoped we would continue to consult whenever the need arose. Bayar agreed, adding that he believed the real strength of NATO consisted of the United States, Great Britain and Turkey, in that order, and it was therefore vital that the three countries work together on policy questions.

*   *   *

The strengthening and broadening of ties between Turkey and the United States that was occurring during this year continued. On several occasions I discussed casually with high-level Turkish officials how Turkey might develop its stagnant oil industry. One day President Bayar mentioned to me mysteriously that he would like to invite me to discuss a 'certain matter'. Finally, on 28 May he asked me to tea at the Marmara Kiosk of Ciflik Farm, an experimental farm originally established by Atatürk.[6] When I arrived I found not only Bayar but Menderes and Köprülü – the three highest Turkish officials – and an interpreter. I had never met with all three before. I was very surprised – and apprehensive. I was not certain what the matter in question would be. Perhaps I had made some gaffe or they wished to raise with me some urgent and serious problem in US-Turkish relations. I guessed it might have to do with petroleum, and as it turned out, I was right.

President Bayar opened the meeting by recalling that Turkey had been exploring for oil for nearly 30 years with relatively little success. Petroleum deposits had been found in the Ramandag area, near the border with Syria, but the other two areas where oil was believed to exist had proved too difficult for the Turks to explore. He said the government believed it to be in the country's national and strategic interest to seek the assistance of US oil companies to ensure that Turkey would have access to indigenous oil. He acknowledged that Turkey possessed neither the capital nor the technical knowledge to discover its oil and said the country was willing to allow foreign companies to enter the market, even if this meant their earning large profits.

Having already given the matter some thought, I told Bayar that I would like to respond to his inquiry in two different capacities – first as an oil man, which I was, and a friend of Turkey, and second as the US ambassador. As an independent oil man in Texas, I had had no ties with the US international oil companies with whom I had competed, and hence no conflict of interest. It was certainly true that Turkey needed to have access to its own supply of oil if the country hoped to continue on its path toward industrialisation. Petroleum had become one of the sinews of the modern state; the United States had been able to develop rapidly in part because of the availability of cheap oil. At present, oil imports were costing Turkey some \$50 million a year of its scarce foreign exchange. If the country continued to grow and develop at the rate foreseen by Bayar, its petroleum requirements would become an even greater drain on the economy.

Developing a petroleum industry, however, is quite different from the development of other mineral resources. The latter can usually be quantified and the quality of the deposits evaluated before the expenditure of large amounts of capital is required. With oil, that is not the case. Most commercially viable deposits are found only after heavy capital investment in exploration and drilling. Although the large international oil companies, mostly US, British and British-Dutch, have access to these large sums, most countries find it difficult to obtain the necessary capital. Even then there is the further question of whether a country is justified in spending public funds on such a risky undertaking as oil exploration.

I pointed out that in most countries that were currently enjoying a large income from oil, such as Venezuela (which earned \$360 million a year), Saudi Arabia (which earned \$150 million), and Kuwait and Iraq (which earned \$100 million), production was in the hands of private international oil companies, which generally had been able to work quite well with the host country. In countries such as Chile, Argentina and Brazil, which for political reasons had attempted to develop their own oil industries, the operations had been unsuccessful. All of those countries continue to be oil importers, despite excellent prospects.

I shared with Bayar, Menderes, and Köprülü my own geologist's opinion of Turkey's prospects for oil exploration. Turkey was largely mountainous, which was not favourable for oil. The two oil fields which had been discovered in the Ramandag area were not strong producers and the oil produced there was of low quality compared with the oil from other Middle Eastern countries. The Adana-Iskenderun area, however, showed much more promise. Seepages and showings of oil indicated the existence of a geological basin containing good quality, high-gravity petroleum, and the location was desirable from the standpoint of sea transport to consumption centres.

I believed US companies would be interested in working in the Adana-Iskenderun area, and also in the other areas where geological conditions, although requiring more exploration, appeared favourable.

Finally, in my capacity as US ambassador to Turkey, I told them that if the Turkish government approached me formally with the proposal suggested by President Bayar, my government would do all it could to help Turkey in the development of its oil resources. We would expect that Turkey would wish to do this by inviting competition among all qualified companies, regardless of nationality. Indigenous oil production not only would assist Turkish economic development but might be available for export to other countries and would ensure that Turkey would not be cut off from petroleum supplies in time of war.

I informed the group that the normal procedure under the circumstances would be for Turkey to pass the necessary legislation (called a petroleum law), as other nations had done, prescribing conditions under which private companies could acquire rights to explore for, produce, refine and market oil in Turkey. Broadly speaking, I said, the basis for foreign participation, starting in Venezuela and spreading to Saudi Arabia and other countries, would be on a 50/50 division of profits with the host country.

If their law was competitive with those in other countries, I was sure that many oil companies, including the major US companies, had a favourable enough view of Turkey's oil prospects to seek participation. The first step the Turkish government must take was to hire one of the international consulting firms specialising in petroleum laws. We would be happy to furnish a list of reputable firms, which could be checked and augmented by their own embassies and experts. Once such a law was passed I believed the oil companies would be knocking at their door.

At the end of the conversation President Bayar declared that I could consider that he had approached me about this matter in my capacity as US ambassador and that he had made his proposals in order that they be communicated to the US government. Although it was several years before a suitable petroleum law was passed by the Turkish Majlis, based on the recommendation of a Denver-based consulting firm that had drafted the corresponding Israeli law, there was an immediate response from the world's oil companies.

The first wave of exploration involved investments of more than $100 million. Unfortunately for Turkey, results were not as favourable as had been anticipated. Mobil Oil made a sizeable find near Adana in southeast Turkey, but only Shell Oil discovered enough resources to make appreciable net profits. At the peak of production only about 30 per cent of Turkey's requirements were met. Nevertheless, Turkey saved what it would have spent in exploration, and the funds expended by the companies for this purpose were much greater and were more expertly applied. The results did alleviate, if not eliminate, Turkey's oil-shortage foreign exchange drain.

8 The Middle East Command: An Idea in the Making, 1951–56

Although military co-operation remained the centrepiece of US-Turkish co-operation, the base had gradually broadened to include discussions on bilateral military aid and training, NATO, the goal of a Middle East defence organisation and the right strategy to pursue with the Arab states. Because of Turkish participation in the Marshall Plan and the European Economic Committee, economic matters were also more frequently on the agenda, and the United States responded to the efforts Turkey was making to liberalise its economic system and attract US investment.

In *Present at the Creation*, Dean Acheson relates that in January 1951 he wrote a letter to General Marshall, then secretary of defense, asking for a study of US interests and policies in the entire area extending from the Mediterranean to India.[1] As US power had waxed and British power had waned, differences between such states as India and Pakistan, according to Acheson, offered increasing opportunity for Soviet intrusion. In addition, no power had been substituted for that of the British in dealing with nationalist movements in Iran and Egypt.

Acheson did not propose relieving the United Kingdom and the Commonwealth of the primary responsibility for providing troops for the defence of the Middle East. Rather, the efforts of the British and the assistance supplied by the United States should be co-ordinated in a plan for the defence of the area as a whole. Various measures should be considered, including small military training missions, placement of Middle East personnel in US military schools, limited equipment for training, and, most important, a US-UK military agency to stimulate and co-ordinate the efforts of all countries involved.

The organisation of such an agency, the State Department hoped, might help solve other problems, such as the British impasse with the Wafd government in Egypt. In addition, the British were also reluctant to accept an American as Mediterranean NATO commander (even though the US Sixth Fleet contributed the principal force in the area), and a joint agency of this type might overcome British hesitation. General Marshall agreed to the study on the condition that Greece and Turkey would be excluded and left to NATO.

By the summer of 1951 the United States and the United Kingdom had concluded that the establishment of a Supreme Allied Command in the Middle East would be a desirable step. In September, while I served as assistant secretary in Washington, I organised a meeting of a British working group and the Pentagon to discuss the question of a Middle East Command (MEC). On 8 September I finally secured agreement between the two on the terms for such an organisation.[2]

This was an idea that had been kicked back and forth across the Atlantic for many months. Its primary purpose was to substitute a British Middle East Command for Britain's fading treaty structure, thereby providing the British with continued troop and base rights in the region. In the form now proposed, a British Allied Command, Middle East, with headquarters in Cairo, would be directed by a Middle East Chief of Staff Committee, which would include Egyptian officers. The British Suez base would be turned over to the Egyptians, who would place it under the new command. British troops beyond those that had been agreed to by Egypt would be withdrawn.

On 25 September President Bayar informed Ambassador Wadsworth that Turkey would welcome a visit to Ankara by General Omar Bradley, Field Marshal Sir William Slim and General Charles Lecheres (representing the United States, Britain and France, respectively) to discuss the MEC,[3] and he promised to help these governments persuade Egypt to join. The Egyptian government, intensely opposed to the MEC concept, summarily rejected the invitation to join in the discussions. When the three generals arrived in Ankara on 13 October the decision was made to present the proposal anyway, in the vain hope that the Egyptians would be influenced by such solidarity. The Egyptian prime minister, Mustafa el-Nahas Pasha, rejected the proposal without reading it. Two days later the Egyptian parliament abrogated Egypt's 1936 treaty with the United Kingdom and the Sudan Condominium Agreement of 1899.

By November the governments of France and Turkey were participating in the US-UK discussions with the knowledge and support of the governments of Australia, New Zealand and the Union of South Africa. Although Egyptian leaders still refused to have anything to do with the group's proposals, the four powers reaffirmed their intention to proceed, with or without Egypt.

On 31 January 1952, after I had taken up my duties as ambassador in Ankara, the British directed a memorandum to the US government in which they noted that, while it had been necessary to defer action on the command until the relationship of Greece and Turkey to the NATO command structure could be finally determined, the time had come to consider what immediate practical steps could be taken to form an embryo Middle East Command organisation.[4] It might not be opportune, the British suggested, to establish a fully operational Supreme Allied Headquarters – such as NATO's SHAPE – but it was time to make a start. The need for co-ordinated planning was urgent. Although the British still hoped that Egypt would decide to participate, they were anxious to begin planning for the command, even without Egypt.

Realising that the Turks might hesitate to join in discussions of the Middle East Command until their membership in NATO had been finalised, the British suggested that politico-military talks be held in London after the Atlantic Council meeting in Lisbon, at which Turkey's admission was to be formalised and Greek and Turkish forces would be assigned to Admiral Carney's southern command. The British proposed that Turkey, at the same time, would receive formal assurances from the three Standing Group powers that its position in relation to the Middle East Command would be identical to that of the United States, France and the United Kingdom – that is, as a full member of NATO, Turkey would collaborate with other NATO powers in arranging for the defence of the Middle East.

'The aim', in the British view, 'should be to set up a nucleus Middle East Command Organization, outside NATO, in accordance with the principles set out in the Quadripartite Declaration'. It would be an effective organisation for 'planning the defence of the Middle East in war'. The British offered Cyprus as a location for this purpose, agreeing that eventually the headquarters might be located elsewhere. They further suggested that the early stages of the command should encompass planning, co-ordinating and liaison only. The MEC should, however, be organised as a command headquarters, to permit its functions to be rapidly expanded if war should break out. The British proposed that, later, when the existing unsettled situation in the Middle East was resolved, the command should evolve in accordance with paragraph 11 of the Paris Declaration into a full-fledged, integrated allied command, with forces assigned or earmarked.

The British also proposed a list of roles that the command should play, in accordance with the Paris Declaration:

- to be a centre of co-operative efforts for defence of the Middle East as a whole;
- to undertake planning and to provide the states of the Middle East, on request, with assistance in the form of advice and training;
- to make plans for the operations in war of all forces within or to be introduced into the area and to co-ordinate them with the operations of the adjoining NATO command in the eastern Mediterranean and Asia Minor;
- to initiate the Middle East Defense Liaison Organization, which should be the link between the command and the countries ready to join in the defence of the area; and
- to reduce such deficiencies as existed in the organisation and its capacity for defending the region.

The British also thought that the Middle East Command would require some form of higher direction on political, military and supply issues. The method of conveying political guidance to the command would require further consideration. A Middle East Military Committee, consisting initially of the seven sponsoring powers, should be organised, but a smaller body, such as a Steering Committee, might also be necessary. Arms supply should come only from the United States, United Kingdom and France. The memo noted that because conflicts might arise with NATO, close contact should be maintained, perhaps by dovetailing the proposed tripartite arms agency for the Middle East into the NATO organisation for co-ordination of supply and production.

I first learned of the British *démarche* regarding the MEC through the British ambassador to Turkey on 5 February.[5] The Foreign Office had told him that Washington's reaction had been favourable. I then asked the State Department to keep me informed and requested that I be permitted to discuss with the Turks US participation in the early meetings on the MEC before any final agreement by the three powers. The British ambassador was as concerned as I that the decision to proceed with the MEC not be presented to the Turks as a *fait accompli*. In my memo to the department I pointed out that many Turks were suspicious that the MEC was a step toward the revival of colonialism, and I stressed the importance of treating the Turks as equals.

In reply the department assured me that Washington was aware of the need to consider Turkish views during talks on the MEC but felt the time not yet ripe for formal four-power talks.[6] It was the department's hope that the Turks would convey through me any general views they wished the United States to consider before a four-power consultation was held. A copy of the US response to Britain was quickly forwarded to me.[7] It stated that the United States 'welcomed' Britain's initiative as set forth in the 31 January memorandum and was 'in general agreement' with British ideas.

The US memo defined the objective of the MEC as 'to strengthen the defenses of the Middle East through the cooperative effort of all states interested in its defense, whether or not territorially part of the area'. In the organisational terms then envisaged, the MEC would consist of two bodies: the command structure, including the Supreme Allied Command, Middle East, and his staff, and a Middle East defence liaison organisation in which all sponsoring and associate members would be represented and which would serve as a link between the command and all the member states.

The purposes of MEC outlined in the department's memo were similar to those pronounced by the British: to develop plans for military operations in the area in time of war or international emergency; to provide advice, training and *matériel* to the countries of the Middle East; and to arrange for the use of facilities by MEC through specific agreements between the command and the individual states providing such facilities. Over the long run, MEC's goal would be to increase the defence capabilities of the states of the Middle East. MEC was not, it was stated, to interfere in problems and disputes arising within the area.

The US memo went on to point out that the sponsoring powers hoped that the MEC proposal would contribute to a compromise solution of the Anglo-Egyptian controversy. However, the Wafd government in Egypt had already, as pointed out, rejected the four-power proposal as an attempt to continue foreign occupation under a new guise, and most Egyptian political factions backed the government's position. King Farouk and the Hilali government in power were reported to be more favourably disposed than the previous government toward association with the West in regional defence, but even they were demanding prior acceptance of the principle of early and complete evacuation of British troops and recognition of Farouk as king of both Sudan and Egypt.

Other Middle East government leaders had shown marked interest in the Middle East Command but had insufficient strength to take a position counter to that expressed by Egypt, for it was an extremely popular position among their respective populations. Israel, although it had expressed willingness to co-operate with the Western powers in the defence of the Middle East against communism, could not openly associate itself with the MEC.

With apparent increased interest in the formation of a Middle East Command, the appropriate departments of the US government prepared a National Intelligence Estimate of the prospects for such an organisation. Completed on 17 March, the report concluded the following:

> A solution of the Anglo-Egyptian controversy is essential to the establishment of any inclusive Middle East defense organization. Egypt will not join until its controversy with the U.K. is settled, and under present circumstances no other Arab nation is likely to if Egypt does not.
>
> A settlement of the Anglo-Egyptian controversy that would permit Egyptian participation in a Middle East defense organization would require British acceptance of at least the principle of early and complete evacuation of British troops from Egyptian soil and on British recognition of Farouk's title as King of the Sudan as well as of Egypt. Egypt will probably not reduce these demands.
>
> While settlement of the Anglo-Egyptian dispute would thus probably make possible the establishment of a regional defense organization capable of channeling Western military aid and advice to the Middle East states and of carrying out some preliminary defense planning and coordination, its development into a more broadly effective organization would remain an extremely difficult task.
>
> Although the evacuation of British forces from Egypt would eliminate a major irritant in Arab-Western relations, Arab fears and suspicions and intraregional rivalries would continue to plague negotiations for development of an effective organization. Public opinion, as well as many leaders, would continue to underestimate, ignore or be fatalistic about the threat of Soviet aggression, which they would regard as far less tangible than the question of Western 'interference' or of the Arab-Israeli dispute. Arab leaders would remain suspicious of Western motives, and would be concerned

lest the defense organization be used as a means of applying collective pressure on them or reestablishing spheres of influence.[8]

On 31 March, two weeks after the NIE's publication, I sent the department a summary of my views on the prospects of the MEC, from my perspective as ambassador to Turkey as well as my overall experience in Middle Eastern affairs.[9] The success of our efforts to build in the Middle East a regional defence against external aggression would, I said, depend on our success in obtaining the co-operation of the individual nations of the region, which in turn hinged on their relations with the four powers both separately and collectively. Therefore, for example, the problem of France's position on Syria would have to be faced squarely, and an appeal made for real four-power co-operation, transcending any remaining rivalries for spheres of influence in the Middle East.

When the United States and Great Britain began co-operative efforts in the Middle East in 1948, I pointed out, it had been agreed that the United States would not try to compete with or displace British responsibilities or interests there. Rather, it would seek to strengthen the British position whenever possible. However, the United States had made clear that it would not recognise any exclusive British spheres of influence. The British had agreed that it would be desirable for the United States to provide financial assistance over and above what they could give wherever there was a common interest. The British had apparently lived up to these agreements and had not opposed constructive contributions by other states, although they had shown a natural desire to protect their interests, especially in Jordan and Iraq. However, the policy of France in recent years seemed to have sought to preserve France's special position in Syria and Lebanon, even at the expense of progress in these countries and four-power co-operation there.

Regarding Turkey, I said, although doubts had been expressed about Turkish participation in military assistance to Arab states (because these countries opposed help from outside powers), Turkey could play a valuable role. The principal complaint against Turkey was believed to result from Turkish solidarity with the Western powers on Middle Eastern questions. The conflicts of Middle Eastern states with France and Britain were far more recent and vivid for the Arab people than their problems with the Ottoman Empire, which might be responsible for some residual anti-Turkish sentiment. About a year before, I recalled, I had spoken with the presidents of

Syria and Lebanon, and both had emphasised that under no conditions would they permit French troops on their soil – in peace or war.

In contrast with these European powers, the Turks had shown no evidence of advanding their own special interests in the Middle East. Turkey had withdrawn from the region following World War I and had no claim to territory or exclusive influence outside its present frontiers. Most Middle Easterners, with the exception of isolated, local groups revived for political reasons by communists and opportunists, now appeared to have respect for and growing confidence in the Turkish leadership. Syria had sent officers and non-commissioned officers to Turkey for training in recent years without any apparent misgivings.

Turkey, I contended, as a neighbour with strong Middle Eastern ties, could play an important role in the development of the Middle East Command. As the only significant military power in the region, Turkey had given other Middle Eastern nations their only real basis of security in the postwar period. Moreover, its admission to NATO and a further build-up of its military strength should give Turkey added prestige.

At the strictly military level, Turkey could provide land defence, in the event of aggression, whereas neither French nor US ground troops would be available and Britain's Middle East forces were pinned down in Egypt and other far-distant Commonwealth countries. Also, Turkey's troops were located at the northern mountain line, the best vantage point for defence of the Middle East against a Soviet invasion. Turkey was also willing and able to provide military training for other Middle East states and to sell them arms. If replacements could be guaranteed, Turkey would be willing to give arms to neighbouring countries.

The Turkish leadership, I concluded, was convinced that assurance against any aggression directed at Middle East states was the first step toward stability in the region. Turkey, now that it was a NATO member, had expressed willingness to play a more active role in the Middle East. Menderes, I told the department, had pledged to take positive steps to allay the suspicions of the Arab states and gain their confidence.

On 16 March I had met with the prime minister and entered into a broad discussion of diplomacy in the Middle East.[10] As I reminded him, the United States' Middle East policy during the past few years had been to overcome the region's tendency toward neutralism and strengthen political and economic stability. Turkey had been a full partner in most of these efforts, and we hoped that with its admission to NATO Turkey would play an even more constructive role, since its own interest in developing stability and military preparedness was even greater.

Menderes, although noting that setbacks had occurred and would probably occur again, had agreed that Turkey would become more and more active in the Middle East. Also, in the interest of proceeding in the Middle East on the basis of full four-power co-operation, Menderes had promised to try to resolve the Turks' differences with the French over the French military attaché's insistence that the co-ordination of assistance to Syria exclude Turkish participation.

During our meeting I asked Menderes what steps he thought Turkey might take to gain the confidence of Arab states. I suggested the possibility of remarks in official speeches or articles, and in editorials in local newspapers, that might make a good impression in the region, and mentioned to him the talks I had held with Köprülü on the broadening of military training in Turkey for officers from other Middle Eastern countries. Further, I suggested that the government might see fit to invite representative leaders of the states concerned to visit Turkey or that top Turkish officials might visit Arab nations.

Menderes was very receptive to these ideas. He agreed to make a major speech indicating Turkey's sympathy with the present situation of the Arab nations and to encourage newspaper articles along the same lines. He also approved of the idea of training Middle Eastern officers in Turkey and promised to see what could be done in this regard. Visits, however, were a more difficult proposition, especially since President Bayar had often been annoyed at the attitude of some of the Arab states, particularly when they criticised Turkey. Although Menderes acknowledged that such criticism must sometimes be ignored or overlooked in order to keep foreign policy on track, convincing Bayar had proved difficult. We agreed, nevertheless, to discuss the matter with President Bayar.

My next conversation with a top-level Turkish official regarding Middle East defence took place on 18 May, when I spoke with Minister Köprülü.[11] The primary topic was Egypt. More than two months previous the Turks had urged a two-week wait before any attempt was made to get the MEC under way, in the hope that some resolution of the situation in Egypt might be forthcoming. Otherwise, some of the countries that wished to join the MEC would be forced to break with Egypt in order to adhere to this new regional defence group.

In our earlier March meeting Köprülü and I had assessed the situation thus: the new Egyptian government was strongly anti-Wafd but, as a consequence, lacked the strong popular support enjoyed by the Wafd. If it made too many concessions to the British, the new government ran the risk of being overthrown. The British also faced problems. The Conservative Party had come to power advocating a stronger British position toward such situations as those in Egypt and Iran, so that it was difficult for them to think in terms of making concessions. A major sticking point continued to be the status of the Sudan, which most Egyptians believed to be the key to any solution of the base issue. Until the British were willing to recognise Egypt's interests there, the Egyptians were likely to balk at settling other questions.

Furthermore, Köprülü and I had agreed that at that point neither Turkey nor the United States was in a position to become directly involved in the Anglo-Egyptian negotiations. Instead our efforts would have to be limited to providing counsel to both sides with the aim of bringing them to an agreement. Köprülü felt that if negotiations failed, there was a good chance that the Wafdists would succeed in overthrowing both the government and the monarchy. In such an event they would come to power with a government sympathetic to the communists, and this would have a strong negative impact throughout the Arab world, particularly in Tunisia and Iran. Although we agreed that a meeting on how to proceed with the MEC was becoming ever more urgent, the decision was made to postpone this step.[12]

Now, on 18 May, a lasting solution to the tension between Egypt and Great Britain was still not in sight, so I asked Köprülü how he viewed the current situation. He replied that two important advantages had been gained by waiting. First, Köprülü said, we had shown Egypt the importance that we attached to its participation in the command and that we did not wish to do anything 'behind Egypt's back'; second, we had shown the other nations of the Middle East that we desired Egypt's participation and had led them to disapprove of Egypt's refusal. Although there was no significant military force among the Arab states, he said, it was nonetheless important to win their friendship as a step toward combating communist propaganda in the region. Köprülü felt that it was time to invite all the Arab states to join the MEC while making it clear that Egypt would always be welcome. He also felt that British influence would ensure the participation of Iraq and Jordan and that US influence would bring in Saudi Arabia.

On 18 June a discussion of Middle East defence was held during a State Department-Joint Chiefs of Staff meeting in Washington.[13] It was estimated that ten divisions would be required to hold the mountains in Iran. Turkey had said it could supply six divisions, and Australia and New Zealand could each supply a division. The United States, however, could not furnish any troops for at least two years. That left two divisions missing.

General Joseph Collins, army chief of staff, declared that in his opinion the real hope of Middle East defence rested with Turkey. With a stable government, however, Iran might be able to exert some force, as might Iraq, if Iran would permit the Iraqis to enter Iranian territory. It was generally agreed that atomic bombs would be ineffective in Iran's mountain passes.

Collins concluded from this analysis that the British must be persuaded to allow Turkey to play a stronger role. So far, he noted, the British had shown interest only in planning defence of the inner ring (the Suez), which made no use of the Turks. The real hope for defence of the region as a whole lay in defence of the outer ring, which would make use of the mountains and the Turkish forces. Without the Turks, there was a danger that the Russians could pass through Iran without involving Turkey. They might, for example, attempt to keep Turkey neutral by promising not to attack it. If such a strategy succeeded, Collins noted, the Russians could easily squeeze the United States out of the Middle East.

All those present at the meeting agreed that US influence in the Middle East was waning. The United States was simply not in a position to supply leadership or troops and *matériel*, since US priorities were Korea, Indochina, the United States itself and NATO, and only then the Middle East. Thus, those present agreed there was no need at the time for a military command in the region but only a planning group that could do some political stocktaking and see what could be done in the future.

On 27 June the United States and Great Britain agreed that the long-delayed efforts to create a defence organisation for the Middle East should proceed with haste.[14] It was decided that the organisation should also include France, Turkey, Australia, New Zealand and South Africa, and that it should be renamed the Middle East Defence Organisation (MEDO). The two countries felt that the concept of an organisation was more appealing than that of a command, especially to the countries of the Middle East. Despite Egypt's refusal in 1951 to become a founding member, it was agreed that the offer should remain open to Egypt and to the other Arab states, which for the time being would not receive formal invitations. They would be unlikely to join as long as Egypt stayed out. In the meantime it could be made clear to them that they would be welcome when they were in a position to join. Since Arab co-operation would be unlikely if Israel were included, it was also decided not to invite Israel, despite the contribution that country could make.

It was further agreed that the functions of MEDO would remain the same as had been originally outlined in the Paris Declaration. The organisation and structure should be kept small and flexible enough to permit efficient planning and should include a number of countries. This would permit a smooth transition into a military representatives' committee and planning group, which would probably be based in Cyprus.

9 A Turkish Role in Regional Defence, 1952

During the course of discussions on the organisation and goals of the MEC, considerable attention was given to Turkey's role in a regional defence grouping. Consideration was given to Turkey's relations with its Arab neighbours and to the leadership role Turkey might play. The following vignettes provide important glimpses into issues that arose during 1952 and impinged on Turkey's standing in the Arab world and the potential for a successful Middle East defence.

THREE EPISODES IN TURKISH-ARAB RELATIONS

Military Training

As Köprülü noted in a March 1952 meeting, Turkey had a long tradition of offering military training to Middle Eastern states, and Turkish authorities were willing to resume such programmes if they were deemed to be in the common good.[1] The United States at the time was aware that Afghans were being trained by Turkey and that the Turkish government was considering the resumption of training for Syrian officers. After commenting on the importance of Turkey's involvement with other Middle Eastern states in military training, I said that Turkey's effort should supplement, not supersede or compete with, the efforts of others and that efforts involving countries covered by the MEC should be co-ordinated with the other members. I also stressed that the United States did not wish to interfere with what was obviously a matter for the Turkish authorities, but that we did see clear advantages in providing ties to the West while strengthening these countries militarily.

Köprülü had no objection to General Arnold's talking to the appropriate Turkish military training authorities about possible US assistance in the training effort. Shortly thereafter, the foreign minister again discussed with me the possibility of resuming training for Syrian officers in Turkey. Syria, as he had discovered, had begun sending its officers to France, but informal inquiries by the Turkish ambassador in Damascus indicated that the Syrians would be interested in resuming training in Turkey. The US ambassador to Syria had been making similar inquiries and, as I told Köprülü, had also received a favourable reaction. To avoid any appearance of bypassing the four-power MEC mechanism, it would be wise, I suggested, that any new Turkish training programme be in addition to, and not in competition with, France's training programme.[2]

A Pakistani Proposal

When I met with Köprülü on 14 March I told him of my conversation with Sir Muhammad Zafrullah Khan, foreign minister of Pakistan, an old friend of mine who had recently passed through Ankara.[3] I had told Zafrullah that the United States was not in sympathy with his prime objective of establishing an Islamic political bloc. As I explained, Washington believed that factors other than religion – such as geographical proximity, the need for a common defence and economic co-operation – provided a better basis for political unity. Zafrullah had commented that he felt Turkey had not shown proper sympathy for the Arab states, particularly in its votes in the UN where it had appeared on occasion to have deferred to its NATO allies. I was curious to see how Köprülü would respond.

Köprülü quickly denied that Turkey had been responsible for its estrangement with the Arab states and stood by Turkey's UN vote on the Suez issue, which he acknowledged had been a source of tension with Arab leaders. Regarding the Pakistani proposal, he felt that Pan-Islam was not a sound basis for political co-operation and that the proposal was being handled in a very amateurish manner. He further suggested that Pakistan's principal motivation was to develop a political bloc that would help make Pakistan more independent of India.

Pakistan, as Köprülü told me, had approached Turkey in a rather curious fashion. The Pakistani chargé d'affaires in Ankara had asked a Turkish official for his response to Pakistan's idea, apparently presuming that Zafrullah had already spoken to the Turks about it. As it turned out, Khan had never directly approached the Turkish government. Nevertheless, the Turkish official told the chargé that Turkey would not attend a conference on this subject, since it believed such a meeting could serve no useful purpose. Turkey's ambassador to Afghanistan had taken the same position when approached by Afghan officials, and Köprülü felt the Afghans would follow suit and decline the invitation. Lebanese officials had also spoken to the Turkish ambassador in Beirut, calling Zafrullah's proposals 'utopian'.

Köprülü assured me that his government would continue to make the development of friendly relations with neighbouring Arab coun tries a high priority in its foreign relations. To this I responded that I was well aware that much of the cause behind the Arabs' feelings was beyond Turkey's control, but I agreed that Turkey should do everything in its power to effect closer relations in order to play a constructive role in the future of Arab nations. Köprülü went on to tell me that the Iranian government had asked Turkey to attend to the interests of Iranian nationals in Israel (where Iran did not have diplomatic relations), and Turkey had agreed in principle. I commended the minister on this decision, adding that the action was certain to strengthen the ties between Turkey and Iran, to which the United States attached great significance.

The Problem of Special Interests

In our 18 May meeting, shortly before the expected visit of Libya's defence minister, Ali Bey Jerbi, I asked Köprülü his views on the situation in Libya.[4] He responded in an angry tone. He understood that the Libyans wanted to seek Turkish assistance in military matters but were being prevented from doing so by the British.

He followed with his well-known criticism of the attitude of the European powers in the Middle East, which he felt had assumed an 'egotistic' stance and were attempting to derive prestige through domination. Prestige, he continued, could not be obtained artificially: 'It is a shadow that, when you turn to it, disappears'. By attempting to hold on to their position in Syria and Lebanon, the French had only made themselves appear ludicrous and had weakened their position, Köprülü charged. Furthermore, the European countries had also weakened and rendered useless the Arab League, which otherwise might have been able to help solve some of the region's problems.

Köprülü suggested that the United States and Turkey, having no special interests to protect in the Middle East, should try to persuade the other outside powers to give up their special interests in the region. He repeated this argument to Assistant Secretary of State

Henry Byroade during his visit to Ankara a few weeks later.

Secretary General of the Foreign Office Acikalin, a wise and discreet man from an old Turkish family, had raised similar concerns to me some weeks earlier about the negative impact of European special interests.[5] His conclusion was that co-operation in the Middle East would be achieved only with US leadership. Turkey's role would have to be subsidiary. The French were too concerned about their specific interests, and Great Britain, although more objective, still sought to hold on to its preferred position in certain countries. Consequently, the Arabs distrusted both powers. Despite some friction regarding specific situations, Turkey was trusted by most of the Arab states, and there were no fears of Turkish imperialism.

Although I appreciated Acikalin's comments on US leadership, I told him that we were not able to assume single-handedly the leadership of the Arab world, since we had responsibilities elsewhere as well. Nations such as Great Britain, with a longer history and deeper interests and commitments in the region, were in a better position to assume such a role. My feeling was that the only hope for constructive action in the Middle East lay in genuine four-power co-operation. As I told Acikalin, the British, French and Turks needed to iron out their differences if the MEC was to function effectively. Acikalin agreed that Turkey must play a more active role in the area, noting that Middle Eastern stability was vital for Turkey. Adding that he had proposed a multilateral approach similar to the MEC four years earlier, he remarked that the current proposals, although they had come a year too late to solve the problems in Egypt, were certainly better late than not at all.

DISCUSSIONS WITH TURKISH LEADERS

The exploration for a basis for Middle East security initiated in 1949 by the United Kingdom and the United States, in which France joined later and Turkey participated following its admission to NATO in February 1952, continued at a quickening pace. The goal of a Middle East Command having been superseded in June by the new and more appealing concept of a Middle East Defence Organisation, the United States sought to increase Turkey's interest in MEDO and utilise that country's latent influence with the other states of the region. Turkey, which had contemptuously distanced itself from Iran and the Arab states for several decades, accepted this new role with interest, as my discussions with high Turkish officials revealed.

As part of the US effort to understand better Turkey's role in Middle East defence, Frank Nash, assistant to the secretary of defense, visited Ankara in early July and met with Köprülü and the British ambassador. Köprülü began by launching into a lengthy critique of certain Western ideas about the region and its peoples, to begin with, the term 'Arab states'.[6] Iraq, he pointed out, had large Iranian and Turkish minorities and was divided between two Muslim sects. A large Turkish minority was also present in Syria. Lebanon was equally divided between Muslims and Christians and had a large foreign population. Jordan was not a state at all but rather a creation of the British to satisfy King Abdullah. Egypt as well could not be viewed as an Arab state, since many of the people are Copts and the ruling classes were Turks, Balkans and other foreigners. The only true Arab states, Köprülü concluded, were Saudi Arabia and the Yemen, both of which were feudal states living in the past.

The Arab League, he continued, was an equally misleading concept. It was a creation of the British for their own purposes and was not representative of the Arabs. Neither the British nor the French, Köprülü charged, really understood the Arabs at all, despite their colonies and spheres of influence. Their knowledge of the countries was limited to the present leadership, which they themselves had created. In Köprülü's view, among the powers involved in MEDO, only the Turks really understood the Arabs and therefore Turkey was in the best position to approach the Arab states with the idea of the proposed defence organisation. In particular, he said, Turkey could exert a positive influence on Syria and Lebanon.

Köprülü repeated the by then familiar thesis that the defence of the Middle East was essentially the defence of Turkey, since Turkish forces constituted the bulwark of regional defence and since the Soviets would be forced to attack Turkey or neutralise it before launching an attack on Iran and Iraq. Thus, he concluded, the most effective way to increase the defence capability of the Middle East was to increase the strength of Turkish forces. The principal objective of MEDO should be psychological – obtaining the friendship and political co-operation of the nations of the area.

Nash asked Köprülü what tactics he would recommend with respect to the Middle Eastern countries regarding MEDO. He replied that careful thought must be given to the initial stages of the approach and much groundwork must be laid through private conversations prior to a formal approach. The British ambassador,

Sir Alexander Knox-Helm, a most agreeable and co-operative colleague, agreed that the initial approach must be discreet. If not, he feared the Arab countries might feel compelled to reject the organisation publicly, a course that would make it difficult for them to join later on, even if they changed their minds.

One real danger, Köprülü pointed out, lay in the possibility that upon being approached, the Arab leaders would reply that the matter must be considered by the Arab League, which would mean that the proposal would get nowhere. Collectively, the Arab leaders displayed even less courage in making difficult decisions involving issues tainted by colonialism than they showed separately. Köprülü stressed that most of the present leaders in the Arab world had little credibility because they had come to power at a time of colonial rule and therefore owed their positions to foreign powers. Nonetheless, he acknowledged, these were the leaders who had to be dealt with, except in cases where the people were more powerful than their leaders. Köprülü failed to elaborate on which countries he thought would fit into this category.

The US view of MEDO, I told Köprülü, was somewhat different. We conceived of the organisation as a co-operative effort, without a legal basis such as NATO had, largely because the political situation in the Middle East did not appear to permit an organisation such as NATO. The proposal we had in mind was the next best thing to a legal commitment; in the case of the United States, for example, participation in MEDO would not have to be submitted to the Congress, since no treaty would be involved.

Nash asked Köprülü whether he believed that the Arab states should be furnished arms. Köprülü replied that he thought arms should be provided but in small amounts, given the size of the military establishments in the countries in question. He suggested that the supply of arms be accomplished through bargaining, since the Arab states had a 'bargaining mentality' and would be persuaded to assume their obligations only if a quid pro quo was involved. The British ambassador agreed on the basis of his experience in the region.

Köprülü went on to suggest that approaches to the various Arab states be made by the country that held the most influential position *vis-à-vis* each state. For example, the British might approach Iraq and Jordan, the Americans could speak to the Saudis, and Turkey could approach Syria and Lebanon. There was some concern, however, about the French, who also claimed influence with Syria and Lebanon. I was also worried that such an approach would represent an implicit recognition of spheres of influence, which would undermine the multilateral approach we were trying to develop with MEDO. While everyone agreed that a multilateral approach was highly desirable, the other major concern was to prevent MEDO from being referred to the Arab League for consideration.

The British favoured an approach whereby the four powers would 'set up shop', in hopes that the Arab states would ultimately be attracted and become involved. I suggested a different approach: after discreet, private discussions had been held, an open invitation to Arab governments to attend a meeting on Middle East defence should be issued, without any commitment as to what might emerge from such a meeting. This approach would not require Arab leaders to make a momentous decision that would, at least apparently, force them to choose between popular feelings and foreign powers. Even though the meeting might be difficult and give rise to sharply opposing points of view, the mere attendance of the Arab leaders at the meeting would give them a feeling of equal participation in the building of a defence organisation. This in turn, I suggested, would tend to orient them toward the West. Köprülü agreed with my suggestion, but the British ambassador remained tied to the 'setting up shop' approach.

Nash, turning to another matter, stated that he envisaged that MEDO would eventually be managed by a committee of military representatives in which all participating countries – the Arab states and the foreign powers – would be represented and over which there would be a rotating chairmanship. There had also been discussion, he said, of a British chairman to a subsidiary planning organisation of this body. No one, including Foreign Minister Köprülü, raised objections to this.

Closing the meeting, Köprülü emphasised the need for sincere co-operation among the four powers involved in getting MEDO off the ground. He stated clearly that such co-operation had not existed in the past and said – apparently directing himself to the British ambassador – that certain actions that foreign countries had taken in the Middle East had to be discontinued if the organisation were to be successful. All present heartily agreed with his formulation.

During this period I had held many conversations with Köprülü on Middle East defence. In a meeting on 5 July he stressed again the need for real four-power collaboration in Middle East defence – the British and the French should abandon their desire for 'spheres of influence'.[7] He also repeated his doubts as to the likelihood of attracting the Arabs to MEDO, although he agreed that carefully planned, low-key efforts ought to continue. He had heard through contacts in Arab capitals that the British and the French were consistently sabotaging Turkish efforts to carry out a constructive Middle East policy. This, of course, was deeply disturbing to me, and I promised to look into it.

Köprülü then entered into a discussion of the various possible approaches toward the building of MEDO, now that it had been decided to proceed without waiting any longer for Egypt to join. He felt strongly that the initial discussion should take place exclusively among the four powers and that the involvement of other Middle Eastern states should be sought at a later stage. Of course, these initial discussions would have to be extremely confidential, since the approach to other countries would be made more difficult if they knew that the four had worked things out in advance.

When I told Köprülü that the United States was thinking more of a defence organisation than a 'command', he repeated his view, expressed during the talks with Nash, that it would be necessary to provide a legal basis for such an organisation. However, as I explained, the United States believed that the political situation in the Middle East lacked sufficient stability to justify a formal treaty. I also told the foreign minister, in response to his query, that I thought it highly unlikely that the new organisation would become part of NATO, given the difficulty with which many European countries had been persuaded to admit even Greece and Turkey.

Köprülü, however, had been giving serious thought to the situation of Iran and other Middle Eastern states, and was not to be put off. He recalled a conversation we had had two years earlier, when I was assistant secretary of state and Greece and Turkey had not yet been admitted to NATO. At the time, the United States had defended Greek and Turkish entry for strategic reasons. Köprülü maintained that Iran and other Arab states were now in a position similar to that of Turkey and Greece at that earlier time, that is, highly vulnerable to penetration from, or disruption by, the Soviet Union.

Although he agreed that the time was not yet ripe to attempt to bring these countries into NATO, he argued in favour of seeking a means to clarify to NATO the importance of their defence. He also suggested creating a new defence organisation along the lines of the Western Defence Community, which had made possible the inclusion of Western Germany. It might be called the Asiatic Defence Community. In answer to my query he said that Turkey would be willing to be a member of such an organisation if the United States and United Kingdom would be willing to react if the community was attacked.

Around this time members of Turkey's administration were invited to take a cruise with units of the US Sixth Fleet in the interests of increasing good will on their part and demonstrating the striking power of the Sixth Fleet and the support it could give Turkey in the event of war. It was also felt that this might provide some compensation for the fact that it had not been possible to arrange for the Turkish president to visit the United States and might contribute toward the growing *rapprochement* between Turkey and Yugoslavia, with the Sixth Fleet as a common denominator. The idea of extending an invitation to President Bayar and other high Turkish officials emerged from my discussion with the fleet commander, Admiral Cassady, when I met with him in Venice in June. Admiral Cassady had mentioned the possibility of Marshal Tito's visiting the fleet, and it occurred to me that it would be desirable to extend a similar invitation to Bayar and other high Turkish officials.

Apart from President Bayar, the principal Turkish guests included Prime Minister Menderes; General Zekai Okan, deputy chief of the Turkish general staff; General Muzaffer Goksenin, chief of Turkish air forces; Vice-Admiral Sedik Altincan, chief of Turkish naval forces; and Major General Ihsan Orgun, chief of staff to chief of Turkish air forces. The party boarded the aircraft carrier *Wasp* on 6 August, and President Bayar was given a 21-gun salute by all units of the Sixth Fleet. After inspecting the honor guard, he was taken to the flight deck and on an inspection into all parts of the ship, including the engine room. After lunch, Admiral Cassady gave the group a presentation of the composition, organisation and capabilities of the Sixth Fleet. He described the operations of a 'Fast Carrier Task Force', and the projected strength of such a force in the event of war.

The Turkish visitors were greatly impressed with Admiral Cassady's explanations and the striking power of the Sixth Fleet. President Bayar said that what he had seen had exceeded his expectations. He had pressed for Turkish entry into NATO but only now realised fully the advantages of membership.

As it turned out, the visit was the setting for some of the more important top-level discussions regarding Turkey's role in Middle East defence.[8] I began the informal talks with Bayar and Menderes by volunteering my opinion that Turkey had a strong tendency to underplay its position in the Middle East – in relation to the countries of the region and with outside powers as well. President Bayar responded immediately, agreeing that Turkey had been 'timid' in its relations with other nations. He explained that this resulted from the foreign policy inherited from the Republican Party, which, because of its embarrassment in not having lived up to its commitments during World War II, had not wanted Turkey to assert itself in foreign policy since that time. Even recently, Bayar pointed out, the Republicans had opposed initiatives taken by his government, such as the decision to send troops to Korea.

Nonetheless, Bayar said, the Turkish government had taken steps to improve relations with other Middle Eastern countries: some of their leaders, including King Abdallah of Jordan had accepted invitations to visit Turkey. Many of the visits, however, including that of the foreign minister of Egypt, had not materialised. The shah of Iran had at one point shown interest in Turkey as a model for progress in Iran, and Bayar had visited the country himself and would be willing to do so again, he added, if it would be useful. According to Bayar, the shah had made the mistake of not going as far as Turkey had gone, of not carrying through, so his revolution was unsuccessful.

Both leaders agreed that it was important for Turkey to establish closer relations with the Arab states in order to exercise a positive influence over them. However, the government – particularly the foreign minister – was adopting a cautious stance, waiting for the opportune moment. As I knew from previous conversations, Köprülü was also concerned at what he perceived to be French and British opposition to Turkish efforts in the Middle East.

My experience in Middle Eastern affairs, I told the two, had led me to the conclusion that the 'right moment' to make any particular constructive move in the Middle East would very probably never come. That was why the United States had pursued its initiatives more or less on its own, sometimes in spite of British, and particularly French, reluctance to accept US involvement in what they considered to be their spheres of influence. Although some of our efforts had not been as successful as we would have liked, I felt they had at least facilitated some progress toward stability in the region. I suggested to Bayar and Menderes that Turkey might take the initial step by making some sort of public gesture that would demonstrate Turkish sympathy and understanding for the Arab cause.

I cited, as an encouraging precedent for a warming of relations with Middle Eastern countries, the recent visit of Ali Bey Jerbi, the defence minister of Libya. I had met privately with Jerbi, who told me that he was most pleased at the warm reception given him by the president and the prime minister and that he intended to propose to his government that a Turkish officer of Libyan origin be designated as the commander of Libyan forces. President Bayar told me that Turkish-Libyan friendship and co-operation went far back in history and that he had told Ali Bey Jerbi that Turkish willingness to assist Libya was without limits – it was for Libya to draw the line.

Shortly after these discussions aboard the *Wasp*, I met with Secretary-General of the Turkish Foreign Office Acikalin.[9] Recalling to him my conversations with the president and the prime minister, I asked Acikalin what steps the Turks were considering to further a *rapprochement* with other Middle Eastern states. Although Turkish officials generally agreed that this should occur, little concrete progress was evident.

Acikalin replied that a major problem faced by Turkey in such an initiative was the lack of stability of Middle Eastern governments. For example, Turkey had completed a treaty with the Iraqi government, which was later denounced by the parliament. When I asked whether a series of top-level visits had been considered, he replied that this, too, was fraught with difficulties. If a visit was made to a government that was overthrown soon after, the new government would likely be hostile toward Turkey and denounce any agreements made with the previous government. Discussions were being held, he told me in strictest confidence, regarding the possibility of achieving closer relations through private citizens, who would establish relations with their counterparts in other Middle Eastern countries in order to lay a foundation for better understanding and friendship, without incurring a political reaction.

Shortly after this discussion Acikalin asked to see me again to talk about the Middle East defence proposals submitted recently by the British. Because of the close relations between the United States and Turkey, he wanted our advice on certain matters that the Turks viewed as basic to their further consideration of the British memorandum. Their underlying concern, he said, was to understand the real purpose of establishing a Middle East defence organisation and what would be the ultimate relationship among the sponsoring powers. 'I am in the dark as to what is actually planned', Acikalin maintained. Although Turkey had no wish to delay or sabotage the creation of a regional defence organisation, which Turkey also saw as vital, it would not be meaningful unless it was based on solid ground. Given that the British and French were both 'hated' in the Middle East because they came as invaders, the Turkish government felt that unless the United States were to play a leadership role in developing the organisation, it would have little chance of success.

The secretary-general went on to point out that the British memorandum seemed to ignore basic questions, such as the purpose of MEDO and its juridical basis. In the past, he charged, Turkey had been asked to rubber-stamp agreements made between the United States, Britain and France. In this case, since Turkey would be playing a major role in the proposed organisation, Acikalin felt it was crucial that the sponsoring powers be very clear about their respective roles and exactly where they stood with each other. 'The Turkish people and the National Assembly will want to know what commitments Turkey is being asked to assume and what commitments the other powers are making', he declared.

In late August 1952 the Turks submitted to Washington the promised memorandum regarding the British proposals for MEDO. On 5 September I visited Secretary-General Acikalin, bringing with me the State Department reply.[10] In our discussion we both agreed that the overthrow of the government of King Farouk in Egypt, and the establishment of the Maher-Naguib government, would probably improve the prospects for an Egyptian decision to join MEDO. Naguib had clearly stated that he wished to keep Egypt free from foreign domination, I noted, but he was a military man and a strong leader. Involvement in MEDO would be likely to strengthen Egypt militarily, which would be an appealing prospect to him, and he was strong enough to push for acceptance of the proposals if he chose to do so.

Acikalin agreed, adding that the new government had been welcomed by other Arab states. In the case of Egypt and other countries, Acikalin said, the basic problem was to let the Arab countries organise their own armies, independent of control and influence by the former colonial powers. He asked what countries were under consideration as potential MEDO members, to which I responded that current thinking included Egypt, Saudi Arabia, Iraq, Syria, Lebanon and Jordan. Iran and Israel had been considered, but were dropped due to political considerations in the region.

On 7 October, when I spoke with Köprülü, one of the items on our agenda was the participation of Arab states in MEDO. He told me that in private talks Turkey had been urging Arab officials to join MEDO and that many Arab leaders wondered whether this would ensure their receiving US arms. He had told them that he was not in a position to know; however, he thought that their co-operation in Middle East defence plans would be a likely prelude to the furnishing of US military assistance.

I reminded Köprülü that the US Congress had in 1950 authorised the transfer of arms to the Arab states up to a specified amount, in return for their co operation in Middle East defence. Thus far none of these monies had been disbursed. I told Köprülü that I thought it likely that limited amounts of arms could be provided to Middle East countries that joined MEDO.

We also discussed the possibility of including Pakistan in MEDO. Köprülü said Turkey had no problem at all in associating with Pakistan for defence, as long as Pakistan could resolve its differences with India and Afghanistan, which Turkey had for some time been attempting to mediate with little success.[11]

ARAB PERCEPTIONS OF TURKEY

On 10 November 1952 I met with President Bayar, Prime Minister Menderes and Foreign Minister Köprülü to discuss the question of Turkey's relations with the countries of the Middle East.[12] Menderes began by advising me that the Turkish government had decided to go forward with a programme designed to strengthen relations with the Arab nations, mainly through a series of visits by top-level officials and parliamentarians, as well as cultural exchanges. Menderes was quite optimistic about Turkey's chances for success, and he cited a recent letter from Egypt's General Naguib, in which he praised the accomplishments of Turkey under Atatürk. He also quoted favourable comments by Colonel Shishikli of Syria, who had recently expressed satisfaction over the results of the training of Syrian military personnel in Turkish academies.

Although I was pleased that the Turks had decided to make a real effort to improve their relations with the other Middle Eastern countries, when Menderes asked for my assessment of the achievements he had mentioned, I was forced to inject a note of realism. I had recently sent memorandums to US heads of mission in each of the Arab countries, asking them to evaluate the prospects for improved relations between Turkey and the country in which they were located, as well as their views on Turkey's potential for exercising a constructive influence in the area (see appendix). I told the three Turkish leaders of my survey and gave them a frank synopsis of the results.

From the responses I had gathered, I began, the difficulties facing the Turks in developing better co-operation and understanding with the states of the Middle East were far greater than they imagined. Two somewhat interrelated problems, in particular, had emerged: there was a widespread feeling in the nations of the Middle East that Turkey had turned its back on them; at the same time, there were suspicions that Turkey was acting as an agent of the West. Turkey's concentration on improving relations with the West, it appeared, had given other Middle East nations the impression that Turkey had little sympathy for their problems – indeed, that Turkey looked down on them.

Interpreting these findings, I suggested that since Turkey had a potential community of interest with the countries of the area, arising out of historical, religious and geographical factors, the Arab nations expected more of Turkey than they did, for example, from the nations of the West. Just as family members expect more from each other and are often more hostile with each other than with outsiders when expectations are not met, the countries of the Middle East were especially angry that Turkey, in their view, had spurned relations with them in favour of ties with the powerful nations of the West. This feeling had been aggravated, I added, by frequent shows of superiority toward the local people by Turkish officials based in Middle Eastern states. The appointment to diplomatic postings of warm, friendly individuals known to respect the Arab peoples, I suggested, could go a long way toward improving matters on this score.

I proceeded to emphasise again a point I had made previously with all the officials present: the similarities between Turkey's role in the Middle East and the US role in the Western Hemisphere. Both Turkey and the United States were the natural leaders of their respective regions and were fundamentally oriented toward Europe. But both countries lived among smaller, weaker and highly nationalistic countries that were extremely sensitive to questions of independence and prestige. As a result, the United States and Turkey, in their respective situations, needed to make a special effort to convince those countries that relations with them had a high priority and that relations as equals were desired. Although the United States had had many difficulties in its relations with Latin America, it had finally, through the Good Neighbor policy and support for the

Organization of American States, achieved co-operation on a basis of equality. In my judgement, Turkey's problems with the states of the Middle East and the actions needed to resolve them were strikingly analogous to the United States' experience with Latin America.

One of the specific problems that had emerged from the results of my survey, I continued, was Turkey's voting record in the United Nations. The Turks were aware of this, and the foreign minister had mentioned many times that he thought Turkey had made a mistake in supporting the Western powers on the Suez issue. Now discussion was focused on Tunisia, but Turkey's action in support of Tunisian independence had been too late to improve its credibility with the Arab states.

Köprülü, in response, felt that Turkey was in an extremely difficult situation. Earlier, when it was still seeking admission to NATO, Turkey had felt obliged to demonstrate its solidarity with the West. Subsequently, the Turks felt they must be loyal to their new allies. Since the interests of the West so frequently clashed with those of the Middle Eastern countries, it was impossible for Turkey to satisfy everyone, and thus it had decided that its commitment to NATO and the West must be given top priority.

Of course, I told Köprülü, I had not meant to imply that Turkey's solidarity with the United States specifically and the West in general was not both appreciated and expected. In matters of vital interest to the West such co-operation should continue. However, I pointed out, these considerations were not always overriding. For example, although the United States viewed France as a key ally, the administration had felt it necessary to support the inclusion of the Tunisian case before the UN. Turkey had reached a similar conclusion, but in tactical terms, it might have taken better advantage of its decision to help gain confidence among the nations of the Middle East. Although Köprülü continued to take a defensive stance, President Bayar expressed agreement with my remarks, adding that he also thought Turkish policy toward Tunisia had been too timid.

Finally, on a more optimistic note, I told the three government leaders of recent information I had gathered regarding Pakistan, which indicated that the Pakistanis were quite anxious to develop closer relations with Turkey, especially in the military field. In fact, the Pakistanis wanted Turkey to press them hard on this issue, which would make it easier politically for them to accept. I felt that this was an important opening for Turkey, since Pakistan, with its 80 million people, strong army and good prospects for economic development, would represent a strong ally.

During the course of this conversation, President Bayar commented, somewhat scornfully, that the countries of the Middle East had never defended themselves. They had always relied on Turkey or Great Britain for military support. Bayar, Menderes and Köprülü all agreed that because of this the objectives of MEDO were, at least in the short run, really more political than military. If the need arose for defence of the region, the hardware and armed strength would have to come from outside, but it would evidently be preferable for the countries of the region to be prepared to co-operate.

The informal survey I had taken regarding Middle Eastern attitudes toward Turkey had actually shown results even more discouraging than I indicated during the 10 November meeting. From the thoughtful responses sent by other US diplomats, it became clear that much mistrust was still rooted in Turkey's long domination of the region, which had been abandoned only three decades earlier. In some countries there was lingering resentment over boundaries or suspicions that Turkey still harboured territorial ambitions. Added to this was the powerful religious factor. Although the Turks were Muslims, they had consistently declined to take part in any bloc based on Islamic ties. Moreover, Turkey was trading with Israel and had supported Israel's application for membership of the United Nations.

To most of the Arab nations, these factors made Turkey anti-Arab, and the attitude toward Turkey, in turn, was one of suspicion and hostility. In the larger and more powerful countries, such as Saudi Arabia, Turkey's 'indifference' toward the Arab world was returned in kind, and its inclusion as a sponsoring power of MEDO was looked at with something akin to rivalry.

I had also asked the chiefs of mission what steps they thought Turkey might take to improve its relations with the Arab world. Although some countries appeared to be impervious to Turkish overtures at the moment, most of the comments indicated that if the Turks would make the effort, it would be worthwhile. It was important, many of the US mission chiefs stressed, that the Turks convince the Arab nations that they were not simply acting as stand-ins for the West, particularly for the United States. They needed to make a genuine effort, to lend a more sympathetic ear, to be less condescending and to offer something – be it educational exchanges or military hardware – that the Arab countries needed.

Such an effort might not require any change in Turkey's policies, the reports indicated, but would require a change in attitude and a great deal of patience. Although most of the comments indicated that Turkey could strengthen its ties with the Arab world, there was general agreement that Turkey could not, at least at present, play a leadership role in the region, largely because of the suspicion and hostility that characterised most Arab nations' views of Turkey. The messages involved in this survey are given verbatim in the Appendix.

10 Progress Toward a Middle East Defence Organisation and Its Early Demise, 1951–58

AN APPROACH TO THE ARAB WORLD IS DISCUSSED

In mid-October 1952 British and Turkish high-level officials met in London to discuss how to make the initial approach to an Arab country regarding membership in MEDO. On 23 October I met with Foreign Minister Köprülü to hear his views of the meeting's results.[1] In general, he was pleased with the British attitude, which he found to be open to criticism and to changes in the British draft document. During the course of the two meetings devoted to discussions of MEDO, the British and the Turks had reached several agreements, key among which were: to proceed as rapidly as possible toward the organisation of the defence of the Middle East and to do so even if the Arab states remained reluctant to join the proposed organisation.

Both countries agreed that every effort should be made to seek Arab involvement from the beginning; and the British idea of a written proposal was abandoned in favour of more informal, oral invitations by whichever of the sponsoring powers was deemed to have the best chance of success. I commented that the United States favoured an initial 'sounding out' process but was more inclined to dropping a formal MEDO-type organisation if the Arab states were strongly opposed. One touchy point noted by British Prime Minister Anthony Eden was how to convince the French to agree to the individual approach idea, since they were particularly concerned with the prestige considerations raised by such an approach.

Köprülü went on to brief me on a confidential memorandum received from Turkey's ambassador to Egypt regarding the attitude of General Naguib and his government toward MEDO. The Turkish Foreign Office had asked the ambassador to gauge Egyptian opinion on this issue, very informally and subtly. The ambassador had first spoken with Egypt's minister of foreign affairs, who had said bluntly that Egypt would not consider membership in MEDO until the

British removed their troops from the Canal Zone. He then talked privately with Naguib, whose response was similar. Naguib had said that he thought it was in Egypt's interest to join an organisation such as MEDO but that it would be impossible as long as the British were occupying the Canal Zone.

Naguib had added that there were disadvantages in Egypt's participation. In particular, he noted that if Egypt joined MEDO, other Arab states would probably do likewise. But if, at a later date, Egypt no longer found it convenient to remain in MEDO, other smaller and weaker states would probably remain, leaving Egypt isolated. Finally, Naguib had insisted that it was Egypt that should defend the Canal Zone, and if Egypt's armed forces were inadequate to do so, it was the fault of the British. He then promised to give further thought to the issue of Middle East defence and talk again to the ambassador within the month.

Köprülü viewed this conversation as proof of the Turkish belief that an informal, oral approach by a friendly country was the best way of proceeding with the creation of MEDO. While in London Köprülü himself had spoken to the regent of Iraq, who told him that he expected Turkey to defend Iraqi interests during his meetings with the British. In Köprülü's opinion, if Turkey alone had approached Arab nations the previous year about the Middle East Command, it would have been much more effective. Köprülü repeated this discussion during his talks with Eden, which he believed played a role in convincing the British to accept the informal approach.

The Turks and British had then agreed that Iraq should be the next country to be approached about MEDO and that the Turks should undertake to do so, despite Britain's treaty with Iraq. The idea developed during the Turkish-British meetings was that Britain and the United States should let the Iraqi authorities know that they supported Turkey's efforts. The same approach was to be used *vis-à-vis* other countries. For example, when the United Kingdom approached Jordan, Turkey and the United States would privately declare their support; when the United States talked to Saudi Arabia, Turkey and the United Kingdom would back up those efforts.

The problem, I noted at this point, would be with such countries as Lebanon and Syria, because the French, viewing themselves as the natural contact point, would be antagonistic toward the idea of another country assuming a leading role. Köprülü said that the French must be told flatly that they must subordinate their national interest and pride to the larger needs of regional defence. Perhaps, he suggested, Britain's example of acknowledging that Turkey was the best country to approach Iraq would set a good precedent – a notion I found unlikely.

But more important was a difference I saw emerging between the agreements that had come out of the Turkish-British talks and US thinking: namely, which country should be approached first. I told Köprülü that because of Egypt's position in the Arab world, and because it had in the beginning been invited to be a sponsoring power, Egypt should be approached before Iraq. Although the original British proposal had called for a written invitation, and the US government had agreed to this, I felt there would be no opposition to changing to the individual approach suggested by the Turks and now agreed to by the British.

I asked Köprülü how he thought Naguib would react to Iraq's being approached first. He responded that Iraq had been selected because it was the most vulnerable to Soviet aggression and because the Egyptians evidently would not join as long as the British were occupying the Canal Zone. There has been no discussion, during his talks in London, of a possible British withdrawal from Suez. In any case, thinking in Turkish and British government circles seemed to agree that an approach to Iraq might best be made following the Iraqi elections that were scheduled to take place in two months.

Köprülü said he wished to make some additional remarks about his meetings in London. At one of the sessions when Marshal Slim and Marshal Alexander were present, the question of Middle East defence had been discussed. Köprülü had said to the marshals that the defence of the Canal Zone and North Africa did not lie there but in northeastern Turkey. To this both Slim and Alexander had agreed. Köprülü also recalled Marshal Montgomery's statement, which, however, he had not discussed in London: 'If I were responsible I would not hesitate to evacuate troops from the Canal to the Turkish border'.

Köprülü had observed to the British that the defence of the Middle East was to them the defence of the canal and their route to the Commonwealth countries in the east; to the Turks the defence of the Middle East was the defence of Turkey. It was agreed to give an accounting of the conversations to the US government and to urge the United States to agree to the conclusions reached.

On 5 November 1952 the Department of State submitted to the British government a note advising that after careful consideration of British and Turkish views, the US government considered that

Egypt, not Iraq, was the most vital key to the establishment of MEDO.[2] Furthermore, the note said, the United States believed that no other Arab state would be willing to consider participation in a Middle East defence organisation until the difficulties between Egypt and the United Kingdom were resolved. The first step in this process, the note suggested, would be a 'clear and precise offer to Egypt with respect to a prompt settlement of the Suez Canal Base question'. Then, the United States and Britain should offer material assistance to the Naguib government, including whatever arms might be deemed necessary to raise the level of the Egyptian army to the point at which it could play a useful role in the defence of the Middle East.

On 10 November the British agreed that the real priority was Egypt and welcomed the US offer to facilitate negotiations between Britain and Egypt, pledging to produce some initial proposals as quickly as possible.[3] Finally, the British felt that any programme of military or economic assistance should be linked to Egyptian commitments to co-operate with the West on Middle East defence.

In the meantime, the British Foreign Office and the State Department were concerned with the relationship of other countries to MEDO, particularly India and Pakistan. The British wanted to inform Pakistani leaders of the progress made toward organising MEDO thus far and invite them to join at such time as the new organisation became a reality. They felt that Pakistan's strategic position would make it an important MEDO member, even if Pakistani troop strength was currently not impressive. Although the British recognised that the impasse with India over Kashmir would probably prevent Pakistan from associating itself immediately with MEDO, they wanted to leave the door open. Since India's policy of non-alignment prevented that country from joining MEDO, the British proposed that the Indian government be informed of any discussions with Pakistan.

THE JOINT CHIEFS ASSESS FORCE REQUIREMENTS

On 28 November the US Joint Chiefs of Staff held a meeting to discuss a memorandum that had been prepared evaluating the force requirements for holding the Middle East.[4] The military assessment was based on the assumption of a world war in which the Soviet Union would be simultaneously moving against the Middle East, Western Europe and the Far East. Based on current knowledge of

Soviet strength and disposition of forces, it was assumed that out of their total of 175 armed divisions, the Soviets would deploy some 23 or 24 in the Middle East.

The basic concept used in assessing military needs looked toward holding what was known as the outer ring. This involved defending a 'line' based in the west on the Taurus Mountains in southern Turkey and in the east on the Zagros Mountains in Iran and Iraq – the area viewed as the most vital to safeguarding the Middle East's key oil-producing areas. The defence strategy on the ground was one of holding the mountain passes that were viewed as the only Soviet entrance to the Middle East.

The number of passes, the likely strength of the Russian troops that would be involved and the number of Western troops needed to counter them were all calculated. The passes to be defended started with the Cilician Gates of Turkey on the west, and going east to the Malatya Pass, the Ruwandiz Pass, the Senna Pass, the Pavrak Pass, the Khurammabad Pass and Bandar Abbas. The extent of the area to be defended was impressive. The 'line' extended approximately 1780 miles, compared with the 150-mile DMZ that the United Nations was then defending in Korea.

The Joint Chiefs calculated that, at the time, the blocking Western forces available were seriously lacking: the deficit was six infantry and one armoured division, 950 aircraft and 30 to 40 naval aircraft and mine sweepers, as well as an unspecified number of logistical and support troops. The Joint Chiefs concluded that by 1955, as long as there was no increase in Soviet strength in the Middle East, a defence build-up on the part of the West could reduce the deficit to one infantry division, 580 aircraft and the necessary support troops. General Omar Bradley, who made the initial presentation to the JCS, concluded by emphasising the need for the early establishment of a Middle East defence organisation that would undertake the military planning required to defend the area. He also urged that maximum efforts be made to resolve the area's political problems.

In the discussion that followed, Turkey's situation played a prominent role. On the one hand, it was suggested that if the Soviet objective were to seize the Suez Canal or the oil fields in Iran and Iraq, the Soviets might bypass Turkey altogether. On the other hand, with some assistance, Turkey might be able to create six mobile divisions that could serve as a potent threat on the flank of a Russian advance. Moreover, the Turks had proved themselves capable of flying and maintaining aircraft; to teach these skills to the armed forces in other Middle Eastern states would require several years. Thus, air strength in the area had to come from the United States and Turkey. In any case, the military men present at the meeting agreed that it was extremely difficult to plan for a defence of the area without knowing what the Soviet objective would be, and without a clear definition of defence priorities on the part of the US government.

One of the generals present, a specialist in Middle Eastern military affairs, felt strongly that the West would in any event be unable to protect the oil fields of the Middle East. Instead of wasting troop strength there, we should begin immediately to plan for defence without reliance on the oil of the Persian Gulf countries. But, it was argued by a State Department official, if the United States was committed to bringing the Arab countries into MEDO, it must offer some evidence that it was willing to aid in their defence. General Bradley, however, saw the objectives of MEDO as more political than military. The funds authorised thus far for military defence of the Middle East were insufficient, he pointed out. In any case, before a large-scale effort to build up indigenous forces in the area could be undertaken, there would have to be a clear display of interest on the part of the states of the Middle East; that is, the Middle East Defence Organisation would have to be a reality before defence planning could begin.

BRITAIN CONSIDERS HOW TO APPROACH EGYPT

On 31 December 1951 the British government presented the United States with a note sketching the outline of MEDO that they intended to present to the Egyptian government.[5] The establishment of MEDO, the note read, 'would assist and support states willing to join in the defense of the Middle East and develop the capacity of each to play its proper role in the defense of the area as a whole against outside aggression'. The organisation would not, however, become involved in disputes within the region, nor would it affect any existing treaties or other arrangements. The initial membership should include the United Kingdom, the United States, Turkey, France, Australia, New Zealand and South Africa, all of which had indicated that they intended to participate. In addition, the membership of Egypt, Iraq, Jordan, Syria, Lebanon, Saudi Arabia and Yemen would be sought. Once these states formed the organisation, the note went on, membership applications from other states would be considered by the existing members according to criteria developed by them.

MEDO's initial tasks should be to: draw up plans for the defence of the Middle East; provide training and other assistance to the states of the Middle East; co-ordinate requests from the countries of the region for arms and equipment; plan for co-ordination with NATO forces in case of war; and improve the organisational and military capacity of the area for its own defence. Functionally, the organisation would consist of a military representatives' committee and a planning group; the latter would consist of officers from participating countries, under a British chairman, and would be divided into the functional areas required to make the organisation work.

The British note was quite consistent with what they, and the US administration, had been proposing for MEDO in the past. We felt, however, and so advised the British, that their latest approach was somewhat stiff and inflexible and that we preferred negotiations that left more room for input from other countries.

In mid-February 1952 the British advised the United States that, having completed negotiations regarding the Sudan, they were preparing to broach with the Egyptian government the subject of MEDO in concert with the United States.[6] The negotiations were to focus on five issues: a phased withdrawal of British forces from Egypt; the retention of a peacetime base in the Suez Canal Zone; provisions for the air defence of Egypt; Egyptian participation in MEDO; and US and UK military and economic assistance to Egypt. It was acknowledged that the Egyptians might wish to consult other Arab governments before making a final decision to participate in MEDO. Should this prove to be the case, the United States and Britain agreed to approach the Arab governments first, on behalf of the sponsoring powers, so that the Egyptians could discuss the matter with them on the basis that those governments would have an equal opportunity to participate in the organisation.

KÖPRÜLÜ REPORTS ON THE DEVELOPING ARAB ATTITUDES TOWARD COLLECTIVE DEFENCE

The ensuing negotiations between Egypt and the British over MEDO proved lengthy. In May 1952, when Turkish Foreign Minister Köprülü spent six days in Baghdad attending the coronation of King Faisal II, the negotiations were still going on. Upon his return, I spoke with

Köprülü, on 8 May, regarding the results of the trip during which he had talked with numerous Arab leaders.[7] Overall, the conversations indicated that there would be little progress on MEDO until the Egyptians and the British reached an agreement about the canal, although Köprülü sensed that some Arab leaders were developing an awareness of the need for positive steps to build up the defence of the Middle East.

Köprülü told me that he had adopted a cautious attitude during his stay, waiting for Arab leaders to come to him rather than actively pursuing contacts, in order not to appear to be pressing the Arabs on the MEDO issue. In the end, both Iraqi and Iranian officials had sought out Köprülü for private conversations about Middle Eastern policies and defence. Nuri Said Pasha, a leading Iraqi politician who was then minister of defence, proposed a novel plan to Köprülü. Since Iran, Iraq and Turkey were the most important Middle Eastern countries from the standpoint of defence, Nuri said, they should band together in a defence pact. Since Iraq was not in a position to suggest the idea to Iran, Nuri wanted Köprülü to do so.

Köprülü, however, was skeptical of such an idea, particularly since both Iraq and Turkey had close relations and treaties with the United Kingdom, whereas the Iranians had no such relations and were hostile toward the British. They would not be willing to enter into a pact with two countries that had such close British ties. Moreover, the Iranians might fear that such a pact would provoke the Russians. Nuri responded that the pact could be designed in such a way as not to appear to be directed against the Russians. Instead it could appear to oppose intervention in the affairs of the three countries by any outside power. Köprülü insisted that the idea was in any event not practical at the time, largely because of Iran's hostility toward Britain.

Shortly thereafter, Köprülü met with Foreign Minister Fatimi of Iran at Fatimi's request. Fatimi began by complaining bitterly about British activities in Iran, blaming the British for recent riots and asserting that when the Iranians closed Britain's embassies and consulates, the British began directing their agents from Baghdad. He charged that the British were trying to overthrow Prime Minister Mossadegh by economic pressures but said that if Mossadegh were overthrown, only the communists would gain. Köprülü said that he and Fatimi exchanged views very frankly on the danger that the Soviet Union presented for all the countries of the region: Fatimi, he said, was quite aware of the Russian threat to Iran. Nonetheless, it was evident that Iran would not be willing to co-operate in any plan such as Nuri's, which would invoke Iran with two countries closely associated with the United Kingdom.

The last leader Köprülü talked to in Baghdad was the regent of Iraq. Köprülü reported to me that he took a hard line, suggesting to the regent that Arabs saw the whole world through the prism of their relations with Israel and as a result were not developing a realistic, effective foreign policy. The Arab-Asian tactic of forming a neutral bloc in order to gain bargaining power with the Soviet Union and the West, Köprülü told the regent, was not only wrong but dangerous. The regent complained that the United States would not furnish arms to the Arabs, to which Köprülü replied, 'Why should they, when there are no assurances that the arms won't be used against them?' The Arab states, Köprülü stated, must stop engaging in blackmail and join the common front of free nations.

Köprülü told me during our meeting that all the Arab leaders to whom he had presented a similar analysis while in Baghdad had agreed with him, including the Iraqi leaders and the secretary-general of the Arab League. The problem, he said, was that they could not take any action to change things because they were 'prisoners of their own demagoguery'. When I asked him what chances he saw for MEDO if Egypt failed to join, he said that it might be possible to proceed on a smaller scale, including such countries as Iraq, Jordan and Lebanon. Köprülü was relatively pessimistic about the future of the Arab states, although he refused to give up hope despite the grave obstacles.

A NEW US ADMINISTRATION CONSULTS WITH TURKEY

With Stalin's death on 5 March 1953, ending 29 years of dictatorial rule starting with the death of Lenin in January 1924, relations between the Soviet Union and Turkey had taken a new turn.[8] On 30 May the leaders who succeeded Stalin had directed a note to the Turkish government proposing a drastic change in the relationship between the two countries. The Soviets offered a renewal of the 1925 Treaty of Friendship, which they had denounced in 1945, and the abandonment of their claims on the Turkish provinces of Kars and Ardahan. They proposed a general relaxation of tensions, friendly co-operation, increased trade and settlement of existing disputes. Soviet diplomats admitted discreetly to Turkish officials that Stalin had been wrong.[9] But Turkey remained cautious and after a delay replied on 18 July in terms which, according to Vali, were 'frosty, formal and laconic'.[10] The Soviets had been too late. Turkey had opted irrevocably for NATO.

The Eisenhower administration, when it came into office in 1953, undertook a comprehensive survey of existing national security policy, particularly in the Middle East where little progress had been made in building an adequate security system. It was pursuant to this review that Secretary of State John Foster Dulles accompanied by former Governor Harold Stassen, director of the Mutual Security Agency, and a considerable staff, made a visit to the key Middle Eastern and South Asian countries in the spring of 1953. The group arrived in Ankara in late May 1953. Dulles and Stassen stayed at the Embassy residence, where I and the staff gave them a briefing.[11] In his meeting with Menderes, to which I accompanied him, Dulles bluntly told the prime minister that his visit to Turkey was not simply a formality; rather, Dulles sought Turkish leaders' opinions regarding Soviet policy in the Middle East, and ways amd means by which greater unity could be attained in the region. Menderes proceeded to give Dulles a broad overview of Turkey's views, which had gradually become less optimistic.

The world today, Menderes began, is divided into three camps: the Soviets and their satellites, the forces opposing communism, and the countries seeking non-alignment. The Soviets are able to provide leadership and direction for those under their control; the West suffers from its inability to control its constituents, due to frequent clashes of local interests. A greater effort should be made to unify the free world, Menderes suggested strongly. The Suez Canal problem provided a good example, he continued. In Turkey's view, the security of the Suez Canal is not simply a matter to be decided between the United Kingdom and Egypt. The canal was a vital geopolitical space, said Menderes, which was of as much importance to Turkey, to the United States and to NATO as a whole as it was to the two countries currently negotiating. Since Egypt could not defend the canal, the Egyptians must be convinced that the free world depends on leaving British troops there, at least until Egypt's armed forces were significantly strengthened or adequate alternative arrangements could be made. The matter should not be clouded by calls for national sovereignty, which, Menderes claimed, had nothing to do with the real issue at stake.

Issues such as that posed by the Canal Zone, he stressed, ought to be seen from a larger perspective. Just as the British should receive backing from the West as a whole, so the French, in their disputes in North Africa, should be supported. These were areas vital to Western defence and to NATO, and it was in a forum such as NATO, Menderes insisted, that efforts should be made to find solutions satisfactory to national interests, which also protect Western interests.

Turning to the question of Middle East defence, Menderes began by noting that the original idea had been to involve the Arab states in a defence organisation. He believed the sponsoring powers had made every effort to achieve this. At this point, he said, the Turkish government had concluded that hope should be abandoned that the Arabs would join MEDO and a new concept for defence developed. In this case, he said, Turkey would have to serve as the backbone of the plan. Only Turkey, he said, had the political stability, the military strength and the commitment to resist Soviet aggression that were required to put teeth into a regional defence organisation. Turkey would be willing, Menderes declared, to undertake whatever efforts were necessary to help develop such an organisation.

Regarding US military aid to Turkey, Menderes stressed that Turkey's location on the Soviet border required Turkey to expend large amounts on defence. Efforts to improve defence had been intensified in recent years and would continue to go forward. The size of the Turkish armed forces was increasing, the number of junior officers being trained had grown, and new technicians were being trained. A joint analysis by NATO and JAMMAT officials had concluded that by the end of 1953 Turkey would be in a position to absorb some $500 million in additional military equipment. Of course, Menderes acknowledged, such equipment would have to come from the United States, and he was aware that there were many nations worldwide competing for US military aid and equipment. But, he stressed, US officials should be aware that dollars spent for defence in Turkey would yield more than those spent in any other country.

Likewise, increased US economic aid to Turkey would be used to an important purpose, Menderes told Dulles. During the past four years Turkey had, with US assistance, made great progress in economic development. This had been a useful experiment, he said, since much of the world believed that rapid economic progress could take place only under an authoritarian regime. By 1960 Turkey would prove the fallibility of this theory, Menderes declared, providing an example for other developing countries of how 'great progress can be achieved by giving way to free enterprise and economic liberty'.

Although the government sought to increase the standard of living of the Turkish population, Menderes added, another important goal to be fulfilled through economic development would be to increase Turkey's ability to maintain its army from its own resources. In the future, Menderes said, he expected that foreign investment would help to fill any gap created by a falling off of US economic aid. But for now, Menderes concluded, aid was needed to help Turkey play its role of 'guardian of civilisation and an element of security' in the part of the world where Turkey constitutes a bridge between the West and the undeveloped countries of the Near and Middle East.

Dulles, who by agreement had waited for Menderes to finish his presentation before responding, proceeded to answer some of the points raised by the Turkish prime minister. Regarding unity in the West, he said, although Soviet-style unity could be a strength, it could also be a weakness. Countries that became accustomed to operating in such a mode became incapable of independent and resourceful action in case of an emergency. Dulles said he was not dismayed at occasional disagreements among the countries of the free world, but he agreed that they should stand together to maximise their strength and improve their techniques for reaching agreement.

Dulles expressed agreement with the prime minister's remarks regarding the Suez Canal and its importance to the international community as a whole. He said that he had sought to stress this in his talks with General Naguib, but the idea had not seemed to penetrate. He suggested that all of the countries that shared this concern should try, in every way possible, to drive this point home to the Egyptians. There was little to be gained by forcibly holding on to the Suez base if the people who surrounded it were hostile, Dulles commented. Efforts should be concentrated on making Egyptian leaders aware of their responsibility and finding a solution that was acceptable to them.

Turning to the question of MEDO, Dulles agreed with Menderes that Turkey would have to be the backbone of any Middle Eastern defence arrangement. But, he said, there must be flesh surrounding the backbone. The secretary of state expressed surprise that Turkey was ready to disregard the Arab countries in this respect. Although he acknowledged that it might be true that a MEDO-type organisation was not practical for all of the Arab states, or at the present moment, Dulles felt it was also not realistic or wise to ignore the

Arab countries with respect to defence plans for their own area. Perhaps, he suggested, the northern Arab countries, such as Iraq, where Soviet pressures were felt more strongly and there was a sense of danger, could be encouraged to begin equipping themselves to meet the Soviet threat. He expressed interest in pursuing this matter further with Prime Minister Menderes.

Later that day, Dulles met with President Bayar and asked him to elaborate on his government's views on Middle East defence. Bayar responded that Turkey had always been sensitive to Russian policies, as a result of geographical and historical circumstances. At present, he noted, there were no problems along the frontier – not even the minor incidents that used to occur when Turkey and Russia had friendly relations. This had given Turks the impression, said Bayar, that the Russians had no present intentions of bringing pressure to bear on Turkey; but, he added, the Turks did not interpret this as a change of Soviet policy toward Turkey or toward the world as a whole. What it meant, rather, was that the Soviets would compromise when necessary in their larger objective of global domination. As a result, the Turks had no intention of relaxing their defences and would continue to prepare the country to resist Soviet aggression. Other NATO countries, he urged, should do likewise. If the United States, in particular, appeared to be slackening its efforts, this would serve to weaken the resolve of other nations, Bayar declared.

Shifting to the question of MEDO and Middle East defence, Bayar expressed views on Turkey's relations with the Arab states that were, if anything, more negative and pessimistic than those of his prime minister. Explaining that his government had tried for three years to engage the Arab states in a dialogue over creating a defence organisation, Bayar felt further effort was futile. Arab leaders, when brought together in a forum such as the Arab League, seemed only to vie over who was more nationalistic and 'tougher than the next guy'. There were no assurances that if the West gave arms to the Arabs today, they would not turn against them tomorrow, Bayar declared. The Arab states seemed to be entirely unaware of the danger posed by Russia. Thus, he said, we should feel free, in the event of war, to conduct our strategy as the situation dictates.

Dulles asked Bayar if he thought there were any Arab states that were reliable, to which Bayar responded that perhaps Iraq could be counted on. In Syria, Bayar said, any tough guy with a shotgun could take over at will. Syria's Shishikli, he said, had many enemies and might be out of power soon. Although Turkey had been impressed at first by General Naguib, he had not met expectations and now, it was rumoured, was flirting with the Soviets. 'We have lived together with the Arab countries for many years', Bayar told Dulles, 'and we have now concluded that we cannot ally with any of the present governments in the area. In the meantime, Turkey's right flank is exposed and in great danger'. In conclusion, Bayar pledged to go forward with efforts to build MEDO, if that were the policy of Turkey's allies, despite the belief that it would be a wasted effort.

The Soviet's main thrust at present, he concluded, was to prevent the entry of Germany and Japan into the defence system of the free world – a scenario that posed a constant nightmare to Soviet officials. One tactic the Soviet Union might employ to create disunity among the countries of the West, Köprülü predicted, was to propose the admission of Communist China into the United Nations.

THE BAGHDAD PACT EMERGES – AND DIES

It was at the end of his Ankara visit that, in an interview in the Embassy residence with the *New York Times*, Dulles unveiled his 'northern tier' concept of the Middle East defence. It was obvious that he had been greatly influenced in making this decision by his meetings with the Turkish leaders. Upon returning from the area, Dulles announced in mid-June his overall conclusions regarding the security of the area, some of which were not surprising but others of which implied new directions. Dulles recognised the continuing Soviet pressures and threat of aggression to which the Middle East was subject. He concluded that any sound defence of the area must be a result of the wishes of the peoples and governments of the various countries of the region, most of which were not willing to be associated with the West in a defence organisation. The states of the 'northern tier' (those bordering the USSR), he concluded, who best understood the Soviet threat, would be most likely to do something about it and were in the best position to protect the area as a whole. The cornerstone of any such alignment could only be Turkey – the strongest state in the region and the only NATO member.

Dulles, who had been favourably impressed by Menderes and his government during his talks in Ankara, looked to Turkey to take the lead in organising the 'northern tier', and Turkey was willing. The first step was a treaty of friendship and co-operation signed on 3 April 1954, between Turkey and Pakistan, with which Dulles had been conducting military negotiations. Iran, not having sufficiently worked out its relations with the United Kingdom regarding oil, was unable to join. On 24 February 1955 Turkey and Iraq's pro-British Nuri as-Said (prime minister since the previous summer) signed what was to become known as the Baghdad Pact. This proved to be a fatal mistake for Nuri, since it ignored the strong Arab nationalist trend sweeping the Middle East under the leadership of Egypt's popular Prime Minister Gamal Abd al-Nasser and resulted in the break-up of the Arab League.

The British became members of the Baghdad Pact on 4 April, as had been widely expected. Jordan, yielding to popular opposition despite British pressure, opted to stay out. Pakistan, however, joined in September 1955, and the shah of Iran, who turned to the West after the overthrow of his anti-Western Prime Minister Mohammed Mossadeq, signed in October, much to everyone's surprise.

The five members of the pact established a formal organisation in Baghdad, which was chosen as permanent headquarters in November 1955. The structure included a Council of Ministers and committees on military planning, economic co-operation, communications and counter-subversion. Conspicuous by its absence, however, was the United States, whose secretary of state had, more than anyone else, been responsible for the initiative that led to the inception of the pact. Although the United States later established a military liaison and sat on the committees of the pact, its failure to join in 1955, presumably out of concern for the Egyptian reaction and the efforts of the pro-Israel lobby, greatly weakened the pact.

Lord Robert Blake in *The Decline of Power* (1915–69) writes that Dulles and Eden, as the new British prime minister, had been in general agreement on a defensive alliance including the United States and United Kingdom, along with Turkey, Iran and Pakistan. In March 1955, however, Eden had without warning to Dulles signed an alliance with Turkey and Iraq, later called the Baghdad Pact. Although Iran and Pakistan later adhered, the inclusion of Iraq, a member of the Arab League, created serious implications for US-Israeli relations and caused Dulles to withdraw support from the pact. Eden, who Blake said was particularly irritated by Dulles anyway, considered that Dulles had reneged on an agreement. Inclusion of Iraq in the pact also, according to Blake, alienated Egypt and Saudi Arabia, which considered Iraq a British fief. This was another basis for United States reluctance.

The Baghdad Pact, as has been previously described, was destined to have a short life. It fell apart on 14 July 1958, with the overthrow of the regency in Iraq and the assassination of its principal founder, the pro-British Prime Minister Nuri as-Said. Early in 1958 Egypt and Syria had formed a union called the United Arab Republic, which was joined by Yemen; Jordan and Iraq had reacted by joining in what they called the 'Arab Federation'. In the ensuing wave of Arab nationalism there was trouble in Aden and also in Lebanon, where the United States landed troops on 15 July at the request of the Lebanese government. They were to stay until 25 October, a few days before the British retired from Jordan. When, after Nuri's assassination, Iraq withdrew from the Baghdad Pact, an era in US-UK efforts to organise a Middle East defence involving the Arab states had ended – in failure.

A high-level British official, who played an important role in this era, made the point that there was at that time some ambivalence in the United States' attitude between support for Britain as an ally against communism and support for nationalist movements against Britain, as a colonialist or at least a neo-imperialist power. He also emphasised the disturbing and demanding effect at that time of the emergence of the State of Israel on both the United States' and United Kingdom's relations with the Arabs. In this official's view, the British had entered the post-World War II Middle East with the burden of the Balfour Declaration around their necks; the United States had entered more recently and dramatically, bearing major responsibility for the creation of the State of Israel and giving the maintenance of Israel first priority in its Middle East policy. Perhaps with these handicaps it was hopeless from the start for either the United States or Britain to get the Arabs to see greater danger from Russia than from Israel.

The United Kingdom, the same official admits, concentrated its negotiations too much on Egypt. Egypt was, however, the most important country, and the cardinal British objective was to bring about a settlement between the Arabs (led by Egypt) and Israel. These efforts failed because no country (neither the United States nor the United Kingdom) was willing or able to obtain the necessary concessions from Israel, and the effort was too late to tempt Nasser back from his recourse to Russia.

I RESIGN MY POST AS US AMBASSADOR TO TURKEY

In accordance with tradition and as a part of a general reshuffle of ambassadors to reflect the sharp differences in foreign policy of the new Eisenhower administration, on 19 June 1953 I resigned my post as ambassador to Turkey to return to private life. My final telegram to the State Department reflected the state in which the Middle East Defence Organisation was left after more than two years of discussions. A few days earlier I had held a final meeting with Foreign Minister Köprülü, who continued to agree with the British that the original four sponsoring powers should 'set up shop' in the Middle East, in the hope that the Arab states would eventually decide to participate. He also appeared to be distressed by the Dulles theory, as expressed in his 1 June television address in the United States, that defence of the area must come from within, not be imposed from without.

I had assured Köprülü that Dulles' statement should not be taken as the final US word on MEDO and that I personally favoured an approach in which planning would continue, but quietly and without fanfare, among countries that had the forces and the desire to work toward Middle East defence. This way, I said, we would not appear to be flaunting the wishes of the Arab states, and there would be less chance of driving an irreconcilable wedge between ourselves and the Arabs.

Although Köprülü had been unwilling to abandon the 'setting up shop' approach, he mentioned a conversation he had held with the Iraqi leader Nuri as-Said in London, in which Said had said that although Iraq could not break with the Arab League at present, it was possible at some future date that Iraq could do so and join Turkey in creating a nucleus for Middle East defence.

In my last telegram to the department I emphasised the importance of a prompt clarification of the US position on Middle East defence. Continued uncertainty, I stressed, would lead to growing differences among the sponsoring powers and would fuel speculation that Turkey and the United States had a serious divergence of opinion. The Turks' real concern, especially after Dulles' speech, I pointed out, was that the United States was willing to wait indefinitely for the Arabs to agree to a defence organisation. Since they were sceptical that such an agreement would ever be forthcoming, the Turkish authorities wished to move ahead, along with the Americans and the

British, in order to close the dangerous security gap in the Middle East as quickly as possible.

Since such an approach could greatly anger the Arab states, however, it would evidently not further the US political objective of collaboration with the countries of the Middle East. Therefore, I suggested, as I had to Köprülü, that perhaps the United States should support covert ongoing talks and planning between Turkey, Great Britain and the United States – the three powers that actually had military forces in the area. This could have the effect of keeping the concept of MEDO alive and thereby calming Turkish anxieties, while at the same time avoiding a direct flaunting of Arab will.

I had greatly enjoyed my tour of duty as US ambassador in Turkey. I was, however, disappointed on leaving that all our efforts to organise a defence for the Middle East, in which I had on behalf of my country been involved since 1947 – for the most part in close co-operation with Turkey and the British – still remained in such an unsatisfactory state. The failure of the proposed Middle East Command in 1951 and the continued stalemate in creating its successor concept through the Middle East Defence Organisation, spoke for themselves. Although Turkey's greatest security aspirations had been fulfilled when it joined NATO in 1952, the Baghdad Pact, in which Turkey had played such a large role in founding and had joined in 1955, was destined to last only until 1958. The Baghdad Pact failed partly because NATO did not show any interest in establishing a liaison with it.

MEDO was succeeded by the relatively unspectacular Central Treaty Organisation, which lingered on until its recent natural and unlamented death. It did, however, serve for a while as a multinational link between Iran and the West and as means of channelling US and UK development aid into such useful projects as the Turkey-Iran railway, the Turkey-Iran harbour and the improvement of the Trebizon harbour. This seems a meagre return for such extended efforts by so many dedicated people to organise an effective Middle East defence. However, if the cure was never found the disease did not prevail, and the end result is the same. The Middle East with all its woes still remains free of Soviet domination, and is likely to continue so.

11 United States-Turkish Relations, 1953–89

Ties between the United States and Turkey have, since the post-World War II era, become increasingly close. Nevertheless, as one might expect under such complex arrangements between two strong, proud and sovereign nations, US-Turkish relations have also been tested and strained. After 40 years it is surprising that the partnership continues as well as it does. Even given shared interests and similar democratic institutions, the two nations differ in their ethnic, religious, political, geographic and historical background.

Yet the major issues that have developed between us cannot be attributed to these factors, or even to problems arising from our bilateral relationships. Curiously they have mainly been the result of a quite extraneous factor – enmity between Turkey and another country, Greece.

This is a familiar situation in today's world – the only real issues the United States faces with Israel and the Arab states result from their enmity toward each other. Greek-Turkish animosity dates back to centuries of Turkish rule of Greece, which ended after a bitter revolution only 155 years ago. Clashes after World War I fuelled this tradition as Greek forces invaded Turkey, only to be pushed back to Izmir (where most of the Greek population was evacuated), leaving the city in flames.

Greek-Turkish influence on US-Turkish relations has been further aggravated by a politically powerful and well-organised Greek-American minority of 3.5 million, which contrasts with a Turkish-American minority of only 200 000, which has little financial or political backing. Political differences between these two groups are bound to emerge in Congress, to the disadvantage of the Turks. An especially troublesome issue related to US assistance to these countries is that, despite a population ratio of two to ten, Greek and Turkish aid has for many years reflected a seven to ten ratio.

Greek-Turkish differences also stem from such issues as control of airspace, surface navigation and oil rights in the Aegean, where many Greek islands lie within sight of the Turkish coast. The United States seeks to avoid involvement in these disputes; however, its actions or failure to take action are frequently criticized by both sides.

Cyprus

Most dramatically, Greek-Turkish – and consequently US-Turkish – relations worsened following Turkey's invasion of Cyprus on 20–22 July 1974. The origins of this crisis can be found in the Greek-Turkish confrontation over Cyprus in 1963, which could have been predicted as almost inevitable in light of the historical background of these two quite different people. It must be remembered that relations between Greece and Turkey became only tolerable after World War I, as a result of the Venizelos-Inönü separation agreement, which exchanged 1 750 000 Greeks and Turks (a total of 3 500 000 persons) and left only 100 000 of each in the other country.

The 1959 Cyprus agreements provided that the 20 per cent Turkish minority in Cyprus would have certain guaranteed political rights, as a protection from the Greek majority. Cyprus would have a legislature with separate representation for the Greek and Turkish communities, an elected Greek-Cypriot president, a Turkish-Cypriot vice-president and a veto by both sides on major issues. Two extraterritorial British bases would remain in the south. The plan never worked well. In 1963 President Archbishop Makarios proposed the elimination of the provisions involving communal separation. As a result, civil war became almost inevitable; the necessity for separation of Greeks and Turks by some federal solution became urgent.

What followed was something of a turning point in US-Turkish relations, which (as will be described later) were already tense in the aftermath of the Cuban missile crisis and removal of Jupiter MRBMs from Turkey. During 1963 and 1964 the State Department and President Lyndon Johnson had become concerned that the apparent civil war in Cyprus would lead not only to a Turkish but a Soviet intervention. On 15 June 1964 Johnson sent to Inönü a letter that remains to this day a major irritant in US-Turkish relations. First, it cast doubt on the NATO guarantee to Turkey in the event that Turkish intervention in Cyprus, without NATO approval, led to a Soviet reprisal. Second, it stated that the United States would not permit the use of US-supplied equipment in any Turkish intervention. There is a possibility that Johnson over-reacted, attributing too great a danger of Soviet intervention and not recognising the affront to Turkey in threatening the disavowal of our NATO guarantee to Turkey and denying Turkey its legitimate rights under the Zurich-London agreement of 1959.

It was on the justification of these treaties, by which Turkey, Greece and Great Britain had agreed to intervene to restore the government of Cyprus if it was overthrown and the safety of the Turkish minority threatened, that Turkish forces occupied Cyprus in 1974. The occasion was a coup against Makarios by the military dictatorship in Athens which was determined to create a union with Greece. The British had declined Turkey's invitation to join them. Strongly influenced by the Greek-American lobby, the United States responded to Turkey's subsequent consolidation of its positions by imposing an embargo of military supplies to Turkey from February to September 1975, followed by a cap on military aid that remained in effect until 1978. The United States held that Turkey had illegally used US aid material for purposes not intended (a position it should be noted, which it did not take when Israel invaded Lebanon in 1982 using American aid cluster bombs). The Turkish government retaliated by restricting US bases on its territory.

After the successful Vance mission in 1976, the Cyprus issue became less critical. The threat of war was replaced by continuous but unproductive negotiations between the leaders of the Greek and Turkish factions in Cyprus, with occasional inconclusive assistance from the United Nations. Turkey's creation of the Independent Turkish State of Northern Cyprus in 1983 has been universally criticised, and the 'state' is recognised only by Turkey.

The unfortunate history of the Cyprus affair since 1963 has been reviewed thoroughly by historians and is the subject of another authoritative review by former US ambassador to Turkey Parker Hart. I will add only that it still resists a solution. Despite determined efforts by skilled US and UN negotiators, including George Ball, William Fulbright, Dean Acheson and Cyrus Vance, and in 1986 the UN Secretary-General Pérez de Cuéllar, Cyprus remains, unfortunately, a key impediment in the normalisation of Greek-Turkish relations and, because it has been taken up as a major cause by the US-Greek minority, in US-Turkish relations.

Turkish Political Unrest

The 1960s and 1970s were no less tumultuous for Turkey within its own borders. During this period democracy suffered several blows, with the replacement of one government after another, rampant political violence, and harsh methods of control. The deteriorating situation negatively affected US attitudes toward Turkey, and it has also led to accusations of human rights violations.

When it all began in 1960, the Democratic Party was in power, led by Prime Minister Adnan Menderes. Military officers instigated a coup d'état based on accusations that Menderes was using authoritarian methods. The military supplanted the parliamentary regime with an interim military government under General Cemal Gursel and suspended all political activities. In September 1961 Menderes was brought to trial, charged with abuse of power and executed.

After supervising the creation of a new constitution, the military turned control of the country over to the Republican Party leader, Ismet Inönü, who came out of retirement to win a plurality in the 1961 elections. Five years later, however, the electorate gave an overwhelming majority to the Justice Party, which had been formed from the banned Democratic Party. In the political and sectarian violence that followed, violent strikes broke out and assassinations averaged 20 a day. The related martial law and police action have been the targets of some of the human rights accusations mentioned above. In 1971 Süleyman Demirel, unable to cope with the situation, resigned at the demand of the armed forces. These forces, after their peaceful takeover, instituted a period of 'guided democracy' under a government of civilian technocrats deemed by the military to be above party considerations.

When the scholarly Bülent Ecevit became leader of the Republican Party, he set it on a leftward course, aligning the party with the Social Democratic parties of Western Europe and calling for a more independent foreign policy that would stress an improvement in relations with other Muslim countries of the Middle East. The RPP emerged from the 1973 elections as the most popular party in a crowded field, but short of a parliamentary majority. This government, which had to rely on an uneasy coalition with the Islamic National Salvation Party (NSP), was short-lived. Expecting to take advantage of his hero status resulting from his handling of the Cyprus crisis, Ecevit resigned in early 1975 to force an election; however, the NSP reneged on its agreement to support the elections.

The deferral of a return to democratic government, accompanied by thousands of imprisonments without the usual judicial procedures and the continuing imposition of martial law, particularly in the urban areas, inspired widespread European criticism. Neither Democrats nor Republicans could deal effectively with the escalating violence between political extremists, which was killing thousands each year. The government was also still plagued by severe economic ills.

To save the situation, the armed forces General Kenan Evren intervened yet again in September 1980. The military deposed the civilian government, took political leaders into custody and established a military council to rule the country, promising to restore democracy by 1984. Turkey's human rights record again came under attack. Evren continued the radical economic programme initiated in 1980 by Turgut Özal under the Demirel regime. In the meantime, a constituent assembly, whose members represented interests identified with the military, was named to draw up the constitution that was approved in a referendum held in November 1982. General Evren continued as president. In elections held in 1983 Özal, then the right-of-centre leader of the Motherland Party, despite opposition by President Evren, was elected prime minister and took office on 13 December. This series of political events, although resolved, had made an impression on US public opinion and created tensions in the US-Turkish partnership.

Final Efforts at Regional Defence

In 1958, the same year that the United States used Turkish bases without permission to stage its intervention in the Lebanon crisis, the Baghdad Pact failed. Both occurrences were irritants to the US-Turkish relationship, but the pact's disintegration was a greater blow to Prime Minister Menderes' Middle Eastern policy. This was ameliorated somewhat by the Co-operation Agreement signed between the two governments on 5 March 1959, expressing the determination of both countries to resist aggression, direct or indirect. The new name, Central Treaty Organisation, was intended to show the organisation's role as a link with NATO. However, it was never able to provide a strong basis for co-ordinating US bilateral aid with the military, economic and political issues facing the remaining member countries, and, as mentioned earlier, it was finally abandoned in 1978. The only subsequent effort to revive Middle East security co-operation was made by Secretary of State Haig at the beginning of the Reagan administration. Although he tried to create a Middle East 'consensus' on regional defence against the Soviets, this proposal had not been given sufficient study and took too lightly the enmity between Israel and the Arab states to have any hope for success.

Removal of Jupiter Missiles from Turkey

One of John F. Kennedy's initial acts as president was to ask former Secretary of State Dean Acheson to make a general study of US policy toward NATO. I participated as a member of Mr Acheson's supporting committee, whose recommendations included the removal of the MRBMs – the Jupiters – from Turkey and Italy. During a meeting on this problem, the president asked me, presumably because of my experience in Turkey, if I thought the Turks would permit us to take the MRBMs out. I replied that I doubted it, but that we could go into the matter thoroughly and see what could be done.

Consequently, we studied the matter, obtained the advice of the Embassy in Ankara, and Secretary Rusk and I talked with the Turkish foreign minister during a CENTO meeting in Ankara. His reaction was sharply against removal of the MRBMs. The Turks had put a good deal of money into the installation of the Jupiters, which had just come into place. According to the foreign minister it would be difficult for the Turkish people to understand their removal without any compensating additions to their security. Thus, I reported to President Kennedy that, in my opinion, the Turks would not agree to the removal of the MRBMs without some compensation or stronger pressure than would be justified at that time.

Much later the Jupiters were removed, but only when the United States was able to introduce Polaris submarines into the Mediterranean. It would have been preferable if the president's original wish could have been carried out, since the removal of the MRBMs at the later date was widely, and as it now turns out correctly, interpreted as a consideration paid by us for the removal of offensive Soviet missiles from Cuba. In a recent statement, former Secretary of State Dean Rusk revealed that there was a more direct relationship than was admitted at the time between the removal of the Soviet missiles in Cuba, whose presence had been confirmed on 15 October 1962, and the subsequent removal of the US Jupiter missiles from Turkey.

According to Rusk, Robert Kennedy communicated secretly to Soviet Ambassador to Washington Anatoly Dobrynin on 21 October President Kennedy's willingness to remove the Jupiters in Turkey within three to four months of the Soviet removal of missiles from Cuba if this could be done without a public announcement revealing that a deal had been struck. This was accepted by Khrushchev. Rusk also revealed, and this for the first time, that President Kennedy, at the time unbeknown to other high officials except Rusk, had also agreed to an open Cuban-Turkish missile swap if the Soviets insisted. However, Khrushchev's approval of Robert Kennedy's first approach fortunately made this unnecessary.

Although plans were under way to retire the Jupiter missiles in Turkey before the Cuban missile crisis, no final decision had been made by NATO. The Turks had been expected to object; however, when the Jupiters were finally removed pursuant to the Kennedy-Khrushchev decision, there was little Turkish complaint. The Turks had observed the threat of a US attack on Cuba following the Soviet missile emplacement there, and they were just as happy to be relieved of such a threat by the Soviets.

Other Problems

Other issues as well have disturbed US-Turkish relations, leading at times to anti-Americanism in Turkey and even on several occasions the assassination of American citizens. Many of these issues reflect the continuous bargaining process for the amount and terms of US aid on the part of the Turks, and for base and personnel rights on the part of the United States. US-Turkish relations have also occasionally become involved in world trends, including student radicalism, which have no relation to underlying US-Turkish interests. In 1970–71 it was concern over the drug trade that led the United States to demand that Turkey eliminate illegal opium sales, with which Turkey eventually complied after we offered $35 million to cushion the impact on Turkish poppy farmers.

Turkey has also come under criticism for its handling of certain problems. One involves the continued attempts of the Kurdish minority in eastern Turkey, aided by the Iraqi Kurds, to gain autonomy from Turkish rule. Although they have a majority in eight southeastern provinces in Turkey, Kurds represent only 8 per cent of the population. The Turkish effort to quell the Kurdish rebellion, which has included drastic actions in the face of Kurdish terrorism, has created human rights accusations against the Turks. These have been expressed more forcefully in Europe than in the United States, however.

Another problem that involves both American public opinion and congressional action is the continuing effort by persons of Armenian descent to redress incidents that occurred during World War I between Turks and the Turkish-Armenian minority. Although greatly to be regretted, it must be remembered that many of these events involved Armenians accused of collaboration with the Soviets, with whom Turkey was at war, when Turkey was under the sultanate. The Armenians were at that time being encouraged by the Soviets and later by the Western powers who occupied Turkey to set up an independent state. In recent years 30 Turkish diplomats in a number of countries have been assassinated by the Armenian Secret Army for the Liberation of Armenia; in the United States it has sparked Armenian-American propaganda campaigns and lobbying for congressional actions censuring Turkey.

Outlook

Following the lifting of the Cyprus-related arms embargo against Turkey by President Carter in April 1978, which was approved by Congress in September, an effort was made to normalise US-Turkish relations. In January 1979 Under-Secretary of State Warren Christopher undertook the negotiation of a treaty called the US-Turkish Defense and Economic Cooperation Agreement of 1980 (DECA), which was signed early in 1980 with a very salutary effect. The DECA provided for the regulation of US military bases in Turkey and for military and other types of assistance. The DECA was renewed in 1985 and has been recognised by the Özal government.

Turkish-US relations have improved greatly in recent years. The Reagan administration has indicated full appreciation of the important contribution Turkey could make in Western defence and has, within the often severe limits set by Congress, attempted to provide generous military support. In April 1988 Turkey quietly ratified a new base agreement quite acceptable to the United States, which it had held up for some time hoping for more favourable financial terms.

The principal remaining US-Turkish differences might be summarised as follows: the built-in possibility for irritations and conflict stemming from the US and NATO dependence on Turkish military forces and bases, and the continuing Turkish need for US economic and military assistance. These reciprocal needs have required the United States to protect itself from excessive Turkish demands, and the natural Turkish desire to maximise aid and to make as favourable as possible the conditions attached, without putting Turkey in the position of a mendicant or making the United States a 'patsy'. Such a necessity has resulted in difficult, even bitter, negotiations, which have often ended in disappointment and resentment on both sides.

A related category of problems arises out of the necessary involvement of US officials in internal Turkish affairs, as a result of the four decades of US military and economic assistance. The presence of US personnel in Turkey in such large numbers has exaggerated differences between personalities, in customs and living standards and has resulted in the occasional infraction of Turkish law by US citizens. There have also been adverse Turkish reactions to real or imagined arrogance or lack of consideration on the part of US personnel or the attempt to impose US viewpoints. These differences, however, have diminished over time as the two peoples have come to understand each other better and as the numbers of US personnel have decreased. Nevertheless, problems remain between the two countries, which, although not believed critical, still evade satisfactory solutions.

12 Turkey's Role Today

In analysing the importance of Turkey to NATO we must first consider what it is in a position to contribute, not just to the defence of the Middle East, but to the territory of the NATO countries themselves to which the alliance is committed. Turkey's principal role in NATO is to defend itself, which it has always done historically. A land attack would come either through Bulgaria and Thrace, or Turkey's eastern border with the USSR. Turkey could, of course, also be attacked by air or by sea, through the Bosporus or its Black Sea coast. The Turkish forces required for defence, for which they are basically armed and configured, are also available for offence. It has been estimated that they would in time of war pin down perhaps 30 Soviet divisions in the Balkans which would otherwise be available for the central NATO front, plus perhaps half as many in the Transcaucasus. In the event of a war involving the alliance as a whole, Incirlik in eastern Turkey and other Turkish air bases could be used by Turkish, US and other NATO bombers through refuelling, or by tactical fighter bombers.

NATO control of the eastern Mediterranean, which will be of prime importance in the event of a war with the Warsaw Pact, will be dependent on Turkish air and naval forces and other NATO forces using air and naval bases in Turkey. The Mediterranean provides access to NATO Mediterranean members for most of their normal supplies of oil and other imports, as well as the supply for NATO military forces. Turkey would also be valuable to the alliance as long as it controls the Bosporus and Dardanelles, by providing access of NATO vessels to the Black Sea, and to deny Soviet vessels access to the Mediterranean. Half of normal Soviet imports and resupply and replacement of Soviet naval forces must transit the Bosporus. Turkey also provides on its Black Sea coast invaluable forward radio intelligence gathering resources not available anywhere else.

In assessing Turkey's role as a bastion of defence we must also consider its assets in human, economic and military terms. In view of Turkish application for membership in the Common Market, comparisons will be made between Turkey and the average of its four leading members. [Statistics are according to the World Bank's World Development Report, 1988.]

TURKEY'S ASSETS

Turkey's population in 1986 was ɔ1.5 million, 15 per cent less than the average population of 57.5 million in Italy, France, Germany and the United Kingdom. Each of these countries comprises only about a quarter of Turkey's territory. Turkey's rate of 'population momentum' – 1.8 per cent for 1986, down from 2.5 per cent in 1980–85 – greatly exceeds the average of the four countries cited above, which is 1.1 per cent. According to the estimates, Turkey's population will grow to 67 million in the year 2000 compared with the four-country average of 58 million. Turkey's hypothetical ultimate stationary population of 112 million compares with an average for the four of 50 million.

Turkey's gross national product (GNP) per capita in 1986 of $1110 was greatly exceeded by the average of the four European countries cited, which was $10 040 per capita. The Turkish gross domestic product (GDP) growth rate in 1980–85, however, was the largest in the Organisation for Ecomonic Co-operation and Development, Turkey having moved ahead of Japan. Turkey's average annual GNP growth rate for 1965–86 was 2.7, approximately the same as the four major European countries but on a much lower base.

Despite the fact that Turkey's GNP continues to lag behind all of the Common Market countries – the lowest being Greece's $3680 per capita – it shows a great increase over its 1960 figure of $207 per capita. Turkey provides an example of an undeveloped country that has used foreign assistance to achieve a modest economic 'takeoff'. However, Turkey has been unable to control inflation, which averaged 37.3 per cent in 1980–86 compared with an 8 per cent average for the European group.

Compared with the European four, a higher percentage of Turkey's gross domestic product came from agriculture in 1986 – 19 per cent versus 3 per cent, but industry accounted for approximately the same 36 per cent and manufacturing the same 25 per cent. Income from services in Turkey, however, at 46 per cent in 1986 was below the 56 per cent average of the four. Turkey showed a comparatively high 1986 gross domestic investment, at 25 per cent. Energy consumption in Turkey in 1986, however, was very low, at 750 kilograms of oil equivalent per capita, compared with a 3800 kilograms average for the four West European powers.

Turkey was one of the first important countries in recent years to encounter an acute international debt problem when its foreign commitments rose in 1980 to $51.229 billion. Turkey and its international creditors, after long and difficult negotiations managed by the International Monetary Fund (IMF) and the World Bank, assisted by West Germany, arranged a debt restructuring that included loans from the IMF in return for extreme austerity in the Turkish budget. Turkey's debt has since remained virtually constant, with a drop in balance of payments deficit from $2.983 billion in 1980 to $1.528 billion in 1986. External public and publicly guaranteed debt in 1986 was $23.309 billion, with total external debt at $31.808 billion. In the meantime, however, so many other countries have encountered much greater deficits, Brazil and Mexico leading with debts exceeding $100 billion, that the international spotlight has shifted from the Turkish debt.

Turkey has in recent years greatly expanded its external trade, exports having increased from $321 million in 1960 to $7.985 billion in 1986, imports from $468 million to $11.027 billion in 1986. Turkey turned to the outside world to finance its first and now its second bridge over the Bosporus, which will be built by a Turkish-Japanese consortium with US financing. Several US banks have opened branches in Istanbul. For the first time a stock exchange is operating in Istanbul, even though on a limited basis. Starting in 1970, Turkish contractors developed a backlog of jobs, mainly in the Middle East, exceeding $10 billion; however, this has decreased with the erosion of the oil price.

Turkey still has its economic problems. Unemployment stands at 20 per cent, with poor prospects for future job opportunities in the Common Market. Özal has promised to bring down the persistent 60 to 70 per cent inflation rate to 35 per cent; however, this has not yet been achieved. There has been resistance and a political reaction to increased prices for gasoline and other commodities forced by the government, and this will have an influence on the outcome of future elections.

As far as health and nutrition are concerned, however, the daily caloric intake in Turkey is a healthy 3167 calories. Longevity stands at 64 years, halfway between that in the low-income countries of Asia and Africa and that of the European industrial market countries, which average about 54 and 74 years respectively.

Since the Turkish armed forces are so important to the defence of the Middle East, can we be sure they are equal to the task? In 1985 the International Institute for Strategic Studies set the Turkish armed forces at 602 000, of whom 544 000 were conscripts on a 20-month tour of duty. This constituted the largest force among the European members of NATO, a force twice the size of Great Britain's. Of the Turkish forces, 500 000 were in the army, including 475 000 conscripts. The Turkish forces, which were commanded from four army and ten corps headquarters, consisted of: one armoured, two mechanical, and 14 infantry divisions, plus four armoured, four mechanical, and 11 infantry brigades. They had 4352 tanks, principally M–48A1 (currently being upgraded to M–48A5s) and M–113 APC. The army alone had 700 000 reserves, for a total mobilisation potential of 1 300 000.

The Turkish navy of 46 000, including marines and 36 000 conscripts, had 16 submarines, 13 US destroyers, plus 140 auxiliary ships; navy reserves totalled 70 000. The air force comprised 56 000 personnel, 33 000 of whom were conscripts, plus 66 000 reserves. Turkey had 450 combat aircraft in two tactical, 17 fighter, two interceptor, two reconnaissance, and six transportation squadrons.

We must recognise the very substantial investment that the United States has made in the Turkish armed forces, aggregating $8.8 billion between 1946 and 1987. Since 1982 the United States through its Military Assistance Program, Economic Support Fund, and International Military Educational Training Program, has allocated annually to Turkey from $600 to $800 million, averaging $700 million. During the same period Greece has received from $300 to $600 million annually; Spain, $160 to $400 million; and Portugal $100 to $200 million. The United States still maintains rights in six military bases in Turkey: Sinop on the Black Sea, Incirlik, Umurtalik and Iskendrun in South Central Turkey, Beelbasi near Ankara and Diyarbakir in eastern Turkey. These are valuable assets for US defence, as well as for the defence of Turkey and NATO. We cannot, however, take Turkey for granted. A new agreement negotiated in 1986 and signed in March 1987, extending US base rights to 1990, was not ratified until almost a year later because the Turkish government considered we had not lived up to the assurances given on aid levels.

Numbers alone, of course, do not provide a definitive insight into the fighting qualities of a military force. For almost 600 years Turkey sustained through its military might the most extensive empire of its time Although religious zeal for a holy war was cultivated as an important factor, an intense Turkish nationalism, which can be traced back to Turkish origins in central Asia, has always constituted the basic motivation for the Turkish fighting man. Inured to hardship by the severe climate of the Anatolian plateau, and indifferent to personal pain, the Turkish soldier has created over the centuries a unique, worldwide reputation.

Former Ambassador to Turkey Raymond Hare, who is a close observer of the Turks and Turkish history, characterises the Turks as being a military people without being militaristic. Although Turkey is now a democracy, the Turkish armed forces still consider themselves the inheritors of a Turkish military tradition that can be traced to Atatürk and further back to an unbroken line of 39 sultans since 1281. That there is no other comparable remaining national military tradition gives confidence that if the Turkish homeland is threatened or invaded, Turkey's military forces would respond with the same loyalty and vigour they have exhibited over the centuries. Those forces are in place squarely along the only possible Soviet invasion routes into the Middle East, and the Soviets know if they invade, the Turks and all of NATO will be involved. Turkey continues to fulfill its historical role of the 'cork in the bottle' of access to the Middle East.

COMPATIBLE INTERESTS

Authorities have made various interpretations over the years of the changing world role of Turkey and of Turkish relations with the United States, Western Europe, NATO and the Soviet Union. In his thoughtful 1971 study, *Troubled Alliance*, George S. Harris correctly characterised the US-Turkish alliance as a defensive arrangement against what appears to be a waning threat. Seventeen years later, however, this has not resulted in any drastic improvements in Turkish-Soviet relations or any radical changes in Turkey's loyalty to NATO or its strategic position in the alliance.

Various commentators have also cited the long list of US-Turkish disagreements, which I have recognised earlier; however, I do not feel that their net effect is necessarily cumulative. Most problems – such as the annual bickering over aid, the stopping of the flow of Turkish opium, the US-Turkish Status of Forces Agreements, and the use of the Incirlik air base – come and go and are usually forgiven and forgotten. Even the Cyprus issue, although unresolved, has with time receded into the general background of such intractable problems as Northern Ireland. There are, I contend, no issues between us that, like a cancerous cell, have increased progressively in intensity without any remedy having been devised. Let us examine where the United States, the West as a whole, and Turkey stand on the basic issues determining our collective security and well-being.

To begin with basic matters, there is a broad congruity of interests between the United States and Turkey. Turkey has proved the permanence if not the maturity of its democracy. The recent Turkish election that returned Prime Minister Özal to office is recognised as having been a free one, and Özal was permitted to take office even though he was originally opposed by President Kenan Evren, the recognised leader of the Turkish military. The Özal government is clearly committed to the furtherance of a free enterprise market economy. Foreign exchange regulations have been virtually eliminated and the role of state enterprises greatly reduced through the elimination of monopolies and subsidies. US and other foreign investment is welcome. Accusations of civil rights violations, left over from the anarchy that existed in Turkey in the 1970s and from the continuing Kurdish rebellion, have decreased. The European Human Rights Commission recently dropped the suit it has been pursuing against Turkey since 1982.

During a period when the US government has been sensitive to the attitudes of other nations toward the Soviet Union, there is no criticism in the United States of Turkish policy toward communism, the Soviet Union or other communist states. The Communist Party is still outlawed in Turkey. The Turkish attitude, and that of the Islamic world generally toward the Soviet Union was adversely affected by the Soviet occupation of Afghanistan. Turkey's attitude toward Bulgaria has recently worsened as a result of the harsh treatment of the Turkish minority there. Turkey's relations with neighbouring Syria, the principal Soviet client in the Middle East, remain cool. Despite occasional offhand comments by Turkish leaders in response to what they considered unfair European criticism, Turkey has never seriously considered withdrawing its forces from, or reducing its co-operation with NATO.

The virtual anarchy that existed in Turkey in the 1970s, while a product of a number of complex developments, was due, at least in part, to Marxist communism, which influenced leftists among teachers, students and the press and figured in the limited support for the activist Confederation of Revolutionary Trade Unions. Although Turkey has accepted closer economic ties and assistance from the Soviet Union since the later 1970s, there has been no increase in the votes for the only political party that supports Marxist-Leninism, the Turkish Labor Party. From a peak of 3 per cent of the electorate in 1965, its last show of strength was 0.1 per cent.

Law enforcement was reinstated, accompanied by widespread martial law, under the government established after General Evren's coup in 1980. The resulting 1982 constitution and election law removed many of the constitutional defects that had led earlier to widespread disaffection. Marxist communism thus finds a much less fertile ground in which to sow dissent. Rustow, in *Turkey, America's Forgotten Ally*, notes that in eight successive Turkish elections spanning three decades, at least six out of seven Turkish voters have decisively supported political parties advocating gradual democratic change.

MUTUAL EXPECTATIONS

What does the United States expect from Turkey? In the first place, it hopes that Turkey will continue to improve its Western-oriented policies, its development of true parliamentary democracy, and its loyal adherence to NATO in fulfillment of its natural role as protector of the eastern NATO flank and as a barrier to Soviet expansion into the Middle East. The United States also hopes that Turkey will continue to shape its economy increasingly toward a free enterprise market system, combined with a liberal international economic policy, as this is consonant with the US view of democracy and fits in with the world trading system in which America participates.

There are hopes that Turkey will strengthen its influence as a free world military and economic force. The United States would also like to see Turkey exert its latent leadership abilities in the Islamic world, particularly over nations that in recent years have generated conflict among themselves and with the West. America hopes that Turkey, while protecting itself against militant conservative Islamic movements, can take advantage of its membership in the Islamic Conference Organisation, which it joined in 1976, to help blunt the present efforts being made by Iran's Ayatollah Khomeini to desecularise the Islamic world and make it a base for a modern-day religious war against the West.

Although the United States seeks and would welcome a normalisation of relations between Turkey and the Soviet Union, it hopes that the Turks will continue to make it clear to the Soviets that they will not tolerate communist political intrusion into Turkey, or pressure to alter Turkey's borders or its control of the straits, and that they will oppose by force Soviet aggression against NATO or the Middle East.

The fluid situation in Afghanistan since the Soviet withdrawal, the withdrawal of Iran from co-operation with the West, and the uncertainty regarding the Greek NATO commitment leave Turkey as the only reliable element in the northern tier of the Middle East.

Are these goals that the United States can reasonably expect from Turkey? Acknowledging that as a proud, independent nation, these are decisions that only Turkey can make, I see no reason arising from Turkish history, religion or character that need preclude their continued acceptance by Turkey.

And what do the Turks expect that will influence them to follow policies congenial to America and the West? Are Turkish expectations reasonable and fulfillable? In the first place, Turkey can be expected to continue to demand special consideration by the United States, Europe and NATO in light of the unique situation Turkey faces and the unique contribution it is in a position to make. Turkey is located in a dangerous part of the world – and knows it. Turkey has been under constant threat from the Soviets over the centuries, and still is. In aligning itself with the West, it helped greatly in strengthening the NATO line and in creating a barrier against Soviet expansion in the eastern Mediterranean and the Middle East. As a reward for the effort and risks this entails for them, the Turks expect to be given assistance in arms and training and expect supplies and reinforcements in the event of war. Turkey expects that its voice will be heard in NATO councils before important decisions are taken, in accordance with its military strength.

As the least developed member of NATO, Turkey expects continued economic assistance from the United States and particularly from Europe, with which it has a more natural basis for a trading partnership. This could assume the form of grants and loans and access to markets – and in the case of the European Community, access of Turkish labour to reduce unemployment at home and gain remittances of much needed hard currencies. As a suppliant for entry into full membership in the community, in which it became an associate member in 1962, Turkey feels rebuffed. Entry is now forecast to be at least ten years away, if ever – the barriers arising basically from fear of too many Turkish workers; the below-European levels of the Turkish economy; and the competition Turkish imports would provide to the recently admitted South European Community members. There is also the threat of a Greek veto.

European Community entry is, I believe, the greatest potential danger in Turkey's relations with the other NATO countries, although the problems associated with entry are not insurmountable. Yet, if after making a determined effort to join the European Community, Turkey concludes that it has little or no chance of success, it might feel forced to seek an alternative course. Such a decision may not necessarily separate Turkey from the United States, but it would drastically affect Turkey's relations with Western Europe. Turkey, in its frustration, may turn back to the east and seek its future in the Middle East, South Asia and the developing world.

I do not believe this alternative will be attractive to the Turks, except under extreme circumstances. Two tendencies in Turkey, however, should be followed very closely. Many Turks feel that they, particularly their youth, are being subjected to an organised underground attack by Khomeini Shiite proselytisers. Indeed, a prominent Turkish friend considers that this is Turkey's principal current threat. Although Turkey is 99 per cent Islamic, with an overwhelming Sunni majority, there is a 10 to 20 per cent minority of Alevis, who are related to the Syrian Alawis. In general, Turks, as non-Arabs and converts to Islam, have not been subject to the extreme religious radicalism found in Iran and Egypt. However, this could be stimulated by a traumatic national experience, such as a feeling of rejection by the West.

Turks also tend to feel isolated – loners in a hostile Middle Eastern world. This was the topic of a recent speech by a distinguished Turkish admiral, which was widely commented on. Turkey's past relations with Greece, Bulgaria, Syria and the Soviet Union speak for themselves. Iraq, which the Turks once ruled and with which they have since enjoyed good relations, has seemed distant under Hussein. Even the United States appears to the Turks to have turned against them (for example, in the case of the arms embargo), as a result of the political power of the hostile US-Greek minority. In a contest in Congress the Greek minority will always win. Europeans, Turks feel, although they once took millions of Turkish workers and accepted Turkey in NATO, now close their doors, reject Turkey's application for full membership in the European Community and discriminate against Turkish exports.

A Turkish friend, whose opinion I respect, said that he and many Turks want to see the Turkish population continue to increase at the present high rate so that it will grow to 100 million to protect Turkey from its unfriendly neighbours. This, of course, would make almost impossible the Turkish drive to improve living standards. The resulting increased pressure for European jobs for Turkish workers would further increase the obstacles to Turkish acceptance in the European Community.

A VALUABLE ALLIANCE

From the US viewpoint, there is little choice whether it is we or our European allies who can fulfill Turkey's needs and aspirations. Various European powers have exercised strong influence over Turkey in the past from a cultural and educational viewpoint: Germany, whose form of university organisation, language and science Turkey once followed, and France, whose language and culture, particularly in diplomacy and the arts, were widely accepted before the British and Americans came. The French Lycée de Galatasaray in Istanbul was once a popular secondary school for the Turkish élite. The Turks first learned English from the British, but after 1947 Americans exerted a strong influence in higher education through Robert College in Istanbul and Hacetepe University and the Middle East Technical University in Ankara, where instruction is in English.

Progress in other fields in Turkey has resulted from the remarkable advance that has been made in education. Literacy, which was only 33 1/3 per cent in 1950, stood at 69 per cent in 1985. Nine out of ten Turkish children today are in a primary school. Between 1960 and 1975 the graduates of universities and technical schools tripled. With only one exception, the 68 provinces of Turkey have teacher training institutes. In many cases English has given way to German again, because of increased numbers of German tourists, the return of Turkish workers from Germany and Germany's importance as Turkey's lead trading partner. (I remember assuring the German ambassador in 1952 that we would both live to see a renewed German predominance in trade with Turkey, since Germany had a more natural basis for trade than the United States.)

In broad terms, Turkey really has no alternative but to continue its pursuit of association with the West. Only in this way can it find security from the Soviet Union. The Soviet Union's natural desire to control the Turkish Straits and to remove the one remaining obstacle to an unhindered access to the oil and stragetic geography of the Middle East, will always make it a *demandeur* – if not an enemy – of Turkey. In purely economic terms the USSR, its people suffering the economic failure of its system, has little to offer Turkey – especially compared with what the United States and Europe can offer. The cultural rewards to Turkey from a closer association with the USSR, moreover, would be thin compared with what America and Europe provide. With the inevitable decline of oil revenues, most Middle Eastern and other Islamic countries will offer fewer economic opportunities, with little advantage in cultural exchange.

The best way the United States can assist Turkey now, I believe, is by helping it attain membership in the European Community – even if this comes somewhat at the expense of US bilateral trade with Turkey. Association with the West provides Turkey's best hope for the future. The momentum Turkey has acquired in its persistent postwar quest for acceptance by the West is well-nigh irresistible. It has reached a point of no return. Turkey's pull toward the West has in recent years been strengthened by manifold economic ties, including access to finance, technical assistance, imports and markets. The several million Turkish workers who have returned from Germany provide additional links. Turkey can make a contribution and profit by acting as middleman in trade and transit between Europe and the Middle East, but this role – as well as further Turkish economic development – depends on the closeness of its connection to the West.

Americans, I believe, are fortunate that we, as a nation, have developed such close ties with Turkey, in light of the sort of country Turkey is and where it is located. If we are to preserve these ties, we must be respectful of Turkey's claims on our partnership. We must place Turkey high on the priority list of nations we are willing to assist. We must contest efforts to relate through some mechanistic formula the aid we give to Turkey to what we give to Greece. We must restrain the Armenian-American groups that seek to revive age-old issues at the expense of current relations with the Turks. We must seek restraint for those who would leave Turkey to bear the full brunt of a Gramm-Rudman-type aid reduction while Israel and Egypt continue to receive almost half of all US foreign aid.

Our attitude toward Turkey should not be viewed as altruism, gratitude for past favours, or sympathy because Turkey has lagged in its economic development. It should be based on the role Turkey has played in the past in the world power game – and the role it can play in the future. The Turks are a resolute people willing to fight for their freedom; Turkey lies athwart Soviet access to the world's greatest repository of oil and strategic territory. We must be sure it remains the common interest of Turkey and the United States to maintain Turkey's role.

Notes

This volume is based largely on my personal notes and recollections, which have in most cases been reinforced and added to by the official State Department documents available and covering the period under review. These include memorandums of conversations, telegrams, letters and miscellaneous reports, some drafted by me and some by others. Many of the State Department documents referred to have been declassified and published in *Foreign Relations of the United States*, vol. 5, Near East, South Asia and Africa, for 1946 and 1947; vol. 4 for 1948; vol. 5 for 1949; vol. 5 for 1950 and 1951; and vol. 9 for 1952–54. Material has also been obtained from unpublished documents in the State Department archives, which have at my request been declassified and released for publication.

2 TURKEY IN PERSPECTIVE: HISTORICAL BACKGROUND

1. Karpat, p. 349.
2. Ibid., p. 355.
3. US Department of State, *Foreign Relations of the United States* (hereafter referred to as DOS, *For. Rel.*), 1946, vol. 7.
4. Ibid., 827–39.
5. DOS, *For. Rel.*, 1946, vol. 7, 843–4.
6. Harry S. Truman, *Years of Trial and Hope* (New York: Garden City, 1955).
7. DOS, *For. Rel.*, 1946, vol. 7, 857–8.
8. Ibid., 225.
9. Ibid., 858.

3 THE TRUMAN DOCTRINE: ORIGINS AND SIGNIFICANCE, 1947

1. DOS, *For. Rel.*, 1947, vol. 5, 32–7.
2. Ibid., 44–5.
3. Ibid., 47–55.
4. Ibid., 58.
5. Ibid., 69.
6. Ibid., 88–9.
7. *Assistance to Greece and Turkey*, Hearings before the Committee on Foreign Affairs, US House of Representatives, 80th Cong., 1st sess., on H. R. 2616 (Washington, DC: United States Government Printing Office, 1947).
8. Dean Acheson, *Present at the Creation: My Years in the State Department* (New York: W. W. Norton, 1969), 219.
9. Truman, *Years of Trial and Hope*, 105–6.
10. *Assistance to Greece and Turkey*, 1–62.
11. Truman, *Years of Trial and Hope*, 230.
12. *Assistance to Greece and Turkey*, report to accompany S.938, Report No. 10, p. 21.

13. Michael H. Hunt, *Ideology and U.S. Foreign Policy*, 156.
14. Ibid., 152–5.
15. George F. Kennan, "x," *Foreign Affairs* (Spring 1987).
16. Kenneth Harris, *Attlee* (London: Weidenfeld & Nicolson, 1982), 304–5.
17. Harold Macmillan, *Tides of Fortune* (London: Macmillan, 1969), 111.
18. Alan Bullock, *Ernest Bevin* (New York and London: W. W. Norton, 1983) 241–5.

4 THE BEGINNINGS OF GREEK-TURKISH AID, 1947–51

1. DOS, *For. Rel.*, 1947, vol. 5, 153–4.
2. Ibid., 138.
3. Ibid., 193–4.
4. Ibid., 258–60.
5. Ibid., 258.
6. Ibid., 260.
7. Ibid., 352–3.
8. Ibid., 351.
9. Ibid., 417.
10. *Aid to Greece and Turkey*, Report of the Committee on Foreign Relations, 80th Cong. 2nd sess., on S.2358 (Washington, DC: United States Government Printing Office, 1948), 8.
11. DOS, *For. Rel.*, 1948, vol. 6, 18–21.
12. Ibid., 34–6.
13. Ibid., 3.
14. *Aid to Greece and Turkey*.
15. Ibid., 13.

5 THE UNITED STATES DEVELOPS A MIDDLE EAST POLICY, 1948–52

1. DOS, *For. Rel.* 1947, vol. 5, 575.
2. DOS, *For. Rel.*, 1949, vol. 6, 45–7.
3. Ibid., 50–90.
4. Ibid., 165–79.
5. US Congress, House, H. R. 7797, *Report of the Committee on Foreign Affairs*, Report No. 1802, Part 3 on Foreign Economic Assistance, Supplementary Report of the Committee on Foreign Affairs, Statement by Mr McGhee, March 1950.
6. Ibid., 188–92.
7. Ibid., 193–6.
8. Ibid., 196.
9. Ibid., 217–21.
10. *Report of the Committee on Foreign Affairs*, Report No. 1802, 233–8.
11. Ibid., 563–4.
12. DOS, *For. Rel.*, 1951, vol. 5, 212–26.
13. DOS, *For. Rel.*, 1948, vol. 4, 83–5.

14. Ibid., 134–5.
15. Ibid., 144–5.
16. Ibid., 158–60.
17. Ibid., 172–6.
18. Ibid., 174.
19. Ibid., 215–16.
20. DOS, *For. Rel.*, 1949, vol. 6, 1638–40.
21. Ibid., 1638–40.
22. Ibid., 1647–53.
23. Ibid., 1656–7.
24. Ibid., 1651.
25. Ibid., 1660–70.
26. DOS, *For. Rel.*, 1950, vol. 5, 54–5.
27. Ibid., 61–89.
28. Ibid., 165–79.
29. Ibid., 1258–9.
30. Harry N. Howard, 'The Development of United States Policy in the Near East, 1945–1951', reprint from *The Department of State Bulletin*, 19 November 1951, 815.
31. Ibid.
32. Ibid.
33. Harry N. Howard, 'The Development of United States Policy in the Near East, South Asia, and Africa, 1951–1952', reprint from *The Department of State Bulletin*, 15 December 1952, 941.
34. Howard, 'The Development of United States Policy in the Near East, 1945–1951', 815.
35. Ibid., 815–16.
36. Howard, 'The Development of United States Policy in the Near East, 1945–1951', reprint from *The Department of State Bulletin*, 26 November 1951, 840.
37. Ibid., 1237–8.
38. Ahmad, Feroz, *The Turkish Experiment in Democracy*, 1950–75, 391.

6   TURKISH ENTRY INTO NATO: THE UNITED STATES' ROLE, 1950–51

1. DOS, *For. Rel.*, 1950, vol. 5, 1306.
2. Ibid., 1310.
3. Ibid., 1312.
4. Ibid., 1315.
5. Ibid., 1320.
6. Ibid., 1316.
7. Ibid., 1344.
8. DOS, *For. Rel.*, 1951, vol. 5, 1101.
9. DOS, *For. Rel.*, 1950, vol. 5, 1254.
10. DOS, *For. Rel.*, 1951, vol. 5, 27–42.
11. Ibid., 50–76.
12. George McGhee, *Envoy to the Middle World: Adventures in Diplomacy* (New York: Harper & Row, 1983), 271.

13. DOS, *For. Rel.*, 1951, vol. 5, 1119–26.
14. Ibid., 1169–72.
15. AmEmb Ankara, MemCon, Emb. desp. no. 488, 4 March 1952.

7 THE UNITED STATES HELPS TURKEY ASSUME ITS NATO RESPONSIBILITIES, 1951–55

1. AmEmb Ankara, MemCon, Emb. desp. no. 397, 19 January 1952.
2. Ibid., Emb. desp. no. 424, 1 February 1952.
3. Ibid., Emb. desp. no. 439, 9 February 1952.
4. Ibid., Emb. desp. no. 450, 10 February 1952.
5. Ibid., Emb. desp. no. 637, 6–8 May 1952.
6. Ibid., Emb. desp. no. 669, 28 May 1952.

8 THE MIDDLE EAST COMMAND: AN IDEA IN THE MAKING, 1951–56

1. Acheson, *Present at the Creation*, 562.
2. Ibid., 563.
3. DOS, *For. Rel.*, 1951, vol. 5, 212–36.
4. DOS, *For. Rel.*, 1952, vol. 9, 160–84.
5. Ibid., 184–5.
6. Ibid., 185–8.
7. Ibid., 189–91.
8. Ibid., 195–9.
9. Ibid., 199–203.
10. AmEmb. Ankara, MemCon, Emb. desp. no. 501, 16 March 1952.
11. Ibid., Emb. desp. no. 644, 15 May 1952.
12. Ibid., Emb. desp. no. 487, 7 March 1952.
13. DOS, *For. Rel.*, 1952, vol. 9, 237–47.
14. Ibid., 251–4.

9 A TURKISH ROLE IN REGIONAL DEFENCE, 1952

1. AmEmb. Ankara, MemCon, Emb. desp. no. 485, 6 March 1952.
2. Ibid., Emb. desp. no. 487, 7 March 1952.
3. Ibid., Emb. desp. no. 499, 14 March 1952.
4. Ibid., Emb. desp. no. 644, 15 May 1952.
5. Ibid., Emb. desp. no. 529, 26 March 1952.
6. Ibid., Emb. desp. no. 13, 5 July 1952.
7. Ibid., Emb. desp. no. 13, 5 July 1952.
8. Ibid., Emb. desp. no. 102, 6–7 August 1952.
9. Ibid., Emb. desp. no. 125, 22 August 1952.
10. Ibid., Emb. desp. no. 139, 5 September 1952.
11. Ibid., Emb. desp. no. 219, 7 October 1952.
12. Ibid., Emb. desp. no. 291, 10 November 1952.

10 PROGRESS TOWARD A MIDDLE EAST DEFENCE ORGANISA-
TION AND ITS EARLY DEMISE, 1951–58

1. AmEmb. Ankara, MemCon, Emb. desp. 23 October 1952.
2. DOS, *For. Rel.*, 1952, vol. 9, 311–13.
3. Ibid., 314–15.
4. Ibid., 319–26.
5. Ibid., 331–3.
6. Ibid., 345–6.
7. AmEmb. Ankara, MemCon, Emb. desp. no. 13, 8 July 1952, 8 May 1953.
8. AmEmb. Ankara, MemCon, Emb. 228, 17 August 1952.
9. AmEmb. Ankara, MemCon, Emb. 187, 6 August 1952.
10. Karpat, 393.
11. DOS, *For. Rel.*, 1952–53, vol. 9, 137–54.

Appendix: Survey of Attitudes of Arab States Toward Turkey by US Diplomats

TURKISH RELATIONS WITH THE ARAB STATES AND IRAN

AMEMBASSY, ANKARA   November 15, 1952

TURKISH RELATIONS WITH THE ARAB STATES
AND IRAN

As the Department is aware from my previous reports on the subject, I have on numerous occasions discussed with the President of the Republic, the Prime Minister and the Foreign Minister the problem of Turkish relations with the Arab States and other countries in the Middle East. I have consistently sought to impress on the leaders of the Turkish Government the importance of making a persistent, affirmative effort to improve those relations, which have been, and are, characterized by an attitude of indifference on the part of the Turks and resentment and distrust on the part of the Arab States and Iran.

In an effort to develop a broader perspective on this complex problem, which so directly affects all our efforts to assure the peace and security of this area, I wrote in September to our Chiefs of Mission in the Arab capitals and Tehran to obtain their views. In particular, I sought their reaction on three specific points:

1.   the attitude toward Turkey in each country;
2.   the possible steps that might be taken to improve relations;
3.   the likelihood that Turkey might assume a role of leadership among the states of the Middle East.

As of interest to the Department, there are enclosed copies of my correspondence with our Chiefs of Mission in the Arab States and Iran on this subject, together with a memorandum summarizing the views expressed on the foregoing three points.

As reported in the Embassy's despatch No. 291 of November 13, 1952, I had the opportunity on November 10 to discuss this problem further during a three-hour meeting with the President, the Prime Minister and the Foreign Minister. I was gratified to find that all of them seemed more than ever aware of the importance of undertaking affirmative steps to develop closer and more friendly relations with other Middle East States, and that the Government in fact intends to take such measures.

I expect to have a further discussion with the Foreign Minister today on this subject, which will be reported separately.

s/George C. McGhee
American Ambassador

Enclosures:
1. Memorandum analyzing and summarizing views expressed by Chiefs of Mission in Arab States and Iran on Turkish relations with those countries;
2. Text of letter addressed to Chiefs of Mission in Arab States and Iran in September 1951;
3. Text of replies received from Chiefs of Mission in Arab States and Iran.

Distribution:
Copies sent to: Damascus, Beirut, Cairo, Baghdad, Jidda, Amman, Tehran, London, Paris; ConGen, Istanbul.

MEMORANDUM

Ankara   November 12, 1952

TURKISH-ARAB RELATIONS
Analysis of Views of U.S. Missions in
Arab States and Iran

In letter to our Chiefs of Mission in the Arab States and Iran last September, we solicited their views on Turkish relations with those countries, specifically (1) the attitude in each country toward Turkey, (2) possible steps that might be taken to improve relations, and (3) the likelihood that Turkey might assume a role of leadership among the M. E. States. The latter question involved particularly the possibility of Turkish leadership in obtaining Arab participation in the proposed MEDO.

Summarized below are the replies which have now been received from all of these missions.

1. *Attitude toward Turkey*
All replies agree that the present Arab (and Iranian) attitude toward Turkey is one of resentment and distrust, caused by (a) long-present historical, racial and religious factors, (b) Turkish support of Western Powers in opposition to Arab positions, especially on the Palestine question, and (c) suspicion in some countries (e.g. Iraq, Iran) of possible recrudescence of Turkish territorial ambitions.

Following are pertinent excerpts from indicated countries:
Syria – 'Relations with Turkey may best be described as friendly but not close ... in addition to latent Syrian resentment over the status of Alexandretta, there still exists a heritage of fear and mistrust of the Turks, stemming from the First World War when the latter repressed the Arab nationalist movement.... most important in consideration of this problem, however, is

the fact that Syrian attention is focused southward towards Israel rather than northward or eastward, and that Turkey has failed to support the Arabs in UN voting on Palestine, and has no claim to a place in the "Arab-Asiatic" bloc.'

Lebanon – 'Turkey's attitude of "indifference" toward the Arab States is of course not lost on our Arab friends. While it has served the useful purpose of exonerating the Turks from charges of imperialist ambitions, it has not improved Turkish standing in the Arab world. The attitude here is one of reciprocated indifference and sometimes antipathy.'

Iraq – 'There is considerable anti-Turk propaganda and feeling in Iraq which stems in by far the greatest measure from Turkey's voting record in the UN on such issues as the Suez Canal and Tunisia.... Also in the background but of secondary importance are (a) latent fears that Turkey might some day reoccupy Mosul or all of Iraq, (b) Turkey's determined resistance to joining any political blocs based on Islamic ties, (c) the long-standing grudge held by Iraqi Kurds against the Kemalists who broke up Kurdish communities in Turkey. At the moment there is also some irritation caused by disagreement between the Iraqi and Turk Governments over Turkey's share in Iraq's increased oil revenues. Embassy believes, however, that this anti-Turk feeling on the part of the Iraqis is for the most part genuine and not externally inspired, although it is undoubtedly encouraged and exploited by the Communists.' (Foregoing from Baghdad's telegram 42 of May 28, referred to in letter of September 29, replying to our letter; following excerpts from letter of September 29.)

'Foreign Minister Jamali feels particularly strongly on the subject of Turkey's "anti-Arab" UN activities.... There are other adverse factors of secondary importance such as traditional grudges, Turkey's negative attitude toward Pan-Islamic movements, fear that Turkey will develop expansionist tendencies and its overtly-manifested antipathy toward the Arabs.'

Jordan – 'The Arabs, in Jordan at least, do not like the Turks. Men of middle age have bitter memories of Turkish oppression and Jordanian hostility toward the Turks has been increased in recent years by Turkish trade with Israel, by Turkey's support of Israel's application to join the United Nations and by what the Jordanians consider Turkish support of the Western Powers against Arab and other Moslem States in a series of recent controversies. Here Turkey is considered to be a satellite of the West and Turkey is frequently denounced along with the Western Powers.... I doubt very much whether any very radical and immediate alterations in the attitude of the Arab States toward the Turks is likely to result from anything we may do or anything we can persuade them to do. Arabs don't like Turks. They haven't liked Turks since they first learned to know them in the Eleventh Century and they have had very good reason not to like the Turks. How to bring about friendly feelings and friendly cooperation between the Turks and the Arabs is a problem on a par with the problem of how to bring about friendly feelings and friendly cooperation between Ireland and England or between France and Germany. We are dealing here with fundamental secular antipathies that are not to be substantially or rapidly modified by any changes of policy on the part of any Government.'

Saudi-Arabia – 'As regards Turkey's new interest in the Arab States, as contrasted with its previous policy of "indifference," I should say that, speaking from the Saudi-Arabian viewpoint, this indifference has been reciprocated. Unlike the Arab States to the north, there is little conscious-ness here of the Turkish impact, either immediate or potential. In fact, the only time that Saudi officials have ever mentioned Turkey to me have been in connection with MEDO and MSA. Regarding MEDO, the Saudis definitely had a raised eyebrow when Turkey was made a sponsoring power. I wouldn't say that the reaction of the Saudis was actually hostile, but they were definitely dubious and it was significant to note that in subsequent discussions regarding MEDO they usually only approached ourselves and the British and pretty much ignored the Turks and French. Regarding MSA, the Saudis have consistently maintained that, as a result of having gone so far as to conclude the Dhahran Airfield Agreement, they were entitled to consideration no less favorable than that which we had given the Turks. Of course, there were numerous and sound arguments which we adduced to the contrary, but the Saudis have always remained somewhat disgruntled.

'Speaking more generally of the attitude toward Turkey here, I must admit to a considerable disappointment. I had hoped that, despite Turkey's unfortunate past relations with the Arabian Peninsula, there would develop an appreciation of the great work which Turkey had done in raising itself by its boot straps. There is in fact some such sentiment, particularly among the younger people, but on the whole Turkey's stock is relatively low. The past is not forgotten; Turkey's attitude toward religion is deplorable; Turkey does not have the tie of either language or race which means so much in the Arab countries; Turkey's representatives here have tended to be aloof and even condescending.'

Egypt – 'You will not be surprised when I tell you that the people of Egypt do not like the Turks. For many years they were under Turkish rule. The Egyptians are conscious of being an older country than Turkey and despite the fact that they were also the subjects of other foreign dynasties, the experience of Turkish suzerainty is too recent to cause them to change old attitudes for one of affection.'

Iran – 'The continued vicissitudes of the past few months have only confirmed this Iranian tendency towards xenophobia (mentioned in earlier letter), as a result of which Turkey and the Turks are distinctly unpopular. . . . Iran continues to fear that Turkey had designs on Azerbaijan. Iranians are concerned lest that increased military strength of Turkey in the event of a general war with the USSR may mean an occupation of Azerbaijan which might be made permanent. Soviet propaganda has played up Iranian fears of the loss of Azerbaijan by charging that Turkey and Pakistan have an agreement with the West to partition the country.'

2. *Steps to improve Turk-Arab relations*
Our chiefs of mission in the Arab States agree in general that efforts to improve Turkish relations with the Arab States through the exchange of official visits and intensified cultural interchange are worth making. Howev-er, they are not optimistic; that such measures would make any appreciable effect on basic attitudes, or enable Turkey to exert any real influence over the Arab States. Ambassador Green goes further, and rules out the possibility of

improvement in Turk-Arab relations regardless of anything we or the Turks may do (See Section 1, *Jordan*, above).

Syria – 'Syria might be influenced by Turkish overtures for closer relations if Turkey had something substantial to offer in return. Syria continually seeks to satisfy what it considers to be its basic needs. Turkey could, therefore, become more influential here by making Turkish military equipment available (or by being the channel through which Western military equipment is supplied to Syria) or by re-orienting its policies to support Arab aims. The former course may be feasible, but not the latter because it would often conflict with the policies of the Western Powers. To further our interests in Syria it would therefore seem wisest for Turkey to continue its present policies with increased emphasis on official visits, exchanges of persons, and offers of such up-to-date equipment as can be delivered to Syria with no conditions attached.'

Lebanon – 'It is our belief that if a program of renewed Turkish interest in the Arab world does nothing more than to establish Turkey as a friendly neighbor, it will have served a most useful purpose. Even that neighbourliness would be highly worthwhile, probably essential, in the development of MEDO.... Your suggestions for various measures Turkey might discreetly take to improve Turco-Arab relations are excellent. We might caution, however, against linking their efforts too closely with the Point Four concept. Unfortunately, at this stage of the game, Point Four connotes to many Arabs an invasion of foreigners, and a superimposition of unwanted influence.'

Iraq – 'That Turkey could improve its position here by a more forthcoming attitude toward the Arabs is a distinct possibility.... The Embassy believes we should indeed do all possible to bring about closer relations between Turkey and the Arab countries, if only because we presently envisage that they will both be members of the same defense organization and will need to cooperate in the event of hostilities. We believe your suggestions for the exchange of official visits, a small Turkish "Point IV Program", the intensification of cultural relations, through exchanges of students and professors, and training programs in Turkish military schools are excellent for this purpose. The Iraqis are not so anti-Turkish that they could not be sold, on such programs if they were presented tactfully and if – and this is important – they were previously cleared with the U.K.' Embassy adds, however, 'it would be too much to expect that even under optimum circumstances Turkey could be the intermediary for bringing the Iraqis materially closer to the West.' See Baghdad's comments under Section 3, below.

Jordan – 'I doubt very much whether any very radical and immediate alterations in the attitude of the Arab States toward the Turks is likely to result from anything we may do or anything we can persuade them to do.'

Saudi-Arabia – 'At a time when the British, French and ourselves have been trying in our various ways to make our influence felt in the Arab countries, the Turks have remained supremely indifferent. They have done nothing to smooth over the troubles of the past, nor to cultivate the ground for the future. What they might have achieved if they had adopted a different tactic, I don't know, but I do feel that it would still be worthwhile for them to make the effort. It must, however, be a real effort; they should not endeavour to approach the Arabs as the agents of the West; they must identify themselves with the interests of the area; they must abandon their smugness and rigid adherence to protocol which has so often characterized their relations with the Arab States. On the other hand, I do not think that Turkey can "drastically improve her relations with the Arab States by a strong show of sympathy and understanding." A situation such as this does not, in my opinion, lend itself to ostentatious gestures. But I do think that real progress can probably be made in the improvement of Turkey's relations with the Arab States provided that the approach bears evidence of real sincerity and understanding. Such a policy, however, would have to be very carefully thought out and pursued along many lines. It is not the type of problem which can be met by action of the push-button variety.... At the present time the Turks are so clearly identified with the policies of the West, particularly that of the United States, that they are sometimes regarded by the Arabs as more or less playing the role of stooges. It is this type of impression which they would have to dispel. Frankly, I do not think that this would necessitate any basic policy change so far as the Turks are concerned; it would be more a question of finding ways and means of implementing Turkish policy change so far as the Turks are concerned; it would be more a question of finding ways and means of implementing Turkish policy in such a way as to make the Arabs feel that the Turks are genuinely interested in the area and not just making a façade-like gesture.'

Egypt – 'I believe that Turkey could improve her relations with this country by that show of sympathy and understanding for the Arab States which you suggest. I see no basic antipathy in Turkey undertaking concrete measures to increase friendly relations with the Arab world and at the same time maintaining its present open and direct ties with the West.... All in all, the situation in Egypt is more encouraging than probably Turkish reports would indicate. I, therefore, think your program, such as outlined in the paragraph at the bottom of page 3 of your letter, would meet at first a somewhat politely incredulous and then perhaps a more affirmative response from the present regime in Egypt.'

Iran – No specific comment.

3. *Turkish leadership in Middle East*
Syria – 'There are some doubts (1) that any non-Arab country can furnish effective area leadership in support of Western policies, or (2) that Turkey specifically is in a sufficiently favored position to enable it to influence Syria's decision.... The Turks now appear to occupy no particularly favored position in Syrian eyes and there is, therefore, little basis for optimism regarding the effectiveness of greater Turkish activity here on behalf of Western policies. Nor is it likely, even if Turkey did enjoy such a favored position, that she could sponsor and make more palatable the Western programs and policies which have been proposed but have not yet found favor here. Turkish support of MEDO or a similar organization is not likely to tip the scales in favor of Syrian adherence. The Syrians are inclined to be both cynical and suspicious and they will approach any area defense program cautiously. The normal local reaction to Turkish advances on behalf of

MEDO would be to accuse Turkey of being the errand-boy of the Western Powers.'

Lebanon – 'As far as leadership is concerned, I doubt whether the Arabs would be willing in the foreseeable future to follow the Turks. As we see it from Lebanon, Arabs, like the Turks, consider America the leading power factor of the West, and if there is any leadership which they would be willing to follow it is our own.... To sum up, I believe Turkey should go forward with a discreet program of developing good will among the Arabs, that it should seek to establish itself as a good neighbor, but that it not be encouraged to take MEDO leadership in this area at the present.'

Iraq – 'The Embassy is frankly dubious that Turkey can ever assert leadership here or be used effectively as an instrument in solving the difficulties between Iraq and the Western Powers. Such a maneuver could not even be attempted, for one thing, until the British could be sold on the idea.... It would be too much to expect that even under optimum circumstances Turkey could be the intermediary for bringing the Iraqis materially closer to the West. The Iraqis are looking for satisfaction of their various grievances and solutions of their problems directly to the U.K. and the U.S.' (In later telegram No. 13 of October 24, Embassy Baghdad states, re proposal Turkey approach Iraq on MEDO: 'anti-Turkish sentiment presently so high here that Embassy doubts if Turkish intervention would be fruitful.')

Jordan – 'Undoubtedly Turkey can make a favorable contribution to MEDO but the Turks' role should not be emphasized if MEDO is to be made palatable to the Arabs. It is difficult to see how, in the present circumstances, any considerable Turkish participation in MEDO could be intergrated with Arab participation.'

Saudi-Arabia – 'Any attempts at leadership in this area, including that of the United States, are definitely open to suspicion but there is no question in my mind but that we Americans are less suspect than the others.... The Turks ... are also regarded with suspicion but I am not entirely despondent that something might not be done to remedy the situation.... You ask if it would be possible for Turkey to exercise a constructive influence in the Near East without abandoning its open and direct ties with the West.... To be specific, I do believe that the Turks would have to reorient their overt policy to a considerable decree in connection with any serious effort at basic readjustment of their relations with the Arabs.' (See also comments under Section 2.)

Egypt – 'Despite this general feeling (of antipathy toward the Turks – See Section 1, *Egypt*, above), however, I do not think the Egyptians believe that Turkey harbors territorial ambitions. In consequence, they would view Turkish attempts at leadership not so much with suspicion as with the feeling that after all Egypt has equal claims toward leadership. This would be particularly true under the present military regime. Certainly, if forced to the point, the Egyptians would regard Turkish leadership as preferable substitute for English or French influence. At present, however, U.S. leadership would be the one which they would most desire to have.'

Iran – 'Iran, resentful of Turkey's military strength and economic revival, derived in part from a large-scale American aid to that country of a character denied to Iran, coupled with its exaggerated fears of the loss of Azerbaijan, will not be inclined to take helpful advice or to welcome Turkish influence in adjusting its troubled affairs.'

American Embassy, Ankara
September 18, 1952

The Honorable Jefferson Caffery
American Ambassador, Cairo
(Identical letters sent to other Chiefs of Mission
in Arab States and Iran)

Dear Jeff:

I have for some time been giving thought to the role which Turkey might be able to play in the defense of the Middle East. I have read with much interest your comments on MEDO and particularly on the British MEDO proposals, and would very much like to have your views on how you think Turkey should fit into the Middle East defense picture, with particular reference to its relations with Egypt.

There is no question that the Turks are prepared to defend their own territory against any attack and, furthermore, that they are whole-heartedly committed to NATO. It is not yet clear, however, to what extent they may be disposed to contribute military forces for the defense of the Middle East outside of Turkey, under the MEDO concept, or to assume a degree of general leadership in the Middle East appropriate to their political and military strength.

[Gap]

From the beginning the Turks have emphasized their relationship and responsibilities to NATO. They have, in fact, placed all of their present ground forces under NATO. In the final analysis, the extent to which Turkey may be disposed to commit forces for the defense of the Middle East outside of her own territory will probably depend upon the nature of the comparable commitments undertaken by other countries participating in MEDO, particularly the U.S., and the extent to which we will assist them in expanding the level of their armed forces strength.

The Turks have consistently taken the position that it is essential to obtain the participation of the Arab states in MEDO. For one thing, they consider their participation necessary to assure utilization of their territories, ports and bases by the Allies. They do not like to envisage an invasion of the Middle East by the Allies in the event of war. They tend to look upon MEDO, as we do, as having primarily a political objective in the first instance, and that political objective is to obtain the collaboration of the Arab States.

With respect to the best method of obtaining such collaboration, the Turks feel that the ground must first be prepared very carefully through personal and informal discussions with the responsible leaders of the Arab Governments. The Foreign Minister has, in fact, commented to me that the Turks might be in the best position to make such an informal approach to certain of the Arab States, particularly Syria and Lebanon.

The role that Turkey can play vis-à-vis the Arab States in connection with plans for defense of the Middle East is, of course, directly affected by the status of Turkish relations with those countries. On this point I should much appreciate your comments. In our judgment, the Turkish attitude toward the Arab States as a whole might best be described as one of relative 'indifference.' The Turks have consistently under the Republic looked to the West, and this was of course a cardinal principle of Ataturk's policy. This tendency has naturally been reinforced by the desire to obtain the support of the West, and particularly of the United States, in common measures of defense against potential Soviet aggression. The Turks look to us as the major power factor in opposition to the USSR. Conversely, they tend to look upon all the rest of the Middle East with little enthusiasm as to the military potential of the countries in the area and, with the exception of the United States of the foreign powers now interested in its defense. They have little confidence in the ability of the Arab States to make any effective military contribution to the defense of the area.

It would seem that the development of closer relations between Turkey and the various Arab countries should be our objective in order to obtain the latter's effective collaboration with us in a common defense effort. Furthermore, it would seem essential if Turkey is to be in a position to exercise any constructive influence with these countries. As you know, the Turks have consistently supported us and the other Western powers in the U.N. and elsewhere on such issues as Palestine, the Anglo-Iranian oil controversy, the Suez Canal question, Tunis, etc., and such support has naturally caused a distinctly negative reaction in the Arab States. The Turks feel that French Middle East representatives, and in certain instances U.K. representatives (as distinct from the Governments in Paris and London), are working against them in the Arab States in order to preserve their spheres of influence.

In my discussions of this whole general question with the leaders of the Turkish Government, I have found general recognition of the situation described and an expressed desire to do something to improve relations with the Arab States. In fact this was included in the platform of the Democratic Party when it came to power in 1950 and a start was made in the invitation to King Abdullah before the Turk vote on the Suez issue cooled the Arabs toward Turkey. Among some of the things it has been suggested might be done are the initiation of what might be called a small Turkish Point IV program, the exchange of official visits, the intensification of cultural relations through the exchanges of students and professors, and training programs in Turkish military schools for officers and non-commissioned personnel from various Arab States. (A number of Syrian officers have been attending Turkish schools, and there is a long-standing military training program with Afghanistan.) However, up to now the Turks have been proceeding very cautiously in implementing this kind of a program.

One reason for this caution is, of course, their recognition of the fact that any too obvious approach might have boomerang effects. Thus the Turks have let it be known to the Syrians, for example, that they would welcome a visit by Colonel Shishikli, but they have not extended a formal invitation for fear that this would be misinterpreted. Also, they have in mind that if Shishikli should one of these days disappear from the scene the successor regime in Syria might not recall such a Turkish initiative with pleasure.

In the light of all the foregoing, I would much appreciate your views on the possibility of the Turks playing a more affirmative role in their relations with the Arab States. How do the people of Egypt like the Turks? Do they believe the Ataturk dictum that Turkey has no imperial or territorial ambitions, or do they take this with a grain of salt? We are, of course, fully convinced that the Turks have no desire for territorial expansion of 'spheres of influence' as such. Would they view Turkish attempts at leadership with suspicion, or would they accept it as a preferable substitute for U.S., British or French influence? How does Turkish prestige and good will stand compared with our own or with that of the British or French? Does Turkish support of the West on the controversial issues I have mentioned nullify the influence which they may derive from their geographical position, historical relations with other states of the Middle East, and Turkey's present strong political and military position? Could Turkey drastically improve her relations with the Arabs by a strong show of sympathy and understanding for the Arab States? Would you say that it is possible for Turkey to exercise a constructive influence without abandoning its open and direct ties with the West and support of the West, or do you believe that she can only do so by aligning herself openly with the Arab States and Iran on such issues as Palestine, Tunis and the current difficulties in which Britain and we ourselves are now involved in Iran and Egypt?

I hate to impose this burden on you and your staff, but I would greatly appreciate your frank reply to these questions, which I am directing to our other Chiefs of Mission in the Arab States.

With best personal regards,
Sincerely yours,
s/George C. McGhee

LETTERS FROM CHIEFS OF MISSION
IN ARAB STATES AND IRAN
SYRIA

October 7, 1952

Dear George:

Many thanks for your interesting and informative letter of September 15 concerning the role which Turkey might play vis-à-vis the Arab States in the defense of the Middle East. Your clear statement of Turkish aims and policy will be most useful as background information, particularly should the tempo of MEDO discussions be accelerated.

As you have no doubt seen from our despatches and telegrams, this Embassy also believes that the Arabs must be included from the start in any successful area defense body and that the primary objective of such an organization is political. Efforts to convince the Arabs of the sincerity of our views and of the benefit to be gained by early adherence to such a Western plan, should be encouraged. There are some doubts, however, 1) that any non-Arab country can furnish effective area leadership in support of Western policies, 2) that Turkey specifically is in a sufficiently favored position to enable it to influence Syria's decision.

Syrian relations with Turkey, viewed from Damascus, may best be described as friendly but not close. No major problems currently divided the two countries, and most Syrians, including Colonel Shishikli, admire the rapid progress which Turkey, a Moslem State, has made in its 'Westernization.' However, Turkey's new strength and close ties with the West have certain disadvantages, one of which is a loosening of Turkish bonds with Arab countries. Furthermore, in addition to latent Syrian resentment over the status of Alexandretta, there still exists a heritage of fear and mistrust of the Turks, stemming from the First World War when the latter repressed the Arab nationalist movement.

Most important in consideration of this problem, however, is the fact that Syrian attention is focused southward towards Israel rather than northward or eastward, and Syrian foreign policy is oriented accordingly. Syrians generally feel that Turkey has failed to support the Arabs in UN voting on Palestine; and has no claim to a place in the 'Arab-Asiatic' bloc.

The Turks now appear to occupy no particularly favored position in Syrian eyes and there is, therefore, little basis for optimism regarding the effectiveness of greater Turkish activity here on behalf of Western policies. Nor is it likely even if Turkey did enjoy such a favored position, that she could sponsor and make more palatable the Western programs and policies which have been proposed but not yet found favor here. Turkish support of MEDO or a similar organization is not likely to tip the scales in favor of Syrian adherence. The Syrians are inclined to be both cynical and supsicious, and they will approach any area defense program cautiously. The normal local reaction to Turkish advances on behalf of MEDO would be to accuse Turkey of being the errand-boy of the Western Powers.

The foregoing may sound discouraging. It is not intended to be. It is my belief that Turkey can help or hinder Syrian acceptance of Western plans, in its capacity as one of several MEDO sponsors but not in the role of a special pleader or intermediary. Egypt, it would appear, is the only country in a position to exercise, either by advice or example, an important influence on Syria's future course of action.

On the other hand, Syria might be influenced by Turkish overtures for closer relations if Turkey had something substantial to offer in return. Syria continually seeks to satisfy what it considers to be its basic needs. Turkey could, therefore, become more influential here by making Turkish military equipment available (or by being the channel through which Western military equipment is supplied by Syria) or by reo-orienting its policies to support the Arab aims. The former course may be feasible, but not the latter because it would often conflict with the policies of the Western Powers.

To further our interests in Syria it would therefore seem wisest for Turkey to continue its present policies with increased emphasis on official visits, exchanges of persons, and offers of such up-to-date equipment as can be delivered to Syria with no conditions attached. The French, British, and ourselves, as well as international agencies, have already indicated readiness to furnish various types of technical assistance to Syria. The non-committal Syrian attitude thus far indicates that a similar Turkish offer would only complicate the situation.

I trust that the foregoing will not be too discouraging in any consideration of the role that Turkey can play in achieving Western objectives in this area.

With best personal regards,
Sincerely yours,
s/James S. Moose, Jr.

LEBANON

October 17, 1952

Dear George:

Your thought-provoking letter of September 17 regarding the role Turkey might be able to play in the defense of the Middle East was awaiting me when I returned this week from consultation in Washington. In sending you this unavoidably belated reply, I hasten to assure you that your thinking at Ankara on this challenging problem corresponds in most respects with our thinking here.

Turkey's attitude of 'indifference' toward the Arab States is of course not lost on our Arab friends. While it has served the useful purpose of exonerating the Turks from charges of imperialistic ambitions, it has not improved Turkish standing in the Arab world. The attitude here is one of reciprocated indifference and sometimes antipathy. The latter stems not so much from Ottoman memories as it does from the fact that in their indifference Turkish representatives in Lebanon and elsewhere have frequently taken a supercilious view of the Arabs, a disdain which has not been well camouflaged. It is our belief, therefore, that if a program of renewed Turkish interest in the Arab world does nothing more than to establish Turkey as a friendly neighbor, it will have served a most useful purpose. Even that neighborliness would be highly worthwhile, probably essential, in the development of MEDO.

The Turkish position that it is essential to obtain the participation of the Arab States in MEDO is identical with our view here in Beirut. Although achieving this objective may cause delay in the establishment of MEDO, we believe it to be of utmost importance, particularly, as you note, in view of the fact that the primary objective of MEDO from the start has been political.

As far as leadership is concerned, I doubt whether the Arabs would be willing in the foreseeable future to follow the Turks. As we see it from Lebanon, Arabs, like the Turks, consider America the leading power factor of the West, and if there is any leadership which they would be willing to follow it is our own. We, of course, have a few handicaps, such as Palestine, to offset before our leadership would be acceptable, but we incline to the view that neither the British, the French, nor the Turks have the chances for success that we have. That does not mean that each of the three, including Turkey which has had a cleaner slate in recent years, should not try to improve its own relations within the MEDO family.

Your suggestions for various measures Turkey might discreetly take to improve Turco-Arab relations are excellent. We might caution, however, against linking their efforts too closely with the Point Four concept. Unfortunately, at this stage of the game, Point Four connotes to many Arabs an invasion of foreigners, and a superimposition of unwanted influence. Strict personnel exchanges, such as military visits or even the encouragement of Moslem hadjis (provided better transportation facilities are assured than were in effect this year), can do much to raise Turkey's stock here.

Another suggestion would be to encourage the Turks to greater latitude than previously in the policies to which you refer: Palestine, Tunisia, Suez, etc. If *occasionally* they do not vote with us at UN, and vote with the Arabs, it could do much to improve their prestige and to counteract the charge, now commonly believed, that they are America's 'stooge.' I remember the Suez issue for example. The Turks firmly believed the UN resolution was against their and our interests in the Middle East, but because their vote was needed to carry the day and because they wanted to defer to our wishes, they voted against the Arabs. The one vote caused their prestige heavy damage in Arab circles.

I believe answers to the specific questions in the penultimate paragraph of your letter may have been covered in the foregoing discussion. To sum up, I believe that Turkey should go forward with a discreet program for developing good will among the Arabs, that it should seek to establish itself as a good neighbor, but that it not be encouraged to take MEDO leadership in this area at the present. As its stock as a good neighbor rises, other opportunities for useful influence will materialize.

As occasion arises, I hope you will again share your views with us on this subject. We shall do the same, particularly if we have some useful suggestions as to fields in which Turkish good-will activity might be initiated.

Warmest personal regards,
Sincerely yours,
s/Harold B. Minor
American Ambssador

IRAQ

September 29, 1952

Dear George:

Your thoughtful letter of September 15 regarding Arab-Turkish relations, is very much appreciated. The Embassy staff has explored the question rather fully on a continuing basis. The most comprehensive statement of Iraq's attitude toward Turkey is contained in the Embassy's telegram 1080 of May 28 rptd. to Ankara as 42.

You may find it useful to consult this and also the Embassy's despatches 997 of April 14, 733 of February 16 and 563 of December 17, 1951 (copied to Ankara), all of which deal directly with this subject.

Nothing has occurred since these reports were submitted to lead the Embassy to believe there is any significant change in the Iraqi viewpoint, which is, at the moment, negative toward Turkey.

As the Embassy has emphasized, the Iraq attitude stems primarily from Turkey's UN voting record on Suez and Tunisia. Foreign Minister Jamali, who was Iraq's UN representative at the time, feels particularly strongly on the subject of Turkey's 'anti-Arab' UN activities. In retrospect I believe it would have been better, inasmuch as Turkey's vote on those issues was not decisive, had Turkey abstained.

There are other adverse factors of secondary importance such as tradition-al grudges, Turkey's negative attitude toward Pan-Islamic movements, fear that Turkey will develop expansionist tendencies and its overtly-manifested apathy toward the Arabs.

The British Embassy attributes great importance to Iraqi fears that Turkey will develop expansionist tendencies, and recalls that when the MEC proposals were first put to Nuri Said by the British Ambassador, Nuri's first reaction was to ask if assurances could be given that no Turkish troops would ever be allowed to set foot on Iraqi soil.

There is, indeed, some sincere fear of Turkey, particularly in the Mosul area. This Embassy is inclined to believe, however, that it could be overcome if high Iraqi and Turkish leaders got together more often, such as on the exchanges of visits you suggest, and the firm adherence of Turkey to a non-expansionist policy was made clear to the Iraqis. The Embassy believes, too, that the Iraqis could be convinced that Turkey, because of its geographic position and on-the-spot military strength, is an essential element in a Middle East defense organization.

That Turkey could improve its position here by a more forthcoming attitude toward the Arabs is a distinct possibility, but the Embassy is frankly dubious that Turkey can ever assert leadership here or be used effectively as an instrument in solving the difficulties between Iraq and the Western Powers. Such a maneuver could not even be attempted, for one thing, until the British could be sold on the idea. As you will note from the Embassy despatch 997 of April 14, 1952, they don't presently favor a more positive role for Turkey.

Secondly, the Iraqis, albeit nurturing various grievances against the West, nevertheless want to deal directly with what they consider to be the sources of World power, i.e., the U.K. and U.S. They are not impressed with Turkish power, since they feel it derives only from the United States.

A third important factor is the relatively low caliber of Turkey's diplomatic representation here. Nor, I gather, is Iraq very well represented in Ankara.

To summarize, the Embassy believes we should indeed do all possible to bring about closer relations between Turkey and the Arab countries, if only because we presently envisage that they will both be members of the same defense organization and will need to cooperate in the event of hostilities. We believe your suggestions for the exchange of official visits, a small Turkish 'Point IV program,' the intensification of cultural relations through exchanges of students and professors, and training programs in Turkish military schools are excellent for this purpose. The Iraqis are not so anti-Turkish that they could not be sold on such programs if they were presented tactfully* and if – and this is important – they were previously cleared with the UK.

It would be too much to expect, however, that even under optimum circumstances Turkey could be the intermediary for bringing the Iraqis materially closer to the West. The Iraqis are looking for satisfaction of their various grievances and solution of their problems directly to the UK and US.

If we have any further thoughts on this question I will write you.
Sincerely yours,
s/Burton Y. Berry

---

*The recent Iraqi decision to elevate its Legation in Ankara (Embtel 114 July 25) to an Embassy is indicative of the fact that they are not inflexibly anti-Turk.

JORDAN

October 10, 1952
My dear George:
I acknowledge the receipt of your letter of September 16 in regard to MEDO, asking a number of questions concerning the possibility of closer cooperation between the Turks and the Arab States in connection with this plan for regional defense.

Please excuse my delay in replying to your letter. The difficulty has been that this small post has been growing with leaps and bounds with the increased activities of our Point IV operations and that at the same time the responsibilities of the Chief of Mission have been multiplied, as for instance by the instructions contained in *Field Responsibilities and Relationships for the Point 4 Program.* Unfortunately, the administrative officers of the Department haven't yet realized these facts and I am left so short handed that it is difficult to keep up with the official correspondence.

I was much interested in what you had to say about the attitude of the Turks toward MEDO and their probable policy in case of war. I agree with you that there can be no doubt but that the Turks would defend their own territory. From time immemorial they have fought valiantly in its defense whenever it was directly attacked.

[Gap]

In reply to your specific questions concerning the possibility of the Turks 'playing a more affirmative role in their relations with the Arab States' I suggest consideration of the following:

1.   Undoubtedly Turkey can make a favorable contribution to MEDO but the Turk's role should not be emphasized if MEDO is to be made palatable to the Arabs. It is difficult to see how, in the present circumstances, any considerable Turkish participation in MEDO could be integrated with Arab participation

2.   The Arabs, in Jordan at least, do not like the Turks. Men of middle age have bitter memories of Turkish oppression and Jordanian hostility toward the Turks has been increased in recent years by Turkish recognition of Israel, by Turkish trade with Israel, by Turkish support of Israel's application to join the United Nations and by what the Jordanians consider Turkish support of the Western Powers against Arab and other Moslem states in a series of recent controversies. Here Turkey is considered to be a satellite of the West and Turkey is frequently denounced along with the Western Powers.

3.   I cannot venture to predict the response that the Syrians and the Lebanese might make to the type of approach from the Turks suggested in the penultimate paragraph of page two of your letter. I question, however, whether the Turks take national feeling sufficiently into account if they consider that they have any great influence with Syria or Lebanon. Any such approach to Jordan would amost certainly be rebuffed.

4.   American prestige in Jordan is at a very low ebb, and as the Turks are considered to be acting in concert with the Western Powers and particularly with the United States, Turkish prestige is also low. The Turks will hardly be able to exert any decisive influence here until there is a marked change in Turkish policy toward Israel, whether this change be in concert with the Western Powers, or by separate action on the part of the Turks.

I doubt very much whether any very radical and immediate alterations in the attitude of the Arab States toward the Turks is likely to result from anything we may do or anything we can persuade them to do. Arabs don't like Turks. They haven't liked Turks since they first learned to know them in the Eleventh Century and they have had very good reason not to like the Turks. How to bring about friendly feelings and friendly cooperation between the Turks and the Arabs is a problem on a par with the problem of how to bring about friendly feelings and friendly cooperation between Ireland and England or between France and Germany. We are dealing here with fundamental secular antipathies that are not to be substantially or rapidly modified by any changes of policy on the part of any Government.

In this connection let me recount an amusing illustrative anecdote.

The Turkish Minister here called on me some weeks ago. Talk of the pilgrims passing through Amman on their way to Mecca led to some general discussion of religion and particularly of the Moslem religion. That led the Turk to make some highly disparaging remarks about the Arabs. He warned me against them. He said that the Prime Minister was one of the few Arabs he had ever met who could be trusted; that most of them were unreliable and untruthful; that the Arabs were mere barbarians from the desert; and that I must not be fooled by the European exterior of many of them into imagining that they were European. The Turkish Minister had just left my office when the Minister of Defense called. In order to make conversation I told him that I had just had an interesting conversation with the Turkish Minister on the subject of religion. At that he said, with obvious contempt, that the Turks knew nothing about religion; that they were nothing but barbarians from Central Asia; and that I must not be deceived by the European appearance of some of them into thinking that they were European.

As your letter under acknowledgment was sent to the Chiefs of Mission in other Arab capitals, I am sending copies of this reply to our colleagues in those capitals.

With all good wishes, I am,
Very sincerely yours,
s/Joseph C. Green

SAUDI ARABIA

October 28, 1952

Dear George:

I am afraid that this letter will arrive as the tail-ender to your round robin on the potential role of Turkey in the Near East, but it so happened that I was in Riyadh when it came, trying to calm down the Saudis in their difficulty with the British regarding the status of the Buraimi oasis, a question which was generating a great deal of heat at the time and threatening to develop into another focus for anti-British sentiment. Fortunately, we were able to pour a little oil on troubled waters but I don't know how long it will last. At any rate, it has been kept from making the headlines so far and that, I think, is often a good standard of so-called diplomatic endeavor. However, it did, unfortunately, interfere with my answering your letter and I hereby belatedly hasten to make amends.

[Gap]

As regards Turkey's new interest in the Arab States, as contrasted with its previous policy of 'indifference,' I should say that, speaking from the Saudi Arabian viewpoint, this indifference has been reciprocated. Unlike the Arab States to the north, there is little consciousness here of the Turkish impact, either immediately or potential. In fact, the only times that Saudi officials have ever mentioned Turkey to me have been in connection with MEDO and MSA. Regarding MEDO, the Saudis definitely had a raised eyebrow when Turkey was made a sponsoring power. I wouldn't say that the reaction of the

Saudis was actually hostile, but they were definitely dubious and it was significant to note that in subsequent discussions regarding MEDO they usually only approached ourselves and the British and pretty much ignored the Turks and French. Regarding MSA, the Saudis have consistently maintained that, as a result of having gone so far as to conclude the Dhahran Airfield Agreement, they were entitled to consideration no less favorable than that which we had given the Turks. Of course, there were numerous and sound arguments which we adduced to the contrary, but the Saudis have always remained somewhat disgruntled.

Speaking more generally of the attitude toward Turkey here, I must admit to a considerable disappointment. I had hoped that, despite Turkey's unfortunate past relations with the Arabian Peninsula, there would develop an appreciation of the great work which Turkey had done in raising itself by its boot straps. There is in fact some such sentiment, particularly among the younger people, but on the whole Turkey's stock is relatively low. The past is not forgotten; Turkey's attitude toward religion is deplored; Turkey does not have the tie of either language or race which means so much in the Arab countries; Turkey's representatives here have tended to be aloof and even condescending. For example, the recently departed Turkish Minister here was not a practicing Moslem and was obviously embarrassed when he happened to get into situations where prayers were in order in connection with social activities. He also consistently refused to fly his flag on Friday and told the Foreign Office that he would not even refer to his Government the suggestion that he might fly his flag on both Friday and Sunday. Good Kemalists just didn't do things like that. I think that with a different type of representative, particularly one who is a devout Moslem, something might be done to remedy this situation but it will take some doing. Incidentally, the Minister to whom I referred was an amusing soul and a very good friend of ours, but that is just the point – he was *our* friend and that of other Westerners and Westernized Arabs but he was not a friend of the real Arabs.

In the foregoing comment, I believe I have covered much of the ground raised by your specific questions, but I will now endeavor to treat any points which I passed over. You asked whether the Turks were taken at their word when they say that they have no imperial or territorial ambitions. I have never heard this discussed by the Saudis except when we made our MEDO proposals last year and, at that time, the Deputy Foreign Minister, Shaikh Yusuf Yassin, immediately raised the question whether the basic Turkish motive was not in connection with Turkish territorial ambitions in Syria. Of course, Yassin is a Syrian by origin but he is also the number one political official of the country and the man who, more than any other, has the ear of the King and influences his thinking.

You asked whether Turkey's leadership would be received with less suspicion than that of ourselves, the British or the French. My reply would be that any attempts at leadership in this area, including that of the United States, are definitely open to suspicion but there is no question in my mind but that we Americans are less suspect than the others. The British are in bad odor but they nevertheless enjoy a certain latent prestige. About the best that could be said about the French is that they are regarded with mild contempt.

As regards the Turks, they are also regarded with suspicion but I am not entirely despondent that something might not be done to remedy the situation. At a time when the British, French and ourselves have been trying in our various ways to make our influence felt in the Arab countries, the Turks have remained supremely indifferent. They have done nothing to smooth over the troubles of the past nor to cultivate the ground for the future. What they might have achieved if they had adopted a different tactic, I don't know, but I do feel that it would still be worthwhile for them to make the effort. It must, however, be a real effort; they should not endeavor to approach the Arabs as the agents of the West; they must identify themselves with the interests of the area; they must abandon their smugness and rigid adherence to protocol which has so often characterized their relations with the Arab States. On the other hand, I do not think that Turkey can 'drastically improve her relations with the Arab States by a strong show of sympathy and understanding.' A situation such as this does not, in my opinion, lend itself to ostentatious gestures. But I do think that real progress can probably be made in the improvement of Turkey's relations with the Arab States provided that the approach bears evidence of real sincerity and understanding. Such a policy, however, would have to be very carefully thought out and pursued along many lines. It is not the type of problem which can be met by action of the push-button variety.

Finally, you ask if it would be possible for Turkey to exercise a constructive influence in the Near East without abandoning its open and direct ties with the West. I think that this question has been more or less covered in preceding comments but, to be specific, I do believe that the Turks would have to reorient their overt policy to a considerable degree in connection with any serious effort to basic readjustment of their relations with the Arabs. At present time the Turks are so clearly identified with the policies of the West, particularly that of the United States, that they are sometimes regarded by the Arabs as more or less playing the role of stooges. It is this type of impression which they would have to dispel. Frankly, I do not think that this would necessitate any basic policy change as far as the Turks are concerned; it would be more a question of finding ways and means of implementing Turkish policy in such a way as to make the Arabs feel that the Turks are genuinely interested in the area and not just making a façade-like gesture.

I fear that I have rambled on at some length but the question which you raised was one of a type which opens up many avenues of thought, and, once started, it is hard to put on the brakes. However, I shall do so now and hope you may find these comments of some slight use. Copies of this letter are being sent to our missions in other Arab capitals.

> With kindest regards,
> Sincerely,
> s/Raymond A. Hare

EGYPT

September 24, 1952

Dear George:

Your most interesting letter of September 18 on the role which Turkey might be able to play in the defense of the Middle East arrived this morning. Before answering the specific questions set forth in the penultimate paragraph of your letter, I should like to say that as seen from this vantage point, the observations you make and the conclusions you draw are sound. For example, we concur in the Turkish strategic estimate of their position in a possible war with the USSR. We concur, and have so told the Department, that it is essential to obtain the participation of the Arab States in MEDO and that the ground must first be prepared carefully through personal and informal discussions with leaders of the Arab governments. We likewise agree that by and large the Turks are justified in looking upon the rest of the Middle Eastern countries with little enthusiasm with regard to military potential. However, in the case of Egypt we would make this exception, which is that, given proper equipment and training, the Egyptian armed forces could make some sort of a show. The Egyptian army is very proud of the fact that during the last war it maintained the anti-aircraft gunnery defenses of Egypt and the Canal Zone. With adequate training and equipment, I believe that not only could the ack-ack be manned by Egyptians, but possibly the essential jet fighter defense could be handled as well.

Now coming to your specific questions on page 4 – how do the people of Egypt like the Turks? You will not be surprised when I tell you that the people of Egypt do not like the Turks. For many years they were under Turkish rule. The Egyptians are conscious of being an older country than Turkey and despite the fact that they were also the subjects of other foreign dynasties, the experience of Turkish suzerainty is too recent to cause them to change old attitudes for one of affection. Despite this general feeling, however, I do not think the Egyptians believe that Turkey harbors territorial ambitions. In consequence, they would view Turkish attempts at leadership not so much with suspicion as with the feeling that after all Egypt has equal claims toward leadership. This would be particularly true under the present military regime. Certainly, if forced to the point, the Egyptians would regard Turkish leadership as a preferable substitute for British or French influence. At present, however, U.S. leadership would be the one which they would most desire to have. Without seeming immodest, U.S. prestige in this country at the moment is at its greatest height in recent years and in comparison, Turkish leadership, although second to ours, is far down on the scale.

Nevertheless, I believe that Turkey could improve her relations with this country by that show of sympathy and understanding for the Arab States which you suggest. I see no basic antipathy in Turkey undertaking concrete measures to increase friendly relations with the Arab world and at the same time maintaining its present open and direct ties with the West. After all, what we are all working for in the MEDO concept is exactly that: an effective working relationship between the Middle East and the West for mutual advantages.

[Gap]

I hope that you will continue this fruitful practice of giving us your views on problems of mutual concern. Since I see that you have likewise addressed these questions to other Chiefs of Mission in the Arab States, I am taking the liberty of sending a copy of my reply to our colleagues in other Arab capitals.

With cordial regards, believe me,
Sincerely yours,
s/Jefferson Caffrey

IRAN

October 15, 1952

Dear George:

You may recall in my last letter to you on the subject on April 14 that I was not very hopeful that Turkish influence could at present be helpfully brought to bear on the Iranian internal situation. The continued vicissitudes of the past few months have only confirmed to me this Iranian tendency towards xenophobia, as a result of which Turkey and the Turks are distinctly unpopular. Hence, with regard to the query you raised in your letter of September 18, I can only add that there has been no essential change in the Iranian attitude.

The Iranians are quite well aware of the military strength of Turkey and of its defense commitments under NATO. Under present conditions they resent Turkish strength and their own weakness. Preoccupied with neutrality as the current political concept of their country, various influential leaders of the National Front see Turkey as an obstacle to the successful carrying out of their program of neutrality for the Middle East.

Iran continues to fear that Turkey has designs on Azerbaijan. Iranians are concerned lest the increased military strength of Turkey in the event of a general war with the USSR may mean an occupation of Azerbaijan which might be made permanent. Soviet propaganda has played up Iranian fears of the loss of Azerbaijan by charging that Turkey and Pakistan have an agreement with the West to partition the country. Iran, resentful of Turkey's military stength and economic revival, derived in part from large-scale American aid to that country of a character denied to Iran, coupled with its exaggerated fears of the loss of Azerbaijan, will not be inclined to take helpful advice or to welcome Turkish influence in adjusting its troubled affairs.

[Gap]

The oil negotiations have continued their tortuous way. Literally at this point nothing more is known or said than appears in the papers and in the periodic Department summaries of the problem. The whole subject is so complicated now that I do believe separate telegrams would give you but a fragmentary and confused picture of the entire situation. In any event, at this writing it does not look promising and there is a real possibility that diplomatic relations will be broken with Great Britain, which will thereafter leave us exposed as the prime target for extremists of the right and left. Meanwhile, public administration and internal security of the country maintain their steady decline.

Sincerely yours,
s/Loy W. Henderson

Bibliography

Abdullah, *Memoirs of King Abdullah of Transjordan*, vol. 1, Philip P. Graves (ed.) (New York: Philosophical Library, 1950); vol. 2 (Washington: American Council of Learned Societies, 1954).

Dean Acheson, *President at the Creation: My Years in the State Department* (New York: W. W. Norton, 1969).

Fouad Ajami, *The Arab Predicament: Arab Political Thought and Practice Since 1967* (Cambridge: Cambridge University Press, 1982).

David J. Alvarez, *Bureaucracy and Cold War Diplomacy: The United States and Turkey* (Thessaloniki: 1980).

Feroz Ahmad, *The Turkish Experiment in Democracy, 1950–1975* (London: C. Hurst & Company, published for The Royal Institute of International Affairs, 1977).

George Antonius, *The Arab Awakening: The Story of the Arab National Movement* (Philadelphia: Lippincott, 1939).

Robert Blake, *The Decline of Power, 1915–64* (London: Granada, 1985).

Charles Bohlen, *Witness to History, 1929–1969* (New York: 1973).

Sir Reader Bullard, *Britain and the Middle East* (London: Hutchinson, 1951).

Alan Bullock, *Ernest Bevin, Foreign Secretary* (New York: Norton, 1983).

John C. Campbell, *Defense of the Middle East: Problems of American Foreign Policy* (New York: Praeger, 1960).

Claude Cohen, *Pre-Ottoman Turkey* (London: Sedgwick & Jackson, 1968).

Anthony Cordesman, 'The Middle East and the Politics of Force', *Middle East Journal*, 40: 1 (Winter 1986).

Frederick J. Dobney, *The Selected Papers of Will Clayton* (Baltimore: 1971).

Robert J. Donovan, *Conflict and Crisis: The Presidency of Harry S. Truman, 1945–1948* (New York: 1977).

Robert J. Donovan, *Tumultuous Years: The Presidency of Harry S. Truman, 1949–1953* (New York: 1982).

Anthony Eden, *The Reckoning* (Boston: 1965).

Rached el-Barawi, *The Military Coup in Egypt: An Analytical Study* (Cairo: Renaissance Bookshop, 1952).

Nuri Eren, *Turkey Today – and Tomorrow* (New York: 1963).

Feridun Cemal Erkin, *Les Relations Turco-Soviétiques et la Question des Détroits* (Ankara: 1968).

Thomas H. Etzold, 'The Soviet Union in the Mediterranean', in *NATO and the Mediterranean*, Lawrence S. Kaplan *et al.* (eds) (Wilmington, Del.: Scholarly Resources Inc., 1985).

N. A. Faris and M. T. Husayn, *The Crescent in Crisis: An Interpretive Study of the Modern Arab World* (Lawrence: University of Kansas Press, 1955).

Herbert Feis, *Between War and Peace: The Potsdam Conference* (Princeton: 1960).

Herbert Feis, *From Trust to Terror: The Onset of the Cold War, 1945–1950* (New York: 1970).

W. B. Fisher, *The Middle East: A Physical, Social and Regional Geography* (New York: Dutton, 1950).

Richard N. Frye (ed.), *The Near East and the Great Powers* (Cambridge: Harvard University Press, 1951).

John Gaddis, *Strategies of Containment: A Critical Appraisal of Postwar American National Security Policy* (New York: Oxford University Press, 1982).

Hamilton A. R. Gibb, *Modern Trends in Islam* (Chicago: University of Chicago Press, 1947).

John Gimble, *The Origins of the Marshall Plan* (Stanford: 1976).

John Bagot Glubb, *The Story of the Arab Legion* (London: Hodder & Stoughton, 1948).

Richard Grimmet, 'United States Military Installations in Turkey', Congressional Research Service Report No. 84–221 F, 12 December 1984.

George S. Harris, *Troubled Alliance: Turkish-American Problems in Historical Perspective, 1945–1971* (Stanford: 1972).

Loy W. Henderson, 'American Political and Strategic Interests in the Middle East and Southeast Europe', Department of State *Bulletin* 17 (23 November 1947), 996–1000.

Uriel Heyd, *Foundations of Turkish Nationalism* (London: Luzac, 1950).

Philip K. Hitti, *History of the Arabs*, 6th ed. (New York: St. Martin's Press, 1956).

Halford L. Hoskins, *The Middle East: Problem Area in World Politics* (New York: Macmillan, 1954).

Charles W. Hostler, *Turkism and the Soviets* (New York: Praeger, 1957).

A. H. Hourani, *Syria and Lebanon* (New York: Oxford University Press, for the Royal Institute of International Affairs, 1946).

Harry N. Howard, *The Partition of Turkey, 1913–1923* (Norman: University of Oklahoma Press, 1931).

Harry N. Howard, 'The Development of United States Policy in the Near East, 1945–1951', reprint from *The Department of State Bulletin*, 26 November 1951.

Harry N. Howard, 'The Development of United States Policy in the Near East, South Asia, and Africa', reprint from *The Department of State Bulletin*, 15 December 1952.

Michael H. Hunt, *Ideology and U.S. Foreign Policy* (New Haven and London: Yale University Press, 1987).

J. C. Hurewitz, *Diplomacy in the Near and Middle East* (Princeton: Van Nostrand, 1956).

International Bank for Reconstruction and Development, *The Economy of Turkey* (Washington: IBRD, 1951).

Kemal Karpat, *Turkey's Politics: The Transition to A Multi-Party System* (Princeton: 1959).

George F. Kennan, *Foreign Affairs*, Spring 1987.

Majid Khadduri, *Independent Iraq: A Study in Iraqi Politics since 1932* (New York: Oxford University Press, for the Royal Institute of International Affairs, 1952).

Lord Kinross, *Atatürk: A Biography of Mustafa Kemal, Father of Modern Turkey* (New York: 1965).

George Kirk, *The Middle East*, 1945–1950 (London: 1954).

George Kirk, *The Middle East in the War* (London: 1952).

George Kirk, 'Turkey', in *The War and the Neutrals*, Arnold Toynbee (ed.) (London: 1956).

Bruce R. Kuniholm, *The Origins of the Cold War in the Near East: Power Conflict and Diplomacy in Iran, Turkey, and Greece* (Princeton: Princeton University Press, 1980).

Bruce R. Kuniholm, *The Near East Connection: Greece and Turkey in the Reconstruction and Security of Europe, 1946–1952* (Brookline, Mass.: Hellenic College Press, 1984).

Bruce R. Kuniholm, 'Retrospect and Prospects: Forty Years of U.S. Middle East Policy', *The Middle East Journal*, Vol. 41, No. 1 (Winter 1987).

Bruce R. Kuniholm, 'Rhetoric and Reality in the Aegean: U.S. Policy Options Toward Greece and Turkey', *SAIS Review*, Vol. 6, No. 1 (1986).

Bruce R. Kuniholm, 'The Geopolitics of U.S.-Turkish Relations: Implications for the Future', International Security Studies Program, The Wilson Center (6 June 1988).

Bruce R. Kuniholm, 'Turkey and NATO: Past, Present, and Future', ORBIS 27 (Summer 1983).

Bruce R. Kuniholm, 'Strategies for Containment in the Middle East', in *Containment: Concept and Policy* (Washington, DC: National Defense University Press, 1986).

Ellen Laipson, 'The Seven-Ten Ratio in Military Aid to Greece and Turkey: A Congressional Tradition', Congressional Research Service Report No. 85–79, 15 June 1983; revised 10 April 1985.

Walter Laqueur, *The Soviet Union and the Middle East* (New York: 1959).

George Lenczowski, *Russia and the West in Iran, 1918–1948* (Ithaca: Cornell University Press, 1949).

Bernard Lewis, *The Emergence of Modern Turkey* (London: 1961).

Geoffrey Lewis, *Turkey*, 3rd ed. (London: 1965).

Alfred M. Lilienthal, *There Goes the Middle East* (New York: Devin-Adair, 1957).

Stephen Hemsley Longrigg, *Iraq, 1900–1950* (New York: Oxford University Press, for the Royal Institute of International Affairs, 1953).

Wm. Roger Louis, *The British Empire in the Middle East, 1945–1951* (Oxford: Clarendon Press, 1984).

Harold Macmillan, *The Blast of War, 1939–1945* (New York: 1967).

George McGhee, *Envoy to the Middle World* (New York: Harper & Row, 1983).

George McGhee, *The U.S.-Turkish-NATO Middle East Connection* (London: Macmillan Press Ltd, 1989).

Walter Millis (ed.), *The Forrestal Diaries* (New York: 1951).

Maurice Peterson, *Both Sides of the Curtain* (London: 1950).

William Polk, *The United States and the Arab World*, 3rd edition (Cambridge, Mass.: 1975).

Rouhollah Ramazani, 'The Autonomous Republic of Azerbaijan and the Kurdish People's Republic: Their Rise and Fall', in *The Anatomy of Communist Takeovers*, Thomas Hammond (ed.) (New Haven: 1975).

David Rees, *The Age of Containment: The Cold War, 1945–1965* (New York: 1968).

Richard Robinson, *The First Turkish Republic: A Case Study in National Development* (Cambridge, Mass.: 1963).

Kermit Roosevelt, *Arabs, Oil and History* (New York: Harper, 1949).

Rothwell, *Britain and the Cold War*.

William H. Rowden, 'The Mediterranean Environment of the Sixth Fleet', in *NATO and the Mediterranean*.

Dankwart Rustow, 'Turkey's Liberal Revolution', *Middle East Review* (Spring 1985).

Dankwart Rustow, 'Foreign Policy of the Turkish Republic', in *Foreign Policy in World Politics*, R. C. Macridis (ed.) (N.J.: Englewood Cliffs, 1958).

Harold Saunders, *The Other Walls: The Politics of the Arab-Israeli Peace Process* (Washington, DC: American Enterprise Institute, 1985).

M. V. Seton-Williams, *Britain and the Arab States: A Survey of Anglo-Arab Relations, 1920–1948* (London: Luzac, 1948).

Philip W. Thayer, *Tensions in the Middle East* (Baltimore: The Johns Hopkins Press, 1958).

Lewis V. Thomas and Richard N. Frye, *The United States and Turkey and Iran* (Cambridge: Harvard University Press, 1951).

Max Thornburg *et al.*, *Turkey: An Economic Appraisal* (New York: Twentieth Century Fund, 1949).

Arnold J. Toynbee, *The Western Question in Greece and Turkey* (London: Constable, 1922).

Harry S. Truman, *Memoirs*. Vol. 1: *Year of Decisions*; Vol. 2, *Years of Trial and Hope* (New York: Garden City, 1955).

US Congress, Testimony of George McGhee and Dean Acheson, *The Middle East, Africa, and Inter-American Affairs* (Historical Series), Vol. 16, Selected Executive Session Hearings of the Committee on Foreign Affairs, 1951–56, US House of Representatives (Washington, DC: 1980).

US Congress, 'U.S. Assistance to Turkey: Foreign Aid Facts', Congressional Research Service (updated 16 July 1985), Issue Brief IB 85059.

US Congress, Testimony of Ambassador Parker T. Hart, *Security and Development Assistance*, Senate Committee on Foreign Relations, Hearings (S. Hrg. 98–908), USGPO (Washington, DC: 1984).

US Congress, *Assistance to Greece and Turkey*, Hearings before the Committee on Foreign Affairs, US House of Representatives, 80th Cong., 1st Sess., on H.R. 2616 (Washington, DC: USGPO, 1947).

US Congress, *Aid to Greece and Turkey*, Report of the Committee on Foreign Relations, 80th Cong., 2d Sess., on S. 2358 (Washington, DC: USGPO, 1948).

US Congress, House, H.R. 7797, *Report of the Committee on Foreign Affairs*, No. 1802, Part 3 on Foreign Economic Assistance, Supplementary Report of the Committee on Foreign Affairs, March 1950.

US Department of State, *Foreign Relations of the United States* Vol. 7, 1946; Vol. 5, 1947; Vols. 4 and 6, 1948; Vol. 6, 1949; Vol. 5, 1950; Vol. 5, 1951; Vol. 9, 1952 (Washington, DC).

Freda Utley, *Will the Middle East Go West?* (Chicago: Henry Regnery, 1957).

Ferenc Váli, *Bridge Across the Bosporus: The Foreign Policy of Turkey* (Baltimore: 1971).

Edward Reginald Vere-Hodge, *Turkish Foreign Policy, 1918–1948* (Ambilly-Annemasse: Imprimerie Franco-Suisse, 1950).

C. M. Woodhouse, *Something Ventured* (London: Granada, 1982).

Ahmet Emin Yalman, *Turkey in My Time* (Norman: University of Oklahoma Press, 1956).

Index